THE SORROWS OF THE ANCIENT ROMANS

THE SORROWS OF THE ANCIENT ROMANS

THE GLADIATOR AND THE MONSTER

Carlin A. Barton

PRINCETON UNIVERSITY PRESS

PRINCETON, NEW JERSEY

COPYRIGHT © 1993 BY PRINCETON UNIVERSITY PRESS

PUBLISHED BY PRINCETON UNIVERSITY PRESS, 41 WILLIAM STREET,

PRINCETON, NEW JERSEY 08540

IN THE UNITED KINGDOM: PRINCETON UNIVERSITY PRESS, CHICHESTER, WEST SUSSEX

LIBRARY OF CONGRESS CATALOGING-IN-PUBLICATION DATA

BARTON, CARLIN A., 1948-

THE SORROWS OF THE ANCIENT ROMANS : THE GLADIATOR AND

THE MONSTER /

CARLIN A. BARTON.

P.   CM.

INCLUDES INDEX.

ISBN 0-691-05696-X

ISBN 0-691-01091-9 (PBK.)

1. NATIONAL CHARACTERISTICS, ROMAN.   I. TITLE.

DG78.B37   1992   937—DC20   92-13603

THIS BOOK HAS BEEN COMPOSED IN LINOTRON SABON

PRINTED IN THE UNITED STATES OF AMERICA

3   5   7   9   10   8   6   4

THIRD PRINTING, AND FIRST PAPERBACK PRINTING, 1996

Clarissa

Our common sense makes us see that without paradox
and contradiction our parables will be too simple for a
complex poverty, too consolatory to console. Our study,
like [Shakespeare's] Richard, must have a certain
complexity and a sense of failure. "I cannot do it;
yet I'll hammer it out," he says.
(Frank Kermode, *The Sense of an Ending*)

CONTENTS

ACKNOWLEDGMENTS

I WISH TO THANK the following individuals for reading and criticizing the whole or parts of the manuscript: John Bodel, Peter Brown, Miriam Chrisman, Mark Cioc, Jean Elshtain, Erich Gruen, Thomas Habinek, William Johnston, Ray Keifetz, Elizabeth Keitel, Barbara Kellum, Amy Richlin, Charles Rearick, Nathan Rosenstein, Carole Straw, Richard Trexler, Valerie Warrior, and Patricia Wright. Their help has been deeply appreciated. I would also like to thank the participants of the Five College Social History Group (Smith College, 1986), the New England Ancient History Colloquium (Mount Holyoke College, March 1987), and the Institute for Advanced Studies in the Humanities at the University of Massachusetts (Fall 1988) for their valuable contributions to the development of my ideas.

I would like to thank the University of California Press for permission to reprint "The Scandal of the Arena," which appeared in *Representations* 27 (Summer 1989), and the superintendent of archaeology of the city of Naples for permission to reprint the photograph of the gladiator tintinnabulum.

THE SORROWS OF THE ANCIENT ROMANS

INTRODUCTION

THIS IS A BOOK about the emotional life of the ancient Romans. In particular, it is about the extremes of despair, desire, fascination, and envy, and the ways in which these emotions organized the world and directed the actions of the ancient Romans.

This is a book about the gladiator and the monster, the most conspicuous of the figures through which these extremes of emotions were enacted and expressed.

This is a book about paradox and reciprocity, about boundaries, transgressions, and expiations.

This is a book, finally, about *homo in extremis*, the human being and human society at and beyond the limits of endurance.

I have written in an effort to address some of the darkest riddles of the Roman psyche, because I suspected that they were some of the riddles of my own life and perhaps of human life: the conjunctions of cruelty and tenderness, exaltation and degradation, asceticism and license, erethism and apathy, energy and ennui, as they were realized in a particular historical and sociological setting, the period of the civil wars and the establishment of the monarchy, roughly the first century B.C.E. and the first two centuries C.E.

The purpose of the work has not been to produce a set of conclusions, but rather a "map" of what one reader has called "the uncharted regions of Roman life": those areas of Roman collective psychology that have heretofore largely resisted interpretation on account of the dispersed, contradictory, and troubling sources, and the even more troubling subject matter. I have tried to construct a "physics" of emotions that suffused Roman action without producing in that culture a systematic exegesis, of patterns that so saturated the life of this period that they are difficult to distinguish from consciousness itself, of paradoxes that constituted a kind of "white noise" in Roman culture—pervasive, yet resisting articulation, and so complex as to verge on silence.

This is a work of popularization; I am hoping to attract an audience beyond that of my own discipline of Roman history. But it is by no means intended as a work of simplification. On the contrary, I have tried to present the most complex understanding of which I am capable, the most complex understanding that I can enunciate. My goals have been to organize and clarify, without unduly "rectifying," the masses of entangled and disconnected material in a way that would be agreeable to the generally educated reader and acceptable to the specialist in Roman history.

To achieve the first goal, I have welcomed the guidance of modern theorists: psychologists, anthropologists and sociologists. To achieve the second, I have relied on the patient and careful labors of countless other ancient historians.

My methods may not appear excessively strange to ethnologists and historians of mental life, but they may cause some consternation to ancient historians. I wish, therefore, to anticipate the reactions of some of my readers and address briefly some issues of concern to ancient historians.

There are many types of sources that ancient historians are trained to dismiss or be wary of: literature and professed fictions in general (especially literary *topoi*), "rhetoric" (especially philosophical), and banalities and commonplaces of all sorts. They are the veils or scrims obscuring a reality whose authentic categories are "politics," "economics," and "law" (or "class," "gender," and "age"). But for my purposes, the "truth," "sincerity," or "authenticity" of the ancient statements or stories that I repeat is largely irrelevant. I am concerned with mapping Roman ways of ordering and categorizing their world, and of transgressing, denying, or obliterating those orders. What made things seem real or unreal to a Roman at a particular moment is of greater concern to me than what was (or is) real. As possible clues to the "physics" of the emotional world of the Romans, the metaphor, the fantasy, the deliberate falsehood, the mundane and oft-repeated truism, the literary *topos*, the bizarre world of schoolboy declamations, and the "cultural baggage" taken over from the Greeks are as valuable as a report of Tacitus or an imperial decree. For my purposes, all of the sources are equally true and equally fictive.

Some readers may feel that I have cast my net altogether too widely through the sources. While the center of my field of vision has been the early Empire, particularly the age of Nero (because it is the period I understand best, the one in which the sources are most familiar and the patterns are clearest), the circle of my attention embraces the last century of the Republic and the first two centuries of the Empire, years in which I believe I can see certain patterns emerging and developing. But my peripheral vision often exceeds these limitations in the search for any idea or experience—always privileging the Roman—that can help me illuminate the material on which I am focused. In attempting to "catch" phenomena which suffused the society of ancient Rome in a particular period, but of which there exist few connected analyses in the sources, I have often stretched my time frame past its stated limits or filled in the Roman puzzle with bits and pieces of other far-flung cultures, including my own.

I expect many readers will question the application to ancient behaviors of psychological patterns gleaned from modern thought. There seems to me to be no alternative to this method. As the philosopher Richard Rorty explains, "We shall never be able to have evidence that there exist persons who speak languages in principle untranslatable into English or who hold beliefs all or most of which are incompatible with our own."[1] We have no access to minds other than our own except insofar as we impute to them shared qualities. The psychologist meeting a new patient or the anthropologist encountering a new culture is compelled to assume a certain number of shared qualities—even if they anticipate revising their assessments, and indeed aspire to do so.

I would ascribe to the opinion of another philosopher, Nelson Goodman, that "reality in a world, like realism in a picture, is largely a matter of habit."[2] Because of the eternal absence of the subject and the sparse and fragmentary artifacts that suggest him or her to us, this observation applies even more to the ancient historian than to the psychologist or the anthropologist. We ancient historians are compelled to rely more on our own habits of mind to piece together an alien mentality and an alien reality than the psychologist or anthropologist—and our conventions are less liable to be confounded and emended by the shock of confrontation. To the extent that the "Romans" exist for us, they are created from the bits and pieces of our own experience—including our experience of the artifact and text—and "authorized" by tradition. *This is no less so when we imagine Romans as different from ourselves.* I yearn to see the Romans "differently," but even the antidote to my own assumptions must be built out of the material at hand; I am compelled to build the "strange" Romans from the same materials that served to build the "familiar" ones. I can only look, within these materials, for the artifact, the idea, the category that defies me. I have no way of knowing, finally, whether the Romans experienced desire the way that I myself or my contemporaries experience desire, but the assumption of a provisional comparability of human experience has given me the key to the decipherment of many particular behaviors. I may posit and desire difference, but I require comparability in order to interpret.

Historians and readers of history accustomed to the narrative form may be exasperated by my endlessly taking stories, anecdotes, and bits of text "out of context." It may seem to some that it is "out of context" to juxtapose the testimony of the martyr and that of the gladiator, or to speak of Lucian in the same breath as Cicero. This fragmentation is due, in part, to the lack of connected expositions on my subjects in the ancient texts, compounded by my tendency to atone for the hybris of synthesizing with a humble excess of documentation. But I would also argue that a

[1] Richard Rorty, "The World Well Lost," *Journal of Philosophy* 69 (1972), p. 656.
[2] Nelson Goodman, *Ways of Worldmaking* (Indianapolis, 1978), p. 20.

degree of dissonance and juxtaposition is essential to my project of bringing the paradox and disjunction in Roman life into high relief.

There are, moreover, no "right" contexts for any symbolic expressions; there are only contexts in which the signs "make sense" or appear "fitting" to the observer and contexts in which the occurrence of the sign seems jarring and "senseless." What "makes sense" is, in large part, conventional. We feel that a map is "correct," for example, when it conforms to a traditional perspective and a certain traditional ordering. Looking at maps of the Western hemisphere turned "wrong side up" can disconcert us but also compel us to acknowledge the arbitrariness and inertia of our orientations. Things "out of place" may seem mutilated, like Schliemann's potsherds, broken from the pots to which they were integral. Initially denied any value and discarded, when placed side by side and compared, these shards, torn from their "natural" contexts, were able to articulate patterns and take on value that they could not otherwise. Much of the information I employ in this book has been denied those contexts most familiar and obvious to ancient historians: chronological, narratological, authorial. I am hoping, however, to coax my fragments to illustrate some of the paradoxes of Roman emotional life that they could not while remaining scattered in their more conventional contexts—where they may appear peripheral or be overwhelmed by other patterns. A seemingly casual mention of eye contact in Livy's story of the meeting of Mucius and Porsena, for instance, may not arrest the reader's attention, but when juxtaposed with descriptions of eye contact in his story of the disaster at the Caudine Forks, something about Livy's complex notion of the gaze, never explicated by him in an extended excursus, may begin to emerge.

The patterns of this book, then, are mosaics built from thousands of shards (with many a raw seam and jagged edge). I can only hope the results will refract more light than they obscure. If I succeed, the contexts that I have established for these "misplaced" fragments will begin to appear "fitting."

I am sensitive to the charge of omission. Not only have I not looked at everything relevant, I have not taken sufficiently "seriously" the categories that seem most real and compelling to many of my contemporaries—such as age and class and gender. I have not ignored social divisions in Rome. On the contrary, I have attempted to clarify their relations to particular emotional contexts whenever possible. (It is, however, almost as difficult to extract the world of the cobbler and the wet nurse from the Roman ruins as it is from the Mayan.) But it is in the nature of the emotional paradoxes that I am discussing both to emphasize distinctions and simultaneously to blur them. Class and gender are relevant to every discussion of emotion, but these emotions obliterate class and gender distinctions at the same time that they emphasize them, enforcing and transgressing a myriad of categories. To use class or gender—or indeed *any* categories—as the "real" categories of analysis would undermine my own project, which has been to illuminate the making and unmaking of the Roman world.

My emphasis on the impossible, the intolerable, and the miraculous will disturb many readers who are accustomed to "sober" and "practical" Romans (or better, to "sober" and "practical" Roman historians). I may seem to them to be exaggerating certain qualities of Roman life. Certainly, the dramatic emotions I describe in my book do not begin to exhaust what can be said about Roman emotional life. Not everyone in the culture idolized the gladiator, or envied, or acted cruelly. However, I do think that these behaviors were sufficiently common in the period of the late Republic and early Empire as to merit explanation from even the most reverent student. More importantly, understanding them can help us articulate our own "physics" of despair, desire, fascination, and envy.

It is important to recognize that ancient Romans did not draw lines between what we might label psychology (individual or social), and sociology or politics. Our rigid separation of the emotions from behavior, of the intimate from the public sphere, was not one that the Romans made. "Economics," "politics," "emotions," etc. were intertwined in a way that is bewildering for us and can appear as a failure to discriminate, needing correction. But if we can suspend our own desire to validate our own categories, if we can tolerate what at first seems the most awesome confusion of categories, a dreadful amalgam of "magic" and "science," "sense" and "nonsense," it will allow us a glimpse into a subtle, nuanced, and interconnected world unavailable to those of us who have "clearer" and more distinctly organized divisions of phenomena.

While writing this book I have tried to keep in mind Martin Buber's distinction between an I/Thou relationship and an I/It relationship, between a relationship that respects and confronts and one that digests and "explains away." It has ever been the wonder aroused in me by everything ancient that attracts me to that world. The Romans, in particular, have seemed surpassing strange—the great carnivores of the ancient world— exercising the same fascination as a Siberian tiger or a great white shark. I am astounded by the excesses that animated them, needing simultaneously to understand and to preserve them in their alienness. In approaching them, therefore, I have endeavored to be at once active and passive, apathetic and engaged, to speak in the common tongue of my discipline and my culture but with a dialect that is not arid and empty of the emotions which have occasioned this work and which are its subject.

At times I fear that the rage for order in me is so great that my patterns may be all too carefully drawn—that I may have inadvertently anesthetized the monster that enchants me. I do not want to "solve" the riddles of the Roman psyche by "dissolving" them. At other times I worry that I may have tried to confront and to understand things that should not be understood, to articulate things better left unsaid. I have worried that if one understands horror it is because, in some sense, one is horrible; if one understands sadism it is because, in some sense, one is a sadist. To the extent you understand, you confess. In spending years writing a book, I know that one "writes oneself"—not so much that one writes *about* oneself (although I suspect that we do that despite our intentions), but that one writes oneself in Montaigne's sense, that one creates oneself, one molds one's own life and mind. Undoubtedly my ways of ordering the world have "infected" the ancient Romans portrayed here. But it is also possible that their ways of ordering the world may have "infected" me; I may have become, in the course of writing this book, like that which confounds me.

If I have not set out to "solve" the dark mysteries of Roman life that inspired this book, it is because I believe that there are many riddles of life that grieve us more because we cannot speak them than because we cannot solve them. We, in the late twentieth century, have a very small vocabulary to deal with the impossible, the intolerable, and the miraculous. But sometimes other cultures, quickened in a different time and space, can offer us words, images, and symbols to say something that our own culture has not the means to say. Perhaps this strange, ancient warrior culture can say something *for us*—even if it is not consoling.

THE GLADIATOR

ONE

DESPAIR

THE SCANDAL OF THE ARENA

La scandale qu'est la gladiature . . . une
impensable monstruosité.
(Georges Ville, *La Gladiature*)[1]

All this horrifies us. . . . To say that we condemn this
revolting custom is too little, we cannot even
begin to understand.
(Ugo Paoli, *Rome*)[2]

What is bereft of meaning in one perspective may
find it in another.
(Vincent Descombes, *Le Même et l'autre*)[3]

T HE ROMAN FASCINATION with the gladiator confounds us:
we see him as a twisted "athlete" in a twisted "sport," the embodiment of Roman sadism, brutality and callousness.[4] We can hear
only his scream; we cannot hear the song within the sorrow. The fact that
the surviving evidence, though suggestive and intriguing, is limited and

---

[1] Georges Ville, *La Gladiature en Occident des origines à la mort de Domitien* (Rome,
1981), p. 471.

[2] Ugo Paoli, *Rome: Its People, Life and Customs* (New York, 1958), p. 253.

[3] Vincent Descombes, *Le Même et l'autre* (Paris, 1979).

[4] "The welter of blood in gladiatorial and wild-beast shows, the squeals of the victims
and the slaughtered animals are completely alien to us and almost unimaginable" (Keith
Hopkins, "Murderous Games," in *Death and Renewal: Sociological Studies in Roman History*, vol. 2 [Cambridge, 1983], pp. 1–30, esp. p. 5). "Nichts zeigt so sehr den ungeheuren
Untershied zwischen der Denk- und Empfindungsweise des römischen Altertums und des
heutigen Europa wie die Beurteilung, welche die Schauspiele des Amphitheaters damals und
jetzt bei Gebildeten fanden" (Ludwig Friedländer, *Darstellung aus der Sittengeschichte
Roms*, 10th ed., vol. 2 [Leipzig, 1964], p. 94). "Of the gladiators, it should be said that
while theirs was doubtless a demeaning, cruel, and bloody 'sport,' yet some attained noto-
riety and even wealth" (Henry Boren, *Roman Society* [Chapel Hill, N.C., 1977], p. 207).
"Though Cicero and Pliny the Younger defended the games as educational the real appeals
were sadism and spectacle" (Thomas Africa, *The Immense Majesty: A History of Rome and
the Roman Empire* [New York, 1974], p. 264). "This ocean of hatred . . . this madness of
cruelty which raged with unequalled frenzy in the games of the arena . . ." (Otto Kiefer,
Sexual Life in Ancient Rome [London, 1934], p. 106). "Même ceux qui désapprouvent ou
condamnent le *munus* le font pour des raisons . . . qui laissent échapper, à notre point de
vue, son immoralité fondamentale" (Ville, *La Gladiature*, p. 456).

fragmentary, conflicting and profoundly ambiguous, allows us to pre-serve our bewilderment.[5] If, however, one is willing to risk understanding too much and censoring too little, I believe it is possible to catch the scat-tered references and refuse of the arena into the powerful opera of emo-tions in which the Roman gladiator was the star.

The "Inverse Exaltation" of the Roman Gladiator

Men give them their souls, women their bodies too. . . . On one and the same account, they glorify them and degrade and diminish them—indeed, they openly condemn them to ignominy and the loss of civil rights, excluding them from the senate house and rostrum, the senatorial and equestrian orders, and all other honors or distinctions of any type. The perversity of it! Yet, they love whom they punish; they belittle whom they esteem; the art they glorify, the artist they debase. What judgment is this: on account of that for which he is vilified, he is deemed worthy of merit! (Tertullian, *De spectaculis* 22).[6]

What was it that the Romans saw in the despised gladiator that so deeply affected them? What, in the late Republic and Early Imperial pe-riod, in particular, motivated men and women of the free and privileged classes to identify with, and even assume the role of, the gladiator both publicly and privately?

The gladiator: crude, loathsome, doomed, lost (*importunus, ob-scaenus, damnatus, perditus*) was, throughout the Roman tradition, a man utterly debased by fortune, a slave, a man altogether without worth and dignity (*dignitas*), almost without humanity. Lucilius (2nd century B.C.E.) labels the gladiator Aeserninus, "a low, vile man worthy of that

[5] The material evidence was collected with extraordinary energy and thoroughness by Georges Ville in his *La Gladiature*. Much of this material is also available in Keith Hopkins, "Murderous Games." See also G. Lafaye, "Gladiator," in Daremberg-Salio, *Dictionnaire des antiquités grecques et romaines* (hereafter *D-S*), vol. 2 (1896), cols. 1563ff.; K. Schnei-der, "Gladiatores," in Pauly-Wissowa, *Paulys Realencyclopädie der klassischen Altertums-wissenschaft* (hereafter *P-W*), suppl. vol. 3 (1918), cols. 760ff.; Louis Robert, *Les Gladi-ateurs dans l'orient grec* (Amsterdam, 1940); Friedländer, *Sittengeschichte*, vol. 2, pp. 1–21, 50–112; Michael Grant, *Gladiators* (New York, 1967); Roland Auguet, *Cruelty and Civilization: The Roman Games* (London, 1972); Patrizia Sabbatini Tumolesi, *Gladiato-rum Paria* (Rome, 1980); Monique Clavel-Lévêque, *L'Empire en jeux* (Paris, 1984).

[6] Tertullian, writing in the early third century C.E., marveled at the Romans' peculiar ability to simultaneously exalt and degrade certain characters. He was speaking of the mime and the charioteer as well as the gladiator. I have chosen to limit my discussion to the glad-iator in preference to the mime or charioteer for two reasons: first, because the paradox of simultaneous degradation and exaltation was most acute in the figure of the gladiator; sec-ond, because the gladiator, to a degree unmatched by the actor or the charioteer, served as a powerful metaphorical figure in the surviving texts of the late Republican period and the first centuries of the Empire.

life and estate" (4.172–75). Cicero, in his speech in defence of Milo (52 B.C.E.), remarks on the lack of sympathy that the Romans showed the timid suppliant "in the fights of the gladiators and in the case of men of the lowest type in condition and fortune" (34). In both Seneca's letters and Juvenal's satires (1st century C.E.), to appear on the stage is a fate worse than death for an honorable man, and descending into the arena a still more disgraceful end than the stage: "When his face had been long abraded by a mask, he transferred it to a helmet" (Seneca, *Naturales quaestiones* 7.32.3).[7] According to Calpurnius Flaccus (2nd century C.E.), "There is no meaner condition among the people than that of the gladiator" (*Declamatio* 52).[8]

The combat between gladiators was, in its origin, a *munus mortis*, an offering or duty paid to the *manes*, or shades, of dead Roman chieftains. Adopted from Etruscan and Samnite funeral sacrifices, the first recorded gladiatorial games were given by the sons of Iunius Brutus in 264 B.C.E. to the shade of their dead father. Three pairs fought in this first *munus*. In 174 B.C.E. seventy-four men fought for three days in honor of the dead father of Titus Flamininus. Up to three hundred pairs fought in the games offered by the great warlords of the collapsing Republic, Pompey and Caesar. (Caesar would have offered more, but he was restrained by the senate.) Augustus, freed from interference, boasted in his autobiographical epitaph of combats that involved ten thousand men. A century later Trajan, having conquered Dacia, caused ten thousand men to fight for four months. As the numbers swelled, the chances of death in the arena increased, particularly at the end of the Republic and during the first two centuries of the Empire. The gladiator had perhaps one chance in ten to be killed in any particular bout in the arena in the first century, and much greater chance of death in the following centuries.[9]

In the beginning the battles were fueled by the bodies of the condemned and defeated, the refuse of Rome's wars: Gauls, Spaniards, Arabs, Thracians, Germans, Asians, Syrians, Greeks. Paradoxically, as the numbers of gladiators, the frequency of the games, and the risks of dying increased,

---

[7] Cf. Juvenal, *Satirae* 8.183–99.

[8] But see Calpurnius's "a man of strength and a gladiator" ("vir fortis gladiator" [ibid.]) and Dio 51.7.2.

[9] The risks of dying in the arena were not equally distributed among all combatants. Condemned criminals had little or no chance of surviving. The odds of prisoners of war, slaves, and volunteers varied greatly, depending on their skill and courage and rank, and on the liberality of the producer of the games. A highly skilled voluntary gladiator was an expensive and valued item and would only be sacrificed by a very liberal *editor* (producer) as an act of conspicuous and splendid generosity. See Ville, *La Gladiature*, pp. 318–23. Clavel-Lévêque (*L'Empire*, p. 203n. 256, cf. p. 76) estimates that in the first century C.E. the gladiator had one chance in seven of surviving a career in the arena; his odds were much worse in the following centuries.

Romans and volunteers began enlisting, until, by the end of the Republic, somewhere around half of all gladiators were volunteers.[10] The volunteer gladiator and his companion *bestiarius* (the hunter of the arena) provoked Cyprian, writing in the third century of the common era, to complain querulously:

> Man is killed for the pleasure of man, and to be able to kill is a skill, an employment, an art. . . . He undergoes a discipline in order to kill, and when he does kill, it is a glory. What is this, I ask you, of what nature is it, where those offer themselves to wild beasts, whom no one has condemned, in the prime of life, of comely appearance, in costly garments? While still alive they adorn themselves for a voluntary death, and miserable as they are, they even glory in their sufferings. (*Ad Donatum* 7)

Not only was the volunteer who entered the arena debased, but he was compelled to affirm, to justify, his debasement. He took a frightful oath, the *sacramentum gladiatorium*: he swore to endure being burned, bound, beaten, and slain by the sword ("uri, vinciri, verberari, ferroque necari patior"; [see Petronius, *Satyricon* 117; Seneca, *Epistulae* 71.23]).[11] He forswore all that might ameliorate his condition, and finally, he forswore life itself. By this awful and compulsory vow the condemned emphasized and legitimated his extraordinary position; it became contractual (the *auctoramentum gladiatorum*). Because of the *sacramentum*, the assumption of a solemn obligation,[12] the gladiator's fate became a point of honor. Henceforward *not* to show himself willing to be burned, bound,

---

[10] Ville (*La Gladiature*, p. 255) estimates that by the first half of the first century C.E. more than half the gladiators were free. There gradually developed a program of active recruitment for the arena, and the liberal use of minor offenders in the arena became, in effect, a sort of draft. Despite the continual increase in volunteers, by definition "free" men, the stigma of condemnation clung to them and was perpetuated in their living conditions, their food, their slaughter, etc. Cf. Ville, *La Gladiature*, pp. 301–29.

[11] For variant forms of the gladiator's oath see Horace, *Satirae* 2.7.58–59; Pseudacron, *Scholia in Horatium vetustiora*, ad loc.; Schneider, "Gladiatores," col. 774; Friedländer, *Sittengeschicte*, vol 2., p. 60; Hopkins, "Murderous Games," p. 24; Ville, *La Gladiature*, pp. 248–49.

[12] The *sacramentum* was a sacred oath. It put one's life "on deposit" with the gods of the underworld. If one broke one's oath, one's honor and one's life were forfeit; one became *sacer* (sacred) and liable to execution as a *piaculum*, or expiatory sacrifice, to the offended gods. Petronius's character Giton, like many of the inhabitants of the Petronian demimonde, has adopted and mixed forms of the aristocratic warrior code and the etiquette of the arena. In chapter 80 of the *Satyricon*, Giton bares his throat and announces his readiness to die for having broken the sacrament of friendship (*amicitiae sacramentum*). See Edouard Cuq, "Sacramentum," in *D-S*, vol. 4.2, pp. 951–55; Klingmüller, "Sacramentum," in *P-W*, vol. 1A.2, cols. 1667–74. For the idea that the martyr was bound by a particularly fierce type of soldier's *sacramentum*, see Tertullian, *Scorpiace* 4.5, *Ad martyras* 3.1; J. De Ghellinck, *Pour l'histoire du mot "Sacramentum"* (Louvains, 1924), pp. 49, 66–71, 145–48, 162–63, 226–27.

beaten, and killed would be dishonorable. It is by the gladiator's oath that Petronius's shady freedmen, Encolpius and Giton, shipwrecked and without means, voluntarily assume the role of slaves to Eumolpus in his shifty confidence scheme; with the oath of the gladiator they bind themselves "body and soul" *religiosissime* to their "master" Eumolpus (*Satyricon* 117). By the use of the gladiator's oath to bind themselves as slaves to Eumolpus,[13] they erase the element of compulsion from whatever disgrace or brutalization they might suffer in the service of Eumolpus and his elaborate farce. The gladiator, by his oath, transforms what had originally been an involuntary act to a voluntary one, and so, at the very moment that he becomes a slave condemned to death, he becomes a free agent and a man with honor to uphold. Petronius's vagabonds elevate, even as they legitimate, their degradation.

In all of Roman life there was no more severe commitment that could be made than the gladiator's oath which was unqualified. The gladiator's oath was unconditional, pronounced on enlistment like the soldier's, but infinitely harsher than the soldier's vow.[14] It was a form of dreadful oath sacrifice, closer to the *devotio*, by which the general consecrated himself to a violent death at the hands of the enemy and to the gods of the underworld (the *dii inferi*).[15] The gladiator's oath, however, seems to have been unilateral. The gladiator's oath did not operate on the principle of reciprocity; it demanded nothing from the gods in return for his life.

The Prescriptive Paradigm

Seneca, in his thirty-seventh letter to Lucilius, has made the gladiator's compact ("the most loathsome of contracts," ["turpissimum auctoramentum"]) the most powerful bond ("maximum vinculum") of "the

---

[13] Strictly speaking the *auctoratus* had a unique status: see Antonio Guarino, "I gladiatores e l'*auctoramentum*," *Labeo* 29 (1983), pp. 7–28.

[14] The soldier swore to obey his officers and the regulations of the camp and not to abandon the standards; he consecrated himself, his family, and his possessions to the god(s) in case of his failure to uphold the oath. (The consecration was not always uttered, just as it is not in the modern courtroom when one swears on the Bible, "to tell the truth, the whole truth, and nothing but the truth, so help me god [i.e., or let God strike me dead].") "Le serment une fois prêté, le soldat est enchaîné par un lien religieux. Il ne peut le brisér sans commettre un crime contre les dieux, il encourt leur malédiction et devient *sacer*; on a le droit de le mettre à mort" (Cuq, "Sacramentum," p. 951). See Polybius 6.21; Dionysius of Halicarnassus 10.18, 11.43; Livy 28.27. In the period of the Empire the soldier swore to respect no man above Caesar (Arrian, *Epicteti dissertationes* 1.14). Notice that Epictetus would have one take the soldier's oath to god.

[15] For a more detailed discussion of the *devotio* and its relationship to the arena, see above, pp. 40–46. For the relationship of the *sacramentum* to the *devotio*, see De Ghellink, *Sacramentum*, pp. 145, 148, 227.

good man." (Notice Seneca's conflation of the soldier and gladiator.)[16] The gladiator's oath expresses the highest ideal and commitment of the virtuous man (the philosopher/soldier), a man severe and without hope or illusion; a man who escapes from the humiliation of being under compulsion through enthusiastic complicity:

> You have enlisted [in life] under oath. If any man should say that this is a soft or easy form of soldiering it will only be because he wishes to mock you. But I do not want you to be deceived: the words of this most honorable of compacts are the very same as those of that most foulest of compacts: "to be burned, to be bound, to be slain by the sword." . . . You must die erect and invincible. What difference will it make if you gain a few more days or years? We are born into a world in which no quarter is given. (*Epistulae* 37.1–2)

Seneca's world without quarter is a *munus sine missione*,[17] a particular version of the tournament from which the *editor* (the producer of the games) has determined that no one is to exit alive: "The spectators demand that those who have murdered confront, in turn, those who will murder; they reserve the victor of one bout for but another round of slaughter. Death is the only issue for the men who fight" (*Epistulae* 7.4).

In this world without quarter, this *munus sine missione*, "You *must* die erect and invincible" ("Recto tibi invictoque moriendum est"). Seneca thus, strangely enough, links utter compulsion together with pride and invincibility; the man who has taken the gladiator's oath is compelled to die, but he dies unconquered ("invictus"). The man who takes the gladiator's oath in Epistle 37, moreover, takes it (indeed it must be taken) willingly and freely ("volens" and "libens" [37.2]). Seneca's intention here is to justify the ways of god to men and to release the Powers That Be from any blame or responsibility in the suffering or death of the good man. The universe is an arena where there is no *missio*, no discharge, no hope for mercy or deliverance; nevertheless, through the voluntary contract (*sacra-*

---

[16] This conflation is characteristic throughout the period. Cf. Seneca, *De providentia* 4.4: "Great men, I say, rejoice often in adversity, just as do brave soldiers in war. I once heard Triumphus, a gladiator in the time of Tiberius. . . ." So many Romans, especially in the upper classes, never experience war firsthand during this period that their military language and their experience of the soldier is increasingly modeled on that of the gladiator. See Otto von Regenbogen, "Schmerz und Tod in den Tragödien Senecas," in *Vorträge der Bibliothek Warburg zur Geschichte des Dramas* (Leipzig, 1930), p. 215; Peter Schunck, *Römisches Sterben* (diss., Heidelberg, 1955), pp. 36–39; Frederick Ahl, "Sangre y Arena," in *Lucan: An Introduction* (Ithaca, N.Y., 1976), pp. 82–115, esp. pp. 86, 11–112. Beginning with Marius, even the soldier, ironically, is compelled to model himself on the gladiator: see Theodor Mommsen, *History of Rome* (New York, 1886), vol. 3, p. 246.

[17] For possible references to this type of *munus*, see Livy 41.20.12; Suetonius, *Augustus* 45.3, *Nero* 4.3; Petronius, *Satyricon* 45; Florus 2.8.14; *Corpus inscriptionum Latinarum* (hereafter *CIL*) 10.6012; Lafaye, "Gladiator," p. 1595; Schneider, "Gladiator," col. 765; Friedländer, *Sittengeschichte*, vol. 2, pp. 74–75; Robert, *Les Gladiateurs*, pp. 258–61.

mentum or *auctoramentum gladiatorium*) the murder is changed to an act of mutual complicity, a conspiracy between victim and executioner, gladiator and spectator.[18]

The function of the gladiator's oath in the thirty-seventh letter of Seneca reflects the complex social and psychological role of the figure of the gladiator in the minds of Romans of the late Republic and early Empire. Already in the middle years of the Republic the gladiator had begun to assume a metaphorical role outside of the arena. Terence (2nd century B.C.E.) is the first to infuse the gladiator with a metaphorical weight. In the *Phormio* Terence uses the expression "with the spirit of the gladiator" ("gladiatorio animo") as the equivalent of "without hope or fear," i.e., fierce, unstoppable, irresistible.[19] Six centuries later the metaphor of the *gladiatorius animus* will have approximately the same significance. Augustine, in the *Enarrationes in Psalmos*, compares the ferocious despair of the gladiator to the soul of the sinner (and the Apostle Paul) as the necessary and prerequisite nadir preceding the receipt of God's mercy: "the sinner and unjust man, already despairing of himself, already having the spirit of a gladiator, and thus able to do whatever he wills, since of necessity he must be condemned" ("Unusquisque peccator et iniquus iam de se desperans, iam habens quasi gladiatorium animum, ut ideo faciat quidquid vult, quia necessario damnandus est" [70.1]).[20]

---

[18] Compare Tertullian, *Scorpiace* 6.11, where the author is defending martyrdom and God against the accusation of brutality: "Do you call these remedies, counsels, judgments—spectacles even—the 'savagery' of God? Does God yearn for human blood? I would go so far as to say that he does—if man yearns for the kingdom of God and certain salvation and a second birth. That exchange causes harm and envy to no one in which the reckoning of both benefit and injury is mutual." For Tertullian, martyrdom is a solemn contract, a *sacramentum*, pleasing to both God and man, which one enters voluntarily and with one's eyes open. Therefore the suffering of the martyr is not evidence of cruelty on the part of God. At the same time (cf. 9.6), one *must* endure suffering in following God. The idea of the contract allows Tertullian, like Seneca, to have a benevolent and merciful god who demands and enjoys the spectacle of his devotees' suffering and death.

[19] *Phormio* 964. "Symbolisch für die unerschütterliche Todesbereitschaft und Todesnähe steht für den Römer . . . der Gladiator" (Schunck, *Römisches Sterben*, p. 36). Cf. Ville, *La Gladiature*, p. 47n. 127. See Lucilius, *Satirae* 4.178–81 = Cicero, *Tusculanae disputationes* 4.21 48); Horace, *Satirae* 2.7.96–100; Florus 2.8.14. By the time Horace composed his *Epistles*, the metaphor of the gladiator could be used to express both a fierce ambition *and* a willingness to be completely dependent upon audience and master (both of which Horace declares he has lost [*Epistulae* 1.1, esp. 3–6]). Cyprian's use of the military metaphor for martyrdom (e.g., *Epistulae* 10.5) is based principally on the analogy of the martyr with the gladiator and only secondarily with the legionnaire (cf. 58.8). He compares God looking down with pleasure on the struggles of his soldiers to the emperor and people observing the battles of gladiators. This metaphorical vision of the arena appears already in Paul: "God has exhibited us apostles as last of all, like men sentenced to death [in the arena], because we have become a spectacle to the world, to angels and to men" (1 Cor. 4:9). See John S. Pobee, *Persecution and Martyrdom in the Theology of Paul* (Sheffield, 1985), p. 1.

[20] Cf. *Sermones* 20.3: "With the spirit of a gladiator, since he despairs of his life, he does

In the *Tusculanae Disputationes*, while dismissing the person of the gladiator as worthless and contemptible, "either abandoned men or barbarians" ("aut perditi homines aut barbari"),[21] Cicero allows the gladiator to be (despite himself and through the habit of discipline) one model and paradigm of "the good man," the soldier/philosopher who through his consistent and unflinching fierceness in the face of death and his complete collusion (and even pleasure) in his own powerlessness couples his slavery with honor.[22] It is not a transformation so much as a conjunction; not a reconciliation but a radical dichotomy, an "inverse exaltation."[23]

> Just look at the gladiators, either debased men or foreigners, and consider the blows they endure! Consider how they who have been well-disciplined prefer to accept a blow than ignominiously avoid it! How often it is made clear that they consider nothing other than the satisfaction of their master or the people! Even when they are covered with wounds they send a messenger to their master to inquire his will. If they have given satisfaction to their masters, they are pleased to fall. What even mediocre gladiator ever groans, ever alters the expression on his face? Which one of them acts shamefully either standing or falling? And which of them, even when he does succumb, ever contracts his neck when ordered to receive the blow? (*Tusculanae Disputationes* 2.17.41)[24]

Seneca, in his essay *On Tranquillity* (11.1–6), models his wise man (*sapiens*) after the gladiator. Like the gladiator entering the arena, the wise man enters life having already signed a contract acknowledging that his body is occupied by him only on the sufferance of the master/deity and can be properly demanded of him on a moment's notice.[25] Like the brave gladiator (11.4–5), the wise man, bound by the terms of his con-

---

whatever he can do to satisfy his desires and lusts, just as if he were devoted to death as a sacrificial victim." In the *Ennarationes in Psalmos* (100.1.10), Augustine remarks on the "licentious cruelty" that attends the life of the gladiator.

[21] For "gladiator" or even "noble gladiator" as terms of opprobrium: Cicero, *Pro Sexto Roscio Amerino* 3.8, 6.17; *In Pisonem* 12.28; *In Catilinam* 2.4.7, 4.9; Velleius Paterculus 2.91.3; *Scriptores historiae Augustae, Commodus* 18–19. Septimius Severus comments on the senate's branding Commodus with the epithet "gladiator": "And do none of you fight as gladiators? Why then have some of you bought his shields and those golden helmets of his?" (Dio 76.8.3).

[22] According to Dio (51.7.2), many supporters abandoned Antony and Cleopatra, but their gladiators, "who were among the most despised of people," displayed the utmost valor and fierce loyalty in fighting for them.

[23] See the colorful description of the volatile, ambivalent attitudes that spectators of cruel punishments in the early modern period manifested toward the condemned in part 1 of Michel Foucault's *Discipline and Punish*, trans. Alan Sheridan (New York, 1979).

[24] Cf. Quintilian, *Declamationes* 9.

[25] Cf. Epictetus, *Encheiridion* 11.

tract,[26] must surrender life and limb directly to his divine master, without murmur or hesitation: "I seek not to evade or hang back; you see me prepared to render willingly to you what you gave to me before I was conscious. Away with my life!" (*De tranquillitate* 11.3).

In these passages from Cicero and Seneca (as in Horace's first epistle) it is clear that the gladiator's pleasure is utterly and completely dependent upon the will and pleasure of his master and his audience; it is a result of his intense interaction with them. The gladiator's collusion with the owner/lessor, the producer, and the fans (the *lanista*, the *editor*, and the *amatores*) was not limited to the *sacramentum*; it included cooperation in a rigorous and extended regime of training and discipline, participation in a sacred banquet/inspection of the gladiators on the night preceding the games (the *cena libera*),[27] the festive and colorful parade immediately preceding the games (the *pompa*),[28] and the ritual beating of the new recruits in the arena (Seneca, *Apocolocyntosis* 9.3).[29] This complicity, this attention to the desires of the producer and audience, continued for each fencer through to the climax of the bouts themselves. It was not only the wounded, exhausted, or demoralized gladiator anxiously petitioning for grace who, frozen in anticipation, expected the sign of the audience's pleasure; the victorious gladiator was equally obliged to attend respectfully and patiently the *editor*'s signal to kill. The etiquette of the arena demanded that the victor suspend his attack and regard the *editor* eye to eye until he received the sign. As Georges Lafaye points out, in the language of the arena it was the *editor* or, if present, the emperor or the provincial governor who was said to kill the fallen gladiator, not the victorious combatant who wielded the sword.[30]

Because of his deliberate and scrupulous attention to the will of his masters, on the analogy of the soldier before the eyes of his general, the

---

[26] See esp. *De tranquillitate* 11.4–6.

[27] On the *cena libera*: Ville, *La Gladiature*, p. 366 and n. 47, and p. 455. Ville gives a detailed description of the ceremony of the arena (pp. 386–430) and the extent of collusion demanded in the gladiator's training (p. 227); cf. Friedländer, *Sittengeschichte*, vol. 2, pp. 72–76.

[28] On the *pompa*: Clavel-Lévêque, *L'Empire*, pp. 40–45.

[29] Seneca's Jove proposes that any human credited with being a god should be made over to the *larvae* (persons costumed as the dissatisfied or hungry spirits of the dead) to be beaten by the rod along with the new gladiators.

[30] "Le droit de grâce (*missio*) appartenait à l'*editor*, et autant qu'il semble, à lui seul; aussi en réalité ne dit-on qu'il fait tuer les vaincus, mais qu'il les tue (*occidit*), le vainqueur n'étant que l'instrument de sa volonté" ("Gladiator," col. 1595). Cf. Ville, *La Gladiature*, p. 418 and n. 138; Hopkins, "Murderous Games," p. 18 and n. 27. Both Lafaye and Ville believe that the right of life and death might, in any given instance, be relinquished by the *editor* to the victorious gladiator, e.g., *CIL* 5.5933. For comparisons of god with the *editor* of the games or with the *lanista* see Seneca, *De tranquillitate* 11.5 (where the editor is Fortuna); *Passio Perpetuae* 3.2.

gladiator offered one model for the man of honor.[31] It is important to emphasize that the elevation of the gladiator was not envisaged as an escape or release from collusion with those for whom the suffering and death of the gladiator was a positive pleasure. On the contrary, his "transfiguration" was brought about by that very collusion, by the completeness of that collusion.[32] The most esteemed of the gladiators took pains at the very least to appear to take active pleasure in the struggle right up to the moment of death.[33] The greater the benefit, indeed the pleasure, that the gladiator could find (or appear to his audience to find) in his condition, the more complete was his miraculous transformation into an ideal type of the soldier/philosopher. Now the relationship between the master and slave, executioner and victim, was not one of mutual status but of mutual aid; they provided each other with mutual pleasure, mutual satisfaction, mutual empowerment.[34]

[31] Seneca, in his essay *De providentia* (4.4–16), articulates this position: "Valor is avid for danger . . . since even what it must suffer is a part of glory. Warriors glory in their wounds and jubilantly display their flowing blood. . . . The raw recruit turns pale at the thought of a wound, but the veteran looks undaunted upon his own gore. . . . Just so, god hardens, reviews, and disciplines those of whom he approves, whom he loves. . . . Not a man of these will say . . . 'My general has treated me unjustly,' but rather, 'He thinks well of me.' So those who are called upon to suffer what would make cowards and ignoble men weep may say, 'God has deemed us worthy instruments of his purpose to discover how much human beings can endure.' . . . Do you imagine that the Lacedaemonians hate their children when they test their mettle by lashing them in public? Their own fathers call upon them to endure bravely the blows of the whip, and ask them, though mangled and half-dead, to keep offering their wounded bodies to further wounds."

[32] Cf. the famous greeting offered to Claudius by the "sailors" about to slaughter each other in his mock sea battle in 52 C.E.: "Hail, Emperor; we who are about to die salute you!" ("have imperator, morituri te salutant!" [Suetonius, *Claudius* 21.6]). Minucius Felix, *Octavius*: "How beautiful a spectacle for God when a Christian comes into close quarters with pain, is matched with threats and punishments and tortures, confronts with a laugh the din of death and the hideous executioner. . . . What soldier would not face risks more boldly under the eye of his general?" (37.1–2; cf. 36.8–9). Cyprian, *Epistula* 58.8: "Men are tried and prepared for the secular combat and think it great glory of their honor if it happens to them to be crowned with the people looking on and the emperor present. Behold a sublime and a great and a glorious contest for the reward of the heavenly crown, that God looks upon us struggling and, casting his eyes upon those whom he has deigned to make sons, he enjoys the spectacle of our combat." When Tertullian uses the closely related metaphor of the Greek athletic *agon* for the martyr, God becomes the *agonothetes* (the producer of the games) and the Holy Spirit becomes the *xystarches* (the trainer). See *Ad martyras* 3.

[33] Cf. Aulus Gelius, *Noctes Atticae* 2.27.2. Minucius Felix (37.4–5; see also n. 32 above), like the authors of the *Passio Perpetuae* (e.g., 6.1), emphasizes not just suffering but simultaneous joyful, laughing cooperation. It is the joy that is the victim's revolt and revenge against dishonor and powerlessness. Compare the light banter and nonchalance of the martyrs at the *cena libera* that preceded their martyrdom in the arena in the *Passio Perpetuae* 5.4. Lactantius (*Divinae institutiones* 6.17) speaks of the "happy and unconquered patience" of the martyrs.

[34] Tertullian, *Scorpiace* 6.11 (quoted in n. 19 above). In Josephus's treatise *Contra Api-*

Are you trying to say that to recline at a banquet and to be tortured are equally beneficial? Does that seem strange to you? . . . I assert that the benefits are the same for the man who triumphs and the man who is borne before his chariot unconquered in spirit. . . . Why are you amazed if I claim that there are times when to be burned, to be wounded, to be killed, to be bound, help a man, and at times even please him? (*Epistulae* 71.21–22)

The glory given to the brave gladiator was impossible without the master and without an audience. The brave gladiator was not liberated from, or raised to a level with, his master. On the contrary, he observed his master (who was both lord and spectator) with concentration in order to satisfy him. One can compare this stance with Seneca's personified Virtue, who "like a good soldier endures his wounds, counts his scars, and pierced with projectiles, dying, loves him for whom he falls: the general [or emperor]" ("ut bonus miles feret volnera, numerabit cicatrices, et transverberatus telis moriens amabit eum, pro quo cadet, imperatorem" [*De vita beata* 15.5]).[35] Lucan's extraordinary Scaeva, with his superhuman zest for pain and mutilation, wishes that he might be given the chance to die before the eyes of Caesar (6.158).

While Seneca, in his essay *De constantia sapientis*, remarks that people considered the gladiator a "man of strength" ("vir fortis") only by an abuse of words, he describes the attitude of the "gladiatores fortissimi" to their audience: "Among the gladiators of the greatest fortitude, one suppresses any sign of his wounds and digs in his heels. The other, regarding the clamoring people, signifies to them that his wound is nothing and that he will not tolerate any intercession" (*De constantia sapientis* 16.2).

The gladiator's life could be seen as a model of severe soldierly discipline, of the soldier's *askesis*. Even *observing* the games could be imagined as a form of soldierly training. According to Pliny the Younger (late 1st to early 2nd century C.E.), the emperor Trajan, as the *editor* of splendid games, produced "nothing spineless or flabby, nothing that would soften or break the manly spirit of the audience, but a spectacle which inspired the audience to noble wounds and to despise death, since even in the bodies of slaves and criminals the love of praise and desire for victory could be seen" (*Panegyricus* 33.1).

In Livy's history (21.42–43), Hannibal extends to his prisoners of war the opportunity to fight to the death in single combat before the eyes of

---

onem (2.232–35), the Jewish martyr takes pride in suffering the torments of a death spectacle and compares such a death favorably with the "easy" death of the soldier; death on the sand is, for Josephus, as for Seneca, a particularly harsh form of soldiering calling for exceptional valor. Cf. Lucan 4.277–78: "They will rejoice to shed their blood" ("gaudebit sanguine fuso").

[35] The word *imperator* can stand for either.

his assembled soldiers. The captives eagerly contend for the chance to fight, enabling Hannibal to demonstrate to his soldiers how greatly the glory of winning *or* falling in battle was preferable to the piteous plight of the captive.[36] Livy also tells us that the gladiatorial games introduced to the East by Antiochus IV Epiphanes (after serving fourteen years as a hostage in Rome) kindled in many young men an enthusiasm for arms: "et armorum studium plerisque iuvenum accendit" (41.20). According to Ennodius, the fifth-century bishop of Pavia, the consuls of the year 105 B.C.E., Rutilius and Manlius, put on the first publicly sponsored gladiatorial games so that they might give the plebs, accustomed to peace, a flavor of what occurred on the battlefield.[37] [Julius Capitolinus] informs us that the Roman soldiers destined for battle were obliged to witness gladiatorial combats, with their wounds and steel and stripped-down men springing to the attack, in order to prevent their being terrified of the armed enemy or of wounds and blood.[38] Gladiatorial arenas have been discovered at the headquarters and garrisons of the legions, as at Carnuntum, Sarmizegetusa, and Aquincum.[39] The practice of using the coaches (*doctores*) of the gladiators to instruct the legions began with the consul P. Rutilius (105 B.C.E.), according to the first-century writer Valerius Maximus (2.3.2).

But observing the gladiator was not always or necessarily an inspiring experience. *The failure to cooperate*, the inability or unwillingness of the gladiator to go eagerly to his slaughter, filled the audience with disgust and wrath and deprived the gladiator of his glory. According to Cicero, "In the case of battles between gladiators and in the case [of others] of the lowest condition and fortune of the human race, we are inclined to despise the timid suppliant and those who plead for their lives, but we desire those to live who offer themselves up to death bravely and fiercely" (*Pro Milone* 34.92).[40] "Why are the people angered," inquires Seneca, "and consider themselves injured, when the gladiator does not gladly perish? Rather, they judge themselves to be despised and they turn, in face in gesture and in passion, from spectators to adversaries" (*De ira* 1.2.4).[41]

---

[36] Cf. Polybius 3.62–63.

[37] *Panegyricus dictus regi Theodorico* 213.25 (ed. Vogel).

[38] *Scriptores historiae Augustae* 21.8.7; cf. Ennodius's *Panegyricus* 13.19 (ed. Vogel). Cicero is inclined to agree with those who find the current use of free men and volunteers cruel and inhuman, "but in the days when it was a criminal who crossed swords in the death struggle, there could be no better discipline against pain and death, at any rate for the eye" (*Tusculanae disputationes* 2.17.41).

[39] Cf. Friedländer, *Sittengeschichte*, vol. 2, pp. 57–58, 61.

[40] Cicero goes on to say that if the Romans are willing to spare a brave gladiator who shows no sign of cowardly cringing, so they are obliged to pardon Milo, who is able to show a *firma frons* in the midst of his troubles.

[41] Cf. Lactantius, *Institutiones divinae* 6.20: "I ask now whether they can be pious and

Seneca's thwarted spectators cry: "Kill him, beat him, burn him! Why does he run on the steel so timidly? Why does he slay with so little verve? Why is he such a Scrooge about dying?" (*Epistulae* 7.5).[42]

In his famous description of the noonday games (the *meridianum spectaculum*) in Letter 7 (as in Letter 94), Seneca, a man whose own creative imagination, like that of his nephew Lucan, was filled with erotically luxuriant scenes of violence, expresses an abhorrence of violence. But if one looks at the array of Seneca's uses of, and reactions to, violence, it is possible to assert that what angers Seneca in these two letters is a particular form of violence, that is, violence characterized by naked victimization, the absence of those aspects of collaboration which he himself admired and which he believed ennobled both participant and spectator.[43] The "gladiators" in this offensive spectacle are condemned criminals; they are without defensive armor, and they are whipped into the fatal fray ("plagis agitur in vulnera" [7.5]; cf. "nudus inermisque producitur" [95.33]). The failure of the victim to cooperate broke the contract by which the slave and subject gained their honor. (The Romans' expectations of the brave gladiator were identical to their expectations of the sacrificial victim: the victim in a Roman sacrifice was led to the altar by a slack rope, in order that it might not seem to be dragged by force; any show of resistance on the part of the victim was considered a bad omen.)[44]

---

just men who, not only allow those who are set up under the mark of death and who plead for mercy to be killed, but who even demand it. . . . Why, they even order those struck and lying prostrate to be sought again and have their bodies torn apart by blows, lest anyone delude them by feigning death."

[42] In *De tranquillitate* (11.5) Seneca imagines the goddess Fortuna as the *editor*: " 'Why should I save you,' she said, 'weak and quivering beast? All the more will you be mangled and stabbed because you do not know how to offer your throat.' "

[43] One has only to read, to begin with, *De ira*, *Oedipus*, *Thyestes*, or *Hippolytus* in order to get very strong doses of the violence of Seneca's imagination. Seneca was, like Lucan, and Augustine's Alypius, fascinated and obsessed with the violence he often decries. Like Lucan (and like Tertullian, Lactantius, and Cyprian), Seneca creates luxurious and erotic fantasies of violence starring victims with whom he deeply sympathized. It is a mistake to think that Seneca *simply* abhorred violence. The loathing does not preclude the loving or the need. (One of the most interesting scenes in all of Seneca, and the one which most closely mirrors the psychological strategy of the Christian apologists for martyrdom is the "fair spectacle" of the barbarian gladiator committing suicide as a revolt against the farce and the killing in the arena [*Epistulae* 70.26–27]). It is easy to read both "pagan" and Christian tirades against the arena in a vacuum. But it is important to assess Seneca's reaction to the mid-day spectacle (*meridianum spectaculum*) in relation to his other passages on violence and on the gladiator. For example, the Seneca of the *Consolatio ad Helviam* (17.1) finds in the games a diversion from private anxieties (his only complaint being that they are not sufficiently diverting!).

[44] Cf. Petronius frag. 1 (= Servius, *In Vergiliam commentarius* 3.57); Pliny, *Historia naturalis* 8.183; Servius, *In Vergiliam* 2.104 and 140; Macrobius, *Saturnalia* 3.5.8. Voluntariness in sacrifice was of tremendous importance (even if it was a fiction): "Le sacrifice est

If watching the brave gladiator fight and die was a positive *askesis* for the spectators, watching the gladiator cringe or tremble was a debilitating and shameful experience for them. The absence of cooperation between the actors and the audience turned the witnesses of this uplifting miracle into perpetrators of a sordid spectacle, ugly and nasty for themselves as well as their victims (both clearly and emphatically exposed now as victims).[45] Instead of providing the opportunity, the test, for glory, the games become naked homicides ("mera homicidia"). The people were turned into executioners, revealed as bloodthirsty beasts. Seneca, who often admired the gladiator and identified with him, was disgusted by the sight of this parody of a military encounter. The audience, in the eyes of Seneca, was being punished and humiliated by its participation in these rites of cruelty no less than the *damnati* in the arena. "What have you done," Seneca asks his fellow spectators, "to deserve watching these games?"

The debased gladiator's love of death (*amor mortis*), his enthusiastic cooperation in his own death, redeemed both himself and the audience. His terrors, his panic, his inability or unwillingness to cooperate in the violent ritual revealed to Seneca the artificial and pathetic aspects of the entire display; it reduced the miraculous paradox to bitter irony.

It is necessary then, to separate the increased recognition of, and identification with, the gladiator from any awakening of conscience, any newfound sensitivity to, or revulsion against, violence in Roman society. Compassion for the gladiator was seldom sympathy with the victim. Many factors inured the Roman to bloodshed, as A. W. Lintott has described succinctly in his book *Violence in Republican Rome*.[46] These factors include the practice of decimation, in which the brave and guiltless were executed indiscriminately along with the cowardly and guilty; mass executions of prisoners of war, deserters, and rebels; public and private

d'autant plus certain, les victimes d'autant mieux acceptées par les dieux, que les condamnés sont volontaires" (Aline Rousselle, *Porneia: De la maîtrise du corps à la privation sensorielle* [Paris, 1983], p. 155). See Jan Bremmer, "Scapegoat Rituals in Ancient Greece," *Harvard Studies in Classical Philology* 87 (1983), pp. 307–8; Walter Burkert, *Structure and History in Greek Mythology and Ritual* (Berkeley, 1979), p. 70; *Homo Necans* (Berkeley, 1983), pp. 3–4. Roman criminals were executed in the manner of sacrificial victims, as offerings to the god: see Theodor Mommsen, *Römisches Strafrecht* (1899), pp. 899–905; Kiefer, *Sexual Life in Ancient Rome*, p. 80.

[45] One can compare this to the experience of a modern audience watching a match between two old or debilitated boxers: the members of the audience feel ashamed and embarrassed for themselves as well as for the contestants.

[46] A. W. Lintott, *Violence in Republican Rome* (Oxford, 1960), pp. 41–42. Cf. Hopkins, "Murderous Games," pp. 1–2, 27–30; Kiefer, *Sexual Life in Ancient Rome*, pp. 65–106; T. P. Wiseman, *Catullus and his World* (London, 1985), pp. 5–10. Violence also penetrated the Roman system of education (*disciplina*): Ausonius (*Epistulae* 22.24–25) remarks that the school resounded with cries and thrashings.

executions and chastisements of all sorts (especially of slaves); torture of witnesses (in the imperial period extended to the upper classes); the liability of all the slaves of a household when one slave has committed a serious crime against the master; the pitiless vendetta. The writers of the Neronian period, in particular, gloried in the violence they abhorred. They not only described but created scenes of violence against victims with whom they could simultaneously identify and sympathize. They were at once both victims and spectators.[47]

"One solution alone remains to us: to die with unconquered neck."

The glorification of abasement and pleasure in abasement made its appearance in Rome in the last generation of the Roman Republic and gained intensity in the early imperial period. This phenomenon, which is often rightly associated with early Christianity, had other spheres of operation, other foci apart from the Lamb of God.[48] It was not an isolated or sectarian tendency, nor one based (as one might expect) principally or exclusively in the nonprivileged classes. It was, rather, a widespread social phenomenon, which attracted many members of the free and privileged classes in Rome.

In 46 B.C.E., according to Dio, Roman knights including one son of a praetor, fought in single combat in Caesar's games, alongside captives and men condemned to death. A Roman senator, he adds, petitioned unsuccessfully to be allowed to fight in full armor (Dio 43.23.4–5). Suetonius adds to the list two men of senatorial rank (*Caesar* 39.1). Despite the prohibition (38 B.C.E.) of senatorial and equestrian participation in gladiatorial games after the death of Caesar,[49] a Roman senator, Quintus Vitellius, appeared as a gladiator in the *munus* given by Octavian at the dedication of the temple of Caesar (Dio 51.22.4). We hear again from Dio (56.25.7) that in 11 C.E. Augustus gave permission to the Roman knights to fight in the arena, "since the prohibition was of no use." The dour Tiberius felt compelled to punish those aristocrats who tried to cir-

---

[47] E.g., Lucan, *Bellum civile* 2.173–232, 4.562–70, 8.665–90, 9.766–88; Seneca, *De ira* 3.19.1–5; *Oedipus* 952–79; *Thyestes* 759–74; *Phaedra* 1093–1114; *Epistulae* 14.5.

[48] It is a mistake to think that the opposition of Christians to the gladiatorial games was necessarily or principally a result of their opposition to violence per se or to the public emulation of the bloody figure of the gladiator. As long as martyrdom was of value, violence was of value. The martyr was, in many ways, competing with the gladiator—but under a different *editor*.

[49] Cf. Dio 48.43.3; Friedländer, *Sittengeschichte*, vol. 2, p. 16; Ville, *La Gladiature*, p. 256.

cumvent the prohibitions (Suetonius, *Tiberius* 35.2).[50] Although Tiberius attempted to enforce the ban on *boni* in the arena, we hear that despite his measures two knights fought at the *munus* of Drusus and Germanicus in 15 C.E. (Dio 57.14.3). Dio is again the source for the story that Gaius Caligula put to death twenty-six knights, some for having consumed their patrimony, and others for having engaged in gladiatorial combats (59.10.2).

Under Nero participation in games became particularly attractive (as well as frequently involuntary).[51] Apparently neither the death of Nero nor the senatorial prohibition against participation in gladiatorial *munera* kept the knights and senators away from the arena, for according to Tacitus the emperor Vitellius was compelled to renew the prohibition (Tacitus, *Historia* 2.62.4), and Juvenal, writing under Domitian, mocks a Gracchus in the arena (*Satirae* 8.199ff.). It was not only free men (and women)[52] already lost through poverty or debt, nor victims of imperial whimsy that were attracted to the arena; even prosperous equestrians and senators repeatedly entered the arena, despite the pain of social stigma and/or perpetual political impotence.[53] The gain was somehow considered greater than the loss.

What was it that drew free men to discard community, status, dignity, and power to fight in the arena, in the space allotted to the ruined and condemned?

The appearance of the otherwise unknown aristocrat Gracchus in the arena as a net fighter (*retiarius*) is described in Juvenal's biting account as a shame and a scandal (8.199ff.). The "noble" *retiarius* carried the trident and net, weaponry of the most theatrical kind, and without even the more conventional (and, Juvenal implies, more respectable) arms of some of the other weapons divisions,[54] without even a shield or helmet to hide his disgrace. His face, exposed and lifted up to the audience, was recognized by everyone. Nevertheless, according to Juvenal, Gracchus himself despised the defensive armor and offensive weapons that might have softened his ignominy, or the helmet that might have hidden his shame. Ac-

---

[50] Cf. the *senatus consultum* of 19 C.E., inscribed on a stone discovered near Larino in Italy, which attempts to restrain the well-born from the stage and arena. See Barbara Levick, "The Senatus Consultum from Larinum," *Journal of Roman Studies* 73 (1983), pp. 98–99.

[51] Cf. Ville, *La Gladiature*, p. 259.

[52] E.g., Petronius, *Satyricon* 45; Juvenal, *Satirae* 1.22–23; Tacitus, *Annales* 15.32; Dio 62.17.3–5.

[53] In most cases, the *auctoramentum* kept one from the senate and the equestrian order, from the municipal *curiae* (*Fontes iuris Romanae antiquae* 1.49; cf. Tertullian, *De spectaculis* 22), from appearing as a witness, and often from cemeteries (*CIL* 11.2.6528); cf. Hopkins, "Murderous Games," pp. 23–24.

[54] But see Martial's praise for Hermes, who had served with the weapons of a *retiarius* as well as those of other weapons divisions (5.24).

cording to Suetonius (*Tiberius* 35.2), wild and profligate men of the senatorial and equestrian orders outflanked the obstacles that the senate employed to keep them from the stage or sand and willingly bore the stigma of a sentence bringing infamy ("famosi iudicii notam sponte subibant"). Dio tells us that the Roman knights who descended into the arena "held in contempt their disgrace [*atimia*]" and the loss of civil rights that this entailed (56.25.7).[55] In other words, *they despised their degradation.*[56] "In this way," he writes, "they incurred death instead of disenfranchisement, for they fight just as much as ever, especially since their fights were eagerly witnessed."

Donning the armor of a *retiarius* or a *secutor* or a *Thraex*[57] was an alternative to the strategy of the foremost citizens, who, according to Tacitus, "were compelled to save their grandeur by servility" ("primores civitatis quibus claritudo sua obsequiis protegenda erat" [*Annales* 3.65.2]): "The fiercest had fallen on the line or in the proscriptions [of the civil wars]. As for the rest of the nobles, the prompter each to servility, the higher he was raised in wealth and honor" (*Annales* 1.2). The importance of the social and psychological role of the gladiator among the free and privileged classes in Rome developed apace with the notion that with the failure of the aristocratic republic, *dignitas*, social worth, had become a word whose only content was humiliation. One finds in Roman literature, from Cicero on, a sense that the price exacted for political, social, and economic status (indeed, for life) had become self-abasement and that honor and dishonor had become synonymous. The traditional testimonials of power, freedom, and pride began to signal *as well* powerlessness, enslavement, and humiliation.[58]

---

[55] Cf. the *senatus consultum* from Larinum, lines 11–13 (Levick, "The Senatus Consultum," pp. 98–99, 108–10, 112).

[56] Even those aristocrats who ended up in the arena as a result of bankruptcy (see Seneca, *Epistulae* 99.13 and Michael Winterbottom, ed., *The Minor Declamations Ascribed to Quintilian* [Berlin, 1984], nos. 260.21–24, 302) may have resembled Juvenal's Rutilus (*Satirae* 11.9ff.; cf. 8.199–200), who threw away his fortune with the same spirit of abandon and self-despair with which he threw away his honor. Cf. Tacitus, *Historia* 2.62.10. (Propertius [4.8] enjoys imagining his extravagant rival ending up eating the "fodder" ["sagina"] of a gladiator.) In general, the gladiatorial bands (*familiae*) were recruited from the same sources and were often identical to the supporters of the revolutionary movements and conspiracies of the last years of the Republic. Cf. Lafaye: "Au temps des guerres civiles, l'*auctoratio* attira autour des chefs de partis une foule d'aventuriers prêts à toutes les besognes" ("Gladiator," p. 1574). E.g., Caesar, *De bello civile* 3.21.4; Cicero, *Pro Sulla* 19.54–55; Dio 39.7.2, 8.1, 51.8.2; Appian, *Bellum civile* 5.30 + 33; Friedländer, *Sittengeschichte*, vol. 2, pp. 51, 56–57, 66. Cicero is not speaking metaphorically when he accuses Catiline of being the intimate of gladiators (e.g., *In Catilinam* 2.7 and 9, 2.24).

[57] These are names for gladiators trained and armed in different weapons divisions.

[58] See, for example, Lucan's description of Caesar's "triumphant" entry into Rome during the civil wars (*Bellum civile* 5.381–402).

The concept of "the equal opponent" was fundamental to the Roman warrior's concept of glory. As in a modern boxing match or a bullfight, in an unequal fight both the contestants were debased, regardless of their rank and skills.[59] (The *secutor* who pursued the fleeing Gracchus across the arena was, according to Juvenal, doubly disgraced: he was pitted against a noble, and the noble was at the same time a poor match [8.209–10].) The very same persons, victories, or skills that might find honor in one situation were automatically worthless or debased in another. The Roman aristocrat had been able to compete for and potentially gain honor, glory, and *dignitas* while there had existed the possibility of a relative equality of means and power between himself and the other members of his class. When the contest was decided at Actium in 31 B.C.E. in favor of Octavian, "the prospect of autonomous military commands and consequent glory had been virtually extinguished" (W. G. Runciman).[60] Competition did not cease, but without that matching of forces the possibility of competing with all one's wits and powers against a worthy foe, an equal opponent, was absent, and thus a fundamental condition of *gloria* and *dignitas* was absent. Without the equal opponent there could be no valor. Now one was compelled to elevate oneself by prostration, by kissing feet and other extremities. Lucan traces back the beginnings of this degradation to the contest in the first century B.C.E. between Marius and Sulla and the bloodbath that followed Marius's taking of Rome: "The one hope of salvation that remained was to press trembling lips to that polluted hand. Oh, degenerate people! Though a thousand swords obey these new signals of death, it hardly would befit men to buy long centuries of life at such a price, much less a short and shameful respite till Sulla returns" (*Bellum civile* 2.113–18).[61]

Epictetus discusses at length the price for climbing the social ladder and for becoming "Caesar's friend": " 'How many things must I endure and undergo, to become a distinguished person? How often must I suffer robbery and from how many?' 'You kiss the hands of other people's slaves in order to get those great and splendid honors, becoming the slave of men who are not even free? Then, if you please, you walk in splendor as praetor and consul?' " (*Dissertationes* 4).[62] The philosopher addresses a Roman aristocrat who has been twice consul:

---

[59] Plutarch's Alexander (*De Alexandri magni fortuna* 1.331), though swift of foot, cannot be enticed into entering the Olympic games. If he wins, it will be over common men; if he loses, his opponents will have conquered a king. Therefore he declined, declaring, "The contest was unequal."

[60] W. G. Runciman, "The Sociologist and the Historian," *Journal of Roman Studies* 76 (1980), p. 263.

[61] Dio (59.27.1–2) describes Caligula extending his hand and even his foot for senators to kiss.

[62] Arrian, *Epicteti dissertationes* 4.1.148–49. In the *Encheiridion* 25, the philosopher complains of the sycophancy required to live among the great. Cf. Tacitus, *Annales* 3.65.8:

"You are just as much a slave yourself as those who have been thrice sold."
"How can I be a slave," he says, "my father is free, my mother is free, no one
has bought me; nay I am a senator, and a friend of Caesar, I have been consul
and have many slaves." . . . "Does it seem to you slavery to act against your
will, under compulsion and with groaning?" "I grant that," he says, "but
who can compel me except Caesar, who is lord of all?" "Why, then, your
own lips confess that you have one master. . . . [R]ealize that you are a slave
in a large household. You are just like the people of Nicopolis, who are wont
to cry aloud, 'By Caesar's fortune we are free.' "63

For Epictetus, climbing the social ladder is a gradual descent, and the life
of a senator "the noblest and sleekest slavery of all."64 It was a "topsy-
turvy" universe, where master was slave,65 virtue crime,66 victory defeat,
peace war,67 brother enemy.

The Roman aristocrat's willingness to identify with, and assume, the
role of the gladiator was a result, in part, of his feeling himself to be in a
similar desperate predicament: "Unhappy they who are raised to high
places. . . . They are like victims fattened for sacrifice, and garlanded for
execution" (Minucius Felix, *Octavius* 37.7). The world *outside* the arena,
the political world, came to be perceived as a theatre where every word
was studied, every emotion feigned. "The higher a man's rank," Tacitus

---

"The story is handed down that Tiberius, as often as he left the senate house, used to ex-
claim in Greek to the effect: 'What men are these, so ready to be slaves!' Clearly such abject
servility on the part of the senators disgusted even Tiberius, who was himself no friend of
public liberty."

63 Arrian, *Epicteti dissertationes* 4.1.6–14 (transl. Matheson). Cicero dreams of Octavian
with a scourge (*flagellum*), a weapon usually employed for punishing slaves (Suetonius,
Augustus 94.9). For a succinct description of the often bitter terror and humiliation to which
the still-haughty aristocracy was subject, see Keith Hopkins and Graham Burton, "Ambition and Withdrawal: The Senatorial Aristocracy Under the Emperor," in *Death and Renewal: Sociological Studies in Roman History*, vol. 2 (Cambridge, 1983), pp. 120–23.

64 See Pliny, *Panegyricus* (88.1–2) for a description of "high-handed" imperial slaves and
freedmen bestowing or withholding priesthoods, praetorships, and consulships to aristocrats. Juvenal laments the complicity required for success: "If you want to be anybody now-
adays you must dare some crime that merits Gyara or prison. It is to these crimes that men
owe their pleasure-grounds and palaces, their fine tables and old silver goblets with goats
standing out in relief" (1.73–75; cf. 3.49–50). The nurse of Seneca's Phaedra: "It isn't easy
to dare a crime mandated by another, but truly, whoever fears the orders of a king must
lay aside and drive from his mind all thought of honor; shame ministers poorly to the do-
minion of a king" (*Phaedra* 427–30). Cf. Lucan 4.484–95.

65 "Alas how wretched it is to learn to serve when you have been taught to command!"
(Publilius Syrus 250). For the inversion of the master/slave relationship, see also 224, 363;
Seneca, *Epistulae* 4.8, 9.22.

66 Lucan 1.667–68 (abominable crime is called heroism), 6.148 (virtue is a crime in civil
war), 4.243–55 (glorying in guilt); Tacitus, *Historia* 1.2.14–16.

67 Peace as an illusion cloaking war, or a strategic feint: Lucan 4.204–10, 222, 267–92,
531–33, 5.381–402.

remarks bitterly, "the more eager his hypocrisy" (*Annales* 1.7.1).[68] The higher one climbed, the closer one got to the emperor, the more necessary the duplicity.[69] Moreover, one had the sense that one could not hide one's lost face behind a senator's cloak or the titles of consul or praetor. All knew and saw one's nakedness and humiliation. Prominence meant simply nakedness exposed. Seeing a decorated person very proud of his broad purple stripe,[70] Lucian's Demonax took hold of the cloth and whispered in his ear, "This attire did not make its original wearer anything but a sheep" (41). The former slave Epictetus asks a Roman worthy, "Do I not know how you became praetor, where you got the consulship, who gave it to you?" (Arrian, *Epicteti dissertationes* 4.1.149).[71]

The paradox of the social pariah, the irrevocably socially debased creature, exalted by its commitment to its own annihilation, became increasingly familiar, even insistent, in the literature of the imperial period at the very same time as its inversion (the paradox of the socially and politically elevated person utterly debased by his commitment to life and hope). The first paradox was, in part, a direct response to the second. Seneca despises the caged, mutilated and degraded King Telesphorus of Rhodes for clinging to life at the price of his honor (*Epistulae* 70.6–7; cf. *De ira* 3.17.3–4), and brands his famous aphorism, "Where there's life there's hope," as "effeminatissima."[72] In sharp contrast, he praises the beast fighter (*bestiarius*) destined to the arena who strangles himself with the outhouse sponge: "Oh man of strength, worthy of being given his choice of fates! How bravely he would have wielded the sword, with what spirit he would have leapt into the depth of the sea or off a sheer cliff!" (*Epistulae* 70.21).

"The foulest death," Seneca explains, "is preferable to the fairest slavery" ("Praeferendam esse spurcissimam mortem servituti mundissimae" [*Epistulae* 70.21]).

In a powerful and eloquent scene, Lucan's entrapped Caesarian sol-

---

[68] For the degree of hypocrisy required to survive under Domitian, see Pliny, *Panegyricus* 2.2 + 5, 3.4, 66.3.

[69] Augustine, in the *De civitate dei* (6.10), bitterly reproves Seneca "the actor," worshiping what he censured, performing acts of which he disapproved, and adoring what he condemned.

[70] The *latus clavus* was the broad purple stripe worn on the toga of a man of senatorial status.

[71] The emperor is likewise dishonored by the lack of an equal opponent. His glory is false. "You have entered as a contestant at the Olympic games, but none other besides you; you gain the crown, the victory you do not gain" (Seneca, *De providentia* 4.2). Pliny mocks the false victories of Domitian ("falsae simulacra victoriae" [*Panegyricus* 16.3]) as Suetonius mocks those of Caligula and Nero.

[72] The captive German king Maboduus, once proud, gradually loses his reputation through his "excessive clinging to life (*nimiam vivendi cupidinem]*" (Tacitus, *Annales* 2.63.5). Cf. Marcus Aurelius 10.7.

diers, under the leadership of their commander Vulteius, wait until their captors hold out the hope of pardon and life, and then, devoted to death, commit exceptionally bloody and joyous mutual suicide before the gaze of the Pompeian soldiers (*Bellum civile* 4.402–581).

The Aristeia

In a fundamental way, the arena reconstructed the traditional conditions of honor. Seneca, in his essay *On Providence*, remarks, "A gladiator reckons it ignominious to be paired with his inferior in skill and considers him to have conquered without glory who has conquered without peril" (*De providentia* 3.4). The possibility of a gladiator's victory was not denied, but the victory must be a difficult one, perhaps even an impossible one.[73] The crucial element in the elevation of the gladiator was less a victory than a contest that tested the gladiator's fierce *amor mortis*.[74] Here, on the sand, one could not feign valor and survive by cowardice. According to Tertullian (*Apologeticus* 15.5), a hot iron (*cauterium*) was used in the arena to expose those who cravenly feigned death. Seneca bitterly mocks D. Junius Brutus, who when ordered to bare his throat to the axe exclaimed, "I will bare my throat if only I might live!" For Seneca, Brutus's death was *turpissima*; he behaved so basely that he deserved to live! (*Epistulae* 82.12).[75] The gladiator's struggle was required to be a desperate one in order to gain him honor. Desperation was the condition of his glory. But in that struggle, provided he fought *gladiatorio animo*, with contempt of life and hope, of status and future, he could gain glory.[76] The fierceness of the gladiator was emulated by the philosopher Seneca. Using metaphors drawn from the *ludus* and the arena, Seneca belittles Lucilius for wasting his time on philosophical trifles while ignoring life and death issues: "It is folly to continue to go through the motions when the signal for your bout has been sounded. Away with the practice weapons; you

[73] Concerning the gladiator's epitaph "He fell and he conquered," Robert comments: "On sent l'admiration qu'il y a dans le membre de phrase: *epipton te kai enikon*, ces morts et ces victoires également glorieuses" (*Les Gladiateurs*, 254–55). Cf. Dionysius of Halicarnassus, *Antiquitates Romanae* 3.12.2–3.

[74] Polybius 3.62; Livy 21.42 + 44.

[75] Caligula's demand that the man who devoted himself to the arena for the health of the emperor fulfill his vow may have been motivated by a similar contempt for false bravado (Suetonius, *Gaius* 27.2).

[76] What was required was the fierce offhanded attitude to death of a severe man (*vir acer*), a Mucius Scaevola or a Regulus. Notice Minucius Felix's comparison of the spirit of Christian martyrs facing torture to that of Mucius, Aquilius, and Regulus (Minucius, *Octavia* 37.4–5).

need the kind of weapons that will take you through a fight to the finish" (*Epistulae* 117.25).

In the artistic representations of gladiatorial bouts as much weight is given to the defeated as to the victorious. As Georges Ville points out, it is not the victory but "the moment of truth" which overwhelmingly dominates the large number of artistic representations of gladiatorial bouts (pp. 410, 423–24).[77]

In a passage where Seneca compares the gladiator's (and soldier's) eagerness to engage in battle with the philosopher's desire to engage with an equal and worthy opponent, especially fortune or death, it is not victory but fierceness which is applauded: "Warriors glory in their wounds; they rejoice to display their flowing blood. . . . The man who returns from battle unhurt may have fought as well, but he who returns wounded is held in higher esteem" (*De providentia* 4.4).[78]

A savage *amor mortis* transformed one. Tacitus tells us of the mock sea battle that Claudius waged in 52 C.E. between nineteen thousand forced and unwilling combatants, prevented from fleeing by armed guards. After a faltering start (the men refused to fight), the battle, "although between condemned criminals, was fought with the spirit of free men" (*Annales* 12.56).[79] Compare Florus's description (2nd century C.E.) of the renegade gladiator Spartacus: "Spartacus himself was killed fighting on the front line with great courage, like an *imperator*" (2.8.14). One can compare this with the epitaph of the fallen gladiator Kinyras: "He won, and killed his opponent, but died a valiant hero."[80] The brave gladiator could become, like Martial's (1st century C.E.) hero and gladiator Hermes, "the glory of universal Mars" ("gloria Martis universi" [5.24]).[81]

In the arena the ground rules for glory were reestablished on the model of the Homeric *aristeia* and the romanticized vision of the single combat (so much more aristocratic than the phalanx!) of the early Roman Republic. The warrior had his moment in the spotlight, on center stage, and could fight alone, in splendid single combat, with splendid armor, removed temporarily from the tawdry toiling and moiling of political life.[82]

---

[77] "In dem Shauder und der Entzückung . . . erlebten die Zuschauer auch selbst den Tod der Kämpfer und das Mysterium tremendum des Todes" (A. D. Leeman, "Das Todeserlebnis im Denken Senecas," *Gymnasium* 78 [1971], pp. 322–33). On "the moment of truth," see Werner Rutz, "*Amor Mortis* bei Lucan," *Hermes* 88 (1960), pp. 65n.6.

[78] Cf. Arrian, *Epicteti dissertationes* 1.29.37: The philosopher is eager, like the bold gladiator and the well-trained athlete, for the crisis that will show his mettle. The philosopher has the spirit of the gladiator.

[79] Cf. Dio 61.33; Hopkins, "Murderous Games," p. 10.

[80] Robert, *Les Gladiateurs*, p. 191, no. 191.

[81] An extraordinary testament to the adoration the gladiator was able to inspire in the *amator*.

[82] See Athenaeus's *Deipnosophistai*, where he compares the gladiatorial bouts to the sin-

As in the bullfight or the boxing ring, victory can have a simplicity, a purity and splendor, never achieved outside the limited perimeters of the arena.[83] The positive lure of this simplified and purified soldiery cannot be underestimated; the severe discipline, the *askesis*, the deprivations of the *ludus* (the training camp), coupled with the brilliance of the impersonal ritual, was of utmost importance and not coincidental to the gladiator's fascination. He fought with marvelous weapons amidst an elaborate ceremonial, with the entire physical universe of the arena arranged to display his valor. The arena, which seems to epitomize Roman "decadence" when seen through modern eyes, also offered a stage on which might be reenacted a lost set of sorely lamented values. The act which was totally ineffective politically, the abandonment of the military and political *agon*, the game which was formerly played with all of one's life and powers, was an expression of yearning toward the imagined personal purity and self-vindication that authors such as Livy associated with Rome's "Golden Age."

> I judge you wretched because you have never been so; you have passed through life without an adversary. No one will know what you are capable of—not you yourself. . . . And so there are men who have of their own accord come forward to challenge reluctant misfortune, and sought an opportunity to blazon forth their worth when it was about to pass into obscurity. Great men glory often in adversity, as do brave soldiers in warfare. (Seneca, *De providentia* 4.3).

For some the arena was a real test of valor that the consulate, the praetorship, the imperial throne was not.[84]

---

gle combats of "the Olden Days" (4.155). The introduction in the sixth century B.C.E. of formation fighting, with its emphasis on self-control, discipline, and cooperation, never supplants, in the Roman imagination, single combat, with its emphasis on individual assertion and ostentatious display before an audience. One glance at the early books of Livy, the *Bellum civile* of Lucan, the *Thebaid* of Statius, or the *Punica* of Silius will convince the reader of this enduring romance. Cf. Polybius 6.54.4–55.4; S. P. Oakley, "Single Combat in the Roman Republic," *Classical Quarterly* 35 (1985), pp. 392–410; William Harris, "Roman Attitudes Towards War," in *War and Imperialism in Republican Rome* (Oxford, 1979), pp. 38–39. The *spolia opima* (the spoils offered to the god by a Roman commander who slew his enemy counterpart in single combat) remained an incomparable distinction for a Roman commander (cf. Pliny, *Panegyricus* 17).

[83] For a brilliant modern artistic portrayal of a similar phenomenon, it is possible to compare the film version of middleweight champion Jake Lamotta's struggles in the ring to those outside the ring in Martin Scorsese's *Raging Bull* (1980). Outside the arena, struggle was complex, tainted, sordid, unclear. Inside, though severe and dangerous, the reward was a sense of purity and valor and honor.

[84] It is interesting that Ville locates the end of sympathy with the gladiator in the period when church and state become one, when, "l'Église cesse d'être tendue dans une attitude de résistance héroïque" (*La Gladiature*, p. 471).

But the gladiator's skill and bravery alone were not sufficient to generate his glory. His worth could not come entirely from within; it was neither essential to him nor a necessary product of his person or his skills. It was partially within his power insofar as it was a product of his response to circumstances which were altogether outside of his control, but his glory and his status were given to him by an audience, an audience that was as intent on him as he was on it. The brave and able gladiator showed that he valued the opinion of the people who witnessed his ordeal. Just as the clamoring fans at a football or basketball game like to feel that their team is playing the better for their shouting and that the athlete's strenuous exertions are an expression of the value they place on this esteem, so the gladiator's willingness to die in order to put on "a good show" honored the audience in the extreme. Willingness to die for the pleasure of the audience was a high honor paid to the audience, and glory was the reward that the spectators could give in return. If, descending into the arena metaphorically or physically, the voluntary gladiator abandoned one society, it was not because he despaired of honor and social recognition. Instead of denying the power of the broader community to grant or withhold honor, it affirmed that power.

The gladiator was, thus, *both* a version of the Stoic *sapiens*, offering a metaphor of apathy, independence, and contempt for the opinions of society, *and* an expression of intense interaction with, and acceptance of, others, a longing for esteem and appreciation, in other words, glory.[85]

The gladiator was at first a defeated warrior; but he was also, even at this early stage, a man given a special privilege, like Hannibal's captives: he was allowed another opportunity to redeem his honor and display his valor before the eyes of his enemy (as an alternative to enslavement or execution).[86] Centuries later it still served this purpose for the prisoner of war, but now it was voluntarily resorted to by free Roman citizens. It offered the would-be soldier a sphere of competition in which victory

[85] For the gladiators' concern for glory as expressed in their epitaphs, see Robert, *Les Gladiateurs*, pp. 302–3. Saint Anthony turns his back on the world into which he was born for a life of asceticism and confrontation with the devil; nevertheless (or on that account), God and Athanasius spread his glory throughout the world. See Athanasius, *Vita Antonii*.

[86] Readers of earlier drafts of this chapter noted independently the remarkable similarities between the behaviors and attitudes expected of and directed toward the gladiator and those expected of and directed toward the brutalized prisoner of war in Father Le Jeune's account of the Huron ritual torture of the captive Senecan warrior from the year 1637. (See Anthony F. C. Wallace, *The Death and Rebirth of the Seneca* [New York, 1972], pp. 104–7. The proud Senecan warrior fully and enthusiastically cooperated in his torments and humiliation. This cooperation and attitude resulted in the extension of his torments. (A coward would have been quickly dispatched.) At the same time there is remarkable sympathy and even affection shown and felt by the Hurons for the man they are cruelly and slowly mutilating to death.

with honor was at least possible, and both victory and defeat could be accompanied with honor depending on the gladiator himself, on his self-control, his *firma frons*.

The gladiator was thus, in one aspect, a metaphor of empowerment; the *munus*, a ritual of empowerment.[87] It gave both individual and community a redress against arbitrary and unpredictable fortune and the Powers That Be: the audience could give a man (or woman) honor where fortune had withheld it.[88] To witness the voluntary gladiator play his role to the moment of truth was to witness the victim die *invictus*. It was a parable of hope to every victim.[89] While it was not a pretty picture, any more than the struggles of Anthony with the devil, it was one which offered a pattern of glory to the powerless. If the price of this empowerment was debasement, one paid that price anyway.

The gladiator's existence offered a form of simplified, purified soldiering, a means of gaining honor within a dishonorable situation and a way of transforming one's humiliation into a pattern of self-sacrifice, even while it was clear to the gladiator and to the would-be gladiator that those who would give him honor and glory were the very ones who despised him and who would take positive pleasure in his pain and death as well as in his vindication. As Tertullian states, the games are a delight ("oblectatio") for the audience as well as a solace ("solacium").

The factors that enticed the free and privileged classes not only to identify with and emulate the gladiator but to realize that role in the arena were the very ones that gave the gladiator an enhanced significance for the audience. The higher the status of the gladiator, the more miraculous the ritual of the *munus* for the spectators. The higher the status of the contestant, the greater his debasement, and therefore the greater the in-

[87] This was true for the audience as well as for the gladiators. According to Georges Ville, the empowerment of the audience and the *editor* consisted principally of the power granted to them to give or take life, to give or withhold honor, epitomized in the "moment of truth" depicted with such insistency on lamps and mosaics, paintings and reliefs. I differ from Ville in that he sees the arena as a ritual of empowerment *only* for the audience and minimizes the audience's identification with the gladiator (see p. 424). Ville's interpretation, which makes the gladiator almost exclusively a victim (of the audience or of his own sadomasochism), renders the romantic attraction of the figure of the gladiator and the allure of the arena for men and women of every status all but incomprehensible. For the political aspects of the spectacles (the interaction between the audience and the *editor*), see Paul Veyne, *Le Pain et le cirque* (Paris, 1976), pp. 702–6; Hopkins, "Murderous Games," pp. 16, 18; M. Cornelius Fronto, *Principia historiae* 17 (vol. 2., p. 217 of the Loeb ed.).

[88] The *sacramentum* of the gladiator, like the *sacramentum* of the martyr, provided access to glory for those customarily deprived of an arena for valor. This class would include women, who had few opportunities to display their valor save in childbirth.

[89] One salvation alone remains to us: to die with an unconquered neck ("una salus . . . indomita cervice mori" [Lucan 9.379–80]).

version of the traditional social hierarchy.[90] In general, the higher the status of the gladiator, the higher the level of voluntarism implied. Therefore, the higher the status of the combatant, the less the likelihood of seeing him being flogged into fighting, the less likelihood of the audience being despised and humiliated.[91] Knights were considered a special treat by the audience, but even freedmen were highly appreciated. Petronius's ragdealer, Echion, rejoices at the feast of Trimalchio: "Just think," he says, "we are to be given a superb spectacle lasting three days, not simply a troop of professional gladiators, but a large number of them freedmen [*familia non lanisticia sed plurimi liberti*]" (*Satyricon* 45).

Apart from a sustained interest in the artistry of gladiatorial combat, and the sensuous and erotic pleasure inherent in witnessing another suffer the fate we fear for ourselves—Tertullian's "They found comfort for death in murder" ("Ita mortem homicidiis consolabantur" [*De spectaculis* 12])[92]—the audience's pleasure and sympathy was increased by the gladiator's recruitment from amongst the free. This pleasure and satisfaction was intensified still further by the gladiator's being culled from the privileged classes and his development as a role model for the aristocrat.

The Arena of Civil Discord

The enhanced metaphorical significance of the arena grew apace, not only with the metaphor of the topsy-turvy universe and the perceived political inversion of honor and degradation, but also with the enhanced psychological and metaphorical significance of civil war, a singular preoccupation of Roman thought from the last century of the Republic through the first century of the Empire.[93]

---

[90] According to Zvi Yavetz (*Plebs and Princeps* [London, 1969], pp. 53, 114–15, 139; cf. p. 24), the Roman people delighted in the humiliation and degradation of the mighty. Lintott (*Violence*, p. 46) argues that the sympathy of the Roman populace was accorded in proportion to the status, the *dignitas*, of the sufferer. Both of these conclusions are justified by the sources. For an explanation of this paradox see chapters 5–6 below.

[91] See Ville, *La Gladiature*, p. 252.

[92] Cf. Tacitus's statement in the *Annales*: "The soldiers gloated over the bloodshed as though it gave them absolution" ("et gaudebat caedibus miles tamquam semet absolveret" [1.44]). Lucretius: "It is sweet, when on the great sea the winds trouble its waters, to behold from land another's deep distress" (*De rerum natura* 2.1–2). Cf. G. Rothman, *The Riddle of Cruelty* (New York, 1971), pp. 12–15.

[93] The theme of intimate or internecine war appears so frequently in the literature of the early imperial period that it would be impossible to cite more than a selection of examples: both Petronius's and Lucan's *Bellum civile*, Seneca's *Hercules furens*, *Hercules Oetaeus*, *Thyestes*, *Phaedra*, *Agamemnon*, *Troades*, *Medea*, *De ira* 2.9.2 (= Ovid, *Metamorphoses* 1.144ff.); Tacitus, *Historia* 1.1–2; Statius, *Thebais*. See Paul Jal, *La Guerre civile à Rome:*

In the *Philippics*, Cicero impresses upon his audience the desperation of their situation and the threat posed by Antony to the aristocratic Republic and its values: either liberty or slavery; either princes of all the world and every people—or gladiators ("principes orbis terrarum gentiumque omnium" or "gladiatores"). Even while insisting that there is nothing more detestable than disgrace, nothing more shameful than slavery, he nevertheless remarks: "The noble gladiators take care to perish with honor" ("Gladiatores nobiles faciunt ut honeste decumbant" [*Phillipicae* 3.14.35]).[94] If the ultimate disaster (the "fatum extremum"), the loss of the social structure which gave their lives value and freedom from domination, cannot be avoided, then they must play the role of the noble gladiators. Slavery must, Cicero insists, be avoided at any cost, but if it cannot be avoided, then a death modeled on that of the brave gladiator will alter (*but not efface*) the ignominy of that disgrace. It is the gladiator rather than the soldier who provides the model for Cicero's noble death.

It is the gladiator who represents the *vis mortua*, the stillborn power of the man without hope, the man without country or cause to fight for, and who fights not against a foreign foe, but against his brethren: "We live our lives in the gladiatorial barracks; we fight with the men with whom we share our drink" (Seneca, *De ira* 2.8.2).

The arena was an extraordinarily apt metaphor for civil war:[95] a battlefield within the very heart of the town,[96] an enclosure which was also a prison, a military engagement which was also a civil execution, a punishment which was also an expiation.[97] The inhabitant of this domestic

---

Étude littéraire et morale (Paris, 1963), esp. pp. 255–359; K. Büchner, *P. Cornelius Tacitus: Die historische Versuche* (Stuttgart, 1955), p. 28.

[94] See C. Wooten, *Cicero's Philippics* (Chapel Hill, N.C., 1983), pp. 61–62. Ville (*La Gladiature*, p. 415) interprets the word *decumbere* here and in *Tusculanae disputationes* 2.17.41 as "to submit," "to sue for discharge (*missio*)." But this interpretation goes against the entire sense of the contexts in both passages. In the first passage Cicero wants his audience emphatically *not* to submit to Antony or to rely on his *gratia* or *clementia*; the only honorable alternative to victory was death. Likewise in the second passage: the brave gladiator, however lacerated, will fight to the death to please his master.

[95] It is possible to argue, for example, that the whole of the civil war, for Lucan, was a type of bloody gladiatorial *munus* in which a series of pairs were matched before the eyes of history (e.g., 6.3, 191–92; 7.695–96). See Ahl, *Lucan*, pp. 56, 82–115; cf. Rutz, "Amor Mortis," p. 465 and n. 4: "Das Fechtspaar, auf das sich das Interesse der zuschauenden Götter bisher richtete war das Paar Caesar-Pompeius. . . . [D]er Mensch kämpft, leidet und stirbt zur 'Götterbelustigung.' " In the school exercises of Pseudo-Quintilian, first father and son, and then companions, are pitted against one another in the arena (nos. 258, 305).

[96] See Hopkins, "Murderous Games," p. 5 and n. 6. Well into the first century gladiatorial *munera* continued to be given in the forum itself in Rome (as well as in other less centrally located sites).

[97] For the civil wars as a punishment or suicidal expiation, see Horace, *Carmina* 1.2, 2.1, 3.6; Vergil, *Georgica* 1.501–2; Ovid, *Fasti* 3.697–710; Lucan 1.37–45, 4.788–90.

prison was not a citizen but an inmate. If he was a warrior, he was one who fought without cause, without a family, a hearth, a temple or an ideal to defend; he fought not against a foreign foe but against his brethren. He was compelled to be a warrior without being a soldier. Unlike the hoplite or legionnaire he fought alone, without comrades, or if, for a moment, he was provided with fellows (*commilitones*), they were the men against whom he would be pitted on the morrow. Like Urbiscus, the *secutor* of Milan made famous by his epitaph, he might be killed by the hand he recently spared. (The tomb of Julius Caesar might have carried the epitaph of Urbiscus: "I warn you that you had better kill the man you have defeated" "*Te moneo ut quis quem vic[e]rit occidat*").[98] Victory achieved nothing for the victor but one more day, one more hour, one more bout. Lucan extrapolates the arena into "the war that is more than civil": "The field of war contracts; here is nourished the blood that will flow over every land; here the future victims of the war in Thessaly and Africa are penned up; the madness of civil war seethes within a narrow arena" (Lucan 6.60–63).[99] For Manilius, writing for his patrons Augustus and Tiberius, the gladiatorial games provided a source of foes to conquer when one had run out of enemies (*Astronomica* 4.220).[100] In Dio's account, the arena is an extension of civil war: the Roman populace attributed the bloodletting at Caesar's games in 46 B.C.E. to his lust for slaughter, stimulated but not satiated by the internecine war (43.24.1).

In civil war the man who would be a soldier is reduced, ultimately, to the status and psychology of the gladiator, whose predicament his own closely resembles. Lucan's general Curio, fighting on the side of Julius Caesar in his war against Pompey, compares the situation of his troops to that of the gladiator. Curio bids his soldiers fight without hesitating or thinking: "When the sword is grasped and the dreadful pleasure rises and a helmet hides their shame, who compares leaders or weighs causes? Each man backs the side on which he stands. Just so those who are presented in the deadly arena are not driven to fight by long-cherished anger; they hate whatever man they confront" (*Bellum civile* 4.705–10).

The gladiator provided, for the soldier manqué, for Seneca, as for Cicero, one model and example of the psychological devastation, the hopelessness, of civil war at the same time as it provided a response to this devastation and hopelessness. To escape the inescapable, "The gladiator,

---

[98] *CIL* 5.5933; see Lafaye, "Gladiator," p. 1595; Friedländer, *Sittengeschichte*, vol. 2, p. 94n. 11; Ville, *La Gladiature*, p. 421.

[99] The irony is that at one time Rome condemned warriors from all over the world to fight in her arenas. Now from the arena of civil war, which turns the world upside down, she is exporting her own blood throughout the world. See Horace, *Odes* 2.1.

[100] "Without war, each contrives for himself an enemy" (4.224).

however timidly he may have fought, offers his throat to his adversary and adjusts the straying knife to his neck" (Seneca, *Epistulae* 30.8).

When the executioners sent by the triumvirs overtook Cicero in his litter on December 7, 43 B.C.E., in the gladiator's gesture of defiant complicity he bared and stretched out his throat to their swords.[101]

"Every meal is a delight at the table of a king."

The psychological and metaphorical significance of the gladiator grew apace, not only with the perception that honor and dishonor were inverted in society and with the extrapolation of the social and physical universe into a *bellum civile*, but also with the popularization of the strategy of complete collusion in political life:

> The injuries of the powerful must be borne, not just patiently, but with a glad countenance; for the powerful will strike again if they think that they have once struck home. (Seneca, *De ira* 1.33.1)[102]

> "At the table of a king," he [Harpagus] said, "every meal is a delight." . . . It is possible to hide the anger that arises even from great sufferings and compel ourselves to speak words that contradict our emotions. This restraint of sorrow is necessary, particularly for those whose lot it is to dine at the table of a king. So must they eat in the company of kings, so must they drink, so must they respond, so must they laugh at the funerals of their loved ones (*De ira* 3.15.2–3).

As the notion that the only way to survive politically was through complete (if apparent) collusion grew popular, the gladiator served as a ready paradigm. He offered a script to the man whose only hope for life and for honor depended on his skillful performance within a culture which threatened both his life and honor. Seneca advises Lucilius, if he would take part in public life, to attend to the model of the gladiator. The man in public life must, like the gladiator, at the very least, *appear* to take sides with the powerful: "The wise man takes care to avoid the power that kills, avoiding, above all, that he appear to be avoiding it" (*Epistulae* 14.8). He must, like Seneca's Julius Canus,[103] offer his jugular gladly; it is still his best chance of survival. "You will both live longer and die more

---

[101] Seneca, *Suasoriae* 6.17 (= Livy frag. 50 [Loeb]): "Leaning out from his litter and offering his neck steadily, Cicero's head was cut off." Cf. Cicero, *Pro Sestio* 37.80: "What are you accusing him of? That he cringed from receiving the blade? That he rejected the cut? That he did not, as gladiators are accustomed to be ordered, receive the death blow?" See also Petronius, *Satyricon* 101.1.

[102] Cf. *De ira* 2.33.1.

[103] *De tranquillitate* 14.4.

expeditiously if you receive your death blow valiantly, without cringing or attempting to ward off the blow with your hands" (*De tranquillitate* 11.5).

The gladiator was a skilled dissembler. The gladiator, like the courtier who could not coldly dissemble, who could not hide his unhappiness, his anger, or resentment, was defenceless. "Anger strips the gladiators" ("Gladiatores ira denudat" [*De ira* 1.11.1]). The man who survived at court did so by welcoming the injuries and saying "thank you": "iniurias accipiendo et gratias agendo" (*De ira* 2.33.2). Like the gladiator the courtier relied on his skill and intelligence: "Gladiatores ars tuetur" (*De ira* 1.11.1). His skill consisted in the ability to adapt himself to the exigencies of the moment: "It is an old proverb which says, 'The gladiator takes counsel in the sand.' To the fencer's acute gaze, a look on the face, a twist of the wrist, a certain inclination of the body are enough to give him warning of his enemy's intentions" (*Epistulae* 22.1).

The Damned and the Devoted

The gladiator's psychological significance was increased as well by the existence in Roman thought of a net of powerful and ambiguous concepts of self-sacrifice, a net into which the figure of the gladiator was drawn.

The peculiarly Roman model of the aristocratic voluntary self-sacrifice was the *devotio*. The Roman general Publius Decius Mus, in the Samnite Wars (340 B.C.E.), ceremonially dedicated his own body, through a violent death at the hands of the enemy, to the Earth and the gods of the dead, before and in return for the victory of his beleaguered troops.[104] The *devotio* was a desperate bargain struck by the commander with the hostile Powers That Be in the hope (here successful) that the gods would accept his own life, in addition to the lives of the enemy, as payment in full for the victory of his troops. Livy, like Juvenal,[105] imagines Decius Mus as a sort of expiatory sacrifice (*piaculum*) for the Roman forces

[104] On the *devotio* and its development see Livy 8.6–10, 10.28.12–13; Cicero, *De divinatione* 1.24.51; *De finibus* 2.19.60–61; *De natura deorum* 3.15; *Tusculanae disputationes* 1.37.89–90; *Paradoxa Stoicorum* 1.12; *Pro Sestio* 21.48; A. Bouché-Leclerq, "Devotio," in *D-S*, vol. 2, p. 1; G. Wissowa, "Devotio," *P-W*, vol. 5, cols. 277–80; L. Deubner, "Die Devotion der Decier," *Archiv für Religionswissenschaft* 8 (1904–5), pp. 66–88; H. Wagenvoort, *Roman Dynamism* (Oxford, 1947), pp. 31–34; K. Latte, *Römische Religionsgeschichte* (Munich, 1960), pp. 125–26; H. S. Versnel, "Two Types of Roman Devotio," *Mnemosyne* 29 (1976), pp. 365–410.

[105] "These [the Decii] are deemed by the infernal deities and our parent Earth a fair equivalent for all the legions, and all the forces of the allies, and all the men of Latium" (Juvenal, *Satirae* 8.255–57). "All the threats and menaces of the gods of heaven and hell he drew onto himself alone" (Livy 8.10.7).

which transfers the wrath of the gods (the plague, or *pestis*) to himself and to the enemy. Before the eyes of enemy and comrade, Decius, having devoted himself to death, rushed the enemy with the fierce and suicidal *amor mortis* of a Leonidas at Thermopylae: "P. Decius Mus plunged into the thick of the enemy, a conspicuous figure to both armies, of an aspect more august than human, as though sent from the sky as an expiation for all the anger of the gods, to turn aside the destruction from his own troops to those of the enemy" (Livy 8.9.9–10).

As a result of his *devotio*, P. Decius Mus was a model of frenzied and unstoppable courage. Like Lucan's Vulteius or Scaeva or Cato he was ardent for death. "When he understood that he was to die instantly, he sought that death more ardently than Epicurus thinks we should seek after pleasure" (Cicero, *De finibus* 2.19.61). As a result of his zeal for death he had no fear, and this made him terrible. According to Livy, wherever Decius rode the enemy was terrorized at the general's fury, "as if stricken by some deadly star [*sidus pestiferum*]."

In his treatise *De natura deorum*, Cicero's Academic Cotta responds to Stoic Balbus's opinion that the Decii are expiatory sacrifices. The gods are not so hostile, protests Cotta, as to require the death of good men without sufficient cause: "You [Balbus], however, are of the opinion that the gods were placated by the devotions of the Decii. But how could the sin of the Roman people have been so great that the gods could not be placated without the death of men such as these?" (Cicero, *De natura deorum* 3.15). For Cicero's Cotta, Decius's suicide was a calculated act of selfless *self-will*, a *strategy* designed to inspire the flagging spirits of the troops to imitate their general's contempt for life. If such an act would not have been necessary unless the gods (or luck) had turned powerfully against the Romans, nevertheless Cicero's Cotta is able to imagine the necessity for the *devotio* while simultaneously maintaining the benevolence of the gods. Suffering, however terrible, when contractual, drastically alters the power relations in the universe. The response of Cotta is evidence that *contractual* self-sacrifice is seen as an alternative to, and a radical transformation of, the despair felt at the prospect of the arbitrary hostility of the gods or Fortune. The powerless commander vindicates his self-will in the very act of becoming a victim:

> Decius [the Younger] cried out to his soldiers, "Where were they fleeing?"—
> "What hope could they have in flight?" He tried to stop them as they broke
> and ran; he tried to call them back. When all his exertions proved powerless,
> he cried aloud on the name of his father Publius Decius: "Why," he asked,
> "do I postpone the fate of my house? It has been granted to our family to be
> expiatory sacrifices to avert the public peril. Now I will give myself and the

legions of the enemy to the Earth and the infernal gods to be slaughtered."
(Livy 10.28.12–13)

The fearsome *devotio*, like the *sacramentum* of the gladiator or the
martyr, which it so closely resembles, allows Cicero (or Cicero's Cotta)
to have gods who, though ultimately or fundamentally benevolent, nevertheless accept and find pleasure in the death of the good man. The *devotio* is *either* expiatory sacrifice or free gift or *both*.

Decius's collapse beneath a hail of missiles, according to Livy (8.9.12–
13), frees the spirits of the Roman soldiers from their scrupulous dread
("exsolutis religione animis"), and they attack the enemy with their confidence restored. The *devotio Deciana* was extraordinary; the Romans
knew of no generals's *devotiones* apart from those of the Decii. So the
Romans of the late Republic and the early Empire could imagine no more
honorable fate than that of Decius. "His death," according to Cicero,
"was so glorious that his son yearned for the same" (*De divinatione*
1.24.51).[106]

Part of the power that the story of the Decii had in this period came
from the fact that the general's *devotio* represented a dramatic embrace
by a member of the warrior caste of types of expiatory sacrifice ordinarily
reserved for the lowly, the condemned, and the enemy: the *sacratio* or
consecratio capitis and the closely related *sacratio* (or *devotio*) of an enemy or enemy town.

The *devotio/consecratio* was an ancient form of punishment and ex-
communication inflicted on the criminal (the breaking of the law being
an offence to the gods, requiring expiation). The individuals subject to
the *consecratio capitis* were devoted to the infernal gods by a solemn rite
corresponding very closely to that employed voluntarily by the Decii.[107]
By this rite the devoted were rendered "sacred" (*sacer*) to the infernal
gods, who were then invited to seize them or let anyone who willed con-
summate the sacrifice. The second type of *devotio/consecratio* was a form
of malediction, or *maleficium*, directed at a personal or collective enemy.
The enemy was devoted to the infernal deities in payment for one's own
victory or salvation.

The *devotio* was thus also a curse. Macrobius, in the *Saturnalia*, describes the formula used to devote the enemy: The commanding general,
having evacuated the condemned city of its divine champions, calls on the
infernal gods to fill the city and the army of the enemy with panic and
terror. He calls on the gods of the dead to bear away, "deprive of light,"

---

[106] The Etruscans at Sentinum in 295 B.C.E. are alleged to have given his son Decius Mus
the chance to devote himself to death for his troops, as Pyrrhus at Ausculum in 279 B.C.E.
is thought to have given his grandson.

[107] See Bouché-Leclerq, "Devotio," pp. 113–14.

and consider as consecrated and devoted, the heads and persons of any age who should bear weapons against the Romans ("capita aetatesque eorum devotas consecratasque" [3.10]), or who should inhabit their towns and fields. By virtue of his good faith and magistracy he gives them to the gods as vicarious offerings ("vicarii") for the preservation of the general himself, his faith, his command, the legions, and the army.[108]

Ludwig Deubner makes the important observation that the only difference between the devotion of the enemy and the devotion of the hero is that the hero is joined to the enemy.[109] "By the words of his prayer the devoted general binds himself and the enemy together in an indissoluble unity."[110] *The savior and the accursed object are henceforward inseparable.*

In the arena these two aspects of the *devotio* meet. [Julius Capitolinus], in explaining the origin of the custom of a general's presentation of gladiatorial games before setting out to war, describes the death of the gladiators in the arena as a form of *devotio* offered to Nemesis: "Many say that this *devotio* was made against the enemy by our ancestors in order that Nemesis, that is, the power of Fortune, might be satisfied by the blood of citizens shed as a propitiatory sacrifice in a sort of battle" (*Scriptores historiae Augustae* 21.8.6).

The generals's *devotio*, both because of the high rank of the victims and the voluntariness of the offering, was a form of sacrifice to which much emotion and admiration was attached in this period. Their suicides were viewed as wonderful, terrible responses to otherwise desperate circumstances. They were, to the Roman mind, extreme and splendid examples of the aristocratic self-sacrifice which saturated the imagination of the late Republic and early Empire. The Decii were not alone; they shared the stage with Curtius, Regulus, the senators awaiting the Gauls in 387 B.C.E., Horatius, Lucius Verginius, Cato the Younger, King Codrus, Leonidas, and Socrates, and with women: the daughters of Erectheus,[111] Lucretia,[112] Alcestis, Livia, and others.[113] Petronius simultaneously bears witness to the popularity of this obsession and laughs at it when he has the grand sacrificial gestures of the aristocratic heroes imitated by his vagabonds.[114]

---

[108] See Macrobius, *Saturnalia* 3.9–13.

[109] "Die einzige Unterschied [between the *devotio Deciana* and the *devotio* of the enemy] ist der, dass die Decier nicht nur die Feinde den Unterirdischen weihen, sondern sich selbst dazu, und dies ist kein Untershied des Wesens" ("Die Devotien," p. 79).

[110] "Der Devovierte bindet . . . sich selbst und die Feinde zu einer untrennbaren Einheit zusammen" ("Die Devotien," p. 79).

[111] Cicero, *Pro Sestio* 21.48.

[112] Cicero, *De finibus* 2.20.66.

[113] See Bouché-Leclerq, "Devotio," pp. 117–18.

[114] E.g., *Satyricon* 80, 98, 108.

Walter Burkert[115] and Friedrich Schwenn[116] place the Roman *devotio* within the model of Hittite, Hebrew, Greek, and Roman human "scapegoats" and *pharmakoi*. Burkert notes that there are two principal models for the scapegoat/*pharmakos* in Greek and Roman antiquity: "Either the victim must be termed subhuman, particularly guilty, or even 'offscourings' to be dumped . . . or else he is raised to a superhuman level, to be honored forever. The extremes may even be seen to meet, deepest abasement turning into divinity" (p. 72). P. Decius Mus conforms to Burkert's second model, that of the honored victim, "going voluntarily to his doom while the others passively look on with feelings of awe, admiration, and relief, which makes one of the most moving scenes in legends, in drama, in religion. Think of the citizens of Calais or of Vercingetorix in the brief and momentous passage of Caesar's (*Bellum Gallicum* 7.89). . . . It re-emerges [as a theme] with singular fascination in Christianity: the lamb voluntarily going to its slaughter—overwhelmingly expressed in the Passion music of Johann Sebastian Bach" (p. 71). According to L. F. Janssen, this is the "authentic" paradigm of the *devotio*: "True devotio cannot be brought about by pressure, but it has to be a personal, self-imposed obligation."[117]

The word *devotio*, which Livy applied to the elaborate rite whereby Decius Mus dedicated his life to the infernal gods, is applied by analogy to other self-sacrifices performed without the benefit of the formalizing ritual of consecration. For example, Livy describes as a "devotio" the suicide of the knight Marcus Curtius, who, in obedience to an oracle which demanded of the Romans their most precious resource, came forward unbeckoned and leaped armed and on horseback into a chasm which suddenly opened in the forum (7.6.4). There are also instances of the application of the word *devotio* to the sacrifices of less exalted figures. Ovid, in a passage from his *Ibis* (465f.) refers to the people of Abdera periodically seizing, "devoting," and then stoning a human to death.[118] The scholiast of the *Codex Philippicus* explains this devotion in Ovid as part of a public rite of purification or lustration, in which one man, "devoted for the heads of all, is slain by stones." A similar type of devotion may have served to found the plot of Petronius's *Satyricon*.[119] In Lucan's

---

[115] See Walter Burkert, *Structure and History*, pp. 64–72.

[116] Friedrich Schwenn, *Die Menschenopfer bei den Griechen und Römern* (Giessen, 1915), pp. 42, 154–64, 183–84.

[117] L. F. Janssen, "Some Unexplored Aspects of the *Devotio Deciana*," *Mnemosyne* 4 [34] (1981), pp. 357–81, esp. p. 376.

[118] "Aut te devoveat certis Abdera diebus/saxaque devotum grandine plura petant" (467–68).

[119] Servius (*In Vergiliam* 3.57) refers to a lost portion of Petronius's epic which contained an account of the measures that the inhabitants of Massilia took against a plague. One of their poorer citizens became a voluntary scapegoat, maintained for an entire year at public

epic, moreover, the *devotio* is one of the principal motives ascribed to many of the characters, male and female, aristocrat and common soldier (e.g., *Bellum civile* 2.306–25; 3.307–11; 4.268–72, 533, 695–99; 7.359; 8.86–105, 110–112).[120] Livy, having in mind both of the models of the *devotio* identified by Burkert, applauds the voluntary sacrifice of the Decii at the same time that he recounts (disapprovingly) a *devotio*, accompanied by a fierce *sacramentum*, made by the Samnite elite troops under compulsion (10.38.2–4).

In the imperial period, the object of the devotion became in many instances not the state or the army but a single individual (usually an emperor or god). [Spartianus] relates the surmise that Antinous, Hadrian's beloved, died as a result of "devoting" himself to death for the health and long life of his master (*Scriptores historiae Augustae, Hadrianus* 14.6). But this voluntary *devotio* is often treated with contempt: Dio Cassius relates in disgust the story of a tribune, S. Pacuvius, who devoted himself ("heauton kathosiose") to Augustus before the assembled senate, "in the manner of the Spaniards."[121] "He won," according to Dio, "the competition in flattery" (53.20.2), and compelled many others throughout the city to imitate his action. It was as a result of this episode, according to Dio, that in approaching the sovereign, men are accustomed to use the expression, "We have devoted ourselves to you" (53.20.4). Suetonius (*Gaius* 27.2) and Dio (59.8.3) tell us of Caligula's satellite Afranius "devoting" himself for the emperor's health and Atanius Secundus vowing to enter the arena if Caligula should recover from an illness. Caligula, restored, compelled both to keep their vows. Moreover, we learn from Suetonius that Atanius was not alone in devoting himself to the arena for the salvation of the Emperor (*Gaius* 14.2). Under the emperors even the act of devotion becomes ambiguous; one can debase oneself by self-sacrifice.

The concept of devotion, then, was associated in this period with the most intensely admirable valor, voluntarism, and patriotic self-sacrifice *and* with the curse and condemnation of criminals and enemies; with al-

---

expense and fed a special diet. At the end of that time, after appropriate ceremonies to bring the misfortunes of the city down on his head, he was cast forth. J. P. Sullivan (*The Satyricon of Petronius*, pp. 40–42) argues the strong possibility that the offended god was Priapus and the scapegoat Encolpius himself, the "antihero" of the mock epic, who, for the remainder of his days is pursued by "The Wrath of Priapus." This wonderful plot outline agrees very well with Petronius's incessant parody of the Romans' often humorless fascination with violence, sex, and self-sacrifice.

[120] See M. Rambaud, "L'Apologie de Pompée par Lucain," *Revue des Études Latines* 33 (1955), pp. 258–96; J. Brisset, *Les Idées politiques de Lucain* (Paris, 1964), p. 75.

[121] Cf. Valerius Maximus 2.6.11; Caesar, *De bello Gallico* 3.22. The Spanish soldier's "devotion" placed him under a solemn obligation to share the fate unto death of a friend or commander to whom he had pledged himself. To default on this obligation made him unholy.

truism *and* with servility; with the elevated *and* with the debased. These peculiarities make it possible for both death in the arena and the general's salvation of the troops to be characterized as "devotion." The *devotio* of the general and the *sacramentum* of the gladiator are woven into the same web of invertible values, of simultaneous humiliation and exaltation, that one finds throughout the late Republic and early imperial period.

According to Georges Ville, by late republican times, "the majority of the gladiators were volunteers, attracted by an appetite for gain, the love of glory, the urge to test themselves at arms, and also, assuredly, by some strange character traits: a taste for killing, sadism, suicidal compulsion, a morbid deathwish."[122] Ville is certainly correct in listing these particular attractions of the arena. I would add, however, that these "character traits" are elicited—and not just in the gladiator—by the society in which the games emerge as a powerful force of attraction. They are anything but strange or unusual in the period of the civil wars and the early imperial period. The fascination of Roman society, of Lucan, Seneca, Petronius, Martial, Juvenal, the Roman matron and the Roman schoolboy with the gladiatorial games is not simply a matter of an idiosyncratic inclination to sadomasochism but a response to an intense and excruciating feeling of humiliation and insecurity and an attempt to find compensation, even exaltation, within this feeling of inescapable degradation. It is a response to hopelessness without denying the hopelessness.

In conclusion, for those who lived in a world from whose "reality" the arena was a "diversion," the gladiator—slave, actor, and soldier manqué—was a symbol of utter degradation and despair, his death an empty mockery. For those who lived in a world in which everything outside the arena was a loathsome and bitter burlesque, the gladiator was a living symbol of redemption and self-vindication, the "moment of truth" in the arena a focused and intensified "reality" beyond anything experienced outside. In one framework he was a victim, under the direst compulsion; in the other, a redeemer, both of himself and his audience. To understand the Roman gladiator one has to live, as did many Romans, in both these worlds.

> The pain that kills pain acts as a medicine.
>
> Pro medicina est dolor dolorem qui necat.
>
> (Publilius Syrus 511)

---

[122] "La majorité des gladiateurs sont des engagés volontaires, attirés par l'appât du gain, l'amour de la gloire, l'envie de se battre at aussi, assurément, par des traits caractériels étranges: goût de tuer, goûts sadiques, pulsion suicidaire, goût morbide de la mort" (Ville, *La Gladiature*, p. 227).

TWO

DESIRE

WINE WITHOUT WATER

It is strange that the true source of cruelty should be desire.
(Novalis, *Psychologische Fragmente*)[1]

THE ROMAN "esthétique de l'agonie" was articulated, above all, in the arena. The anguish, the waste, the caprice of Roman life encountered in the arena its aggravating and compensating extremes of severity and violence. In the powerful, erotically charged figure of the gladiator, the Roman romance with death, unendurably intensified and concentrated, met its ultimate and its limits.

The gladiator symbolized many things to the Romans. On the one hand, he was an emblem of hopelessness, and those members of the free and upper classes who entered the arena often did it as the final and ultimate act of a libertine existence, the suicidal culmination of a life of self-indulgence.[2] The gladiators' notorious oath, their *sacramentum* ("to be burned to be bound, to be beaten . . ."), confirmed and advertised that despair; to become a gladiator was to embrace, with a vengeance, cosmic cruelty.

On the other hand, the Romans understood despair of one's life as a prerequisite for courage. "Death summons us all indiscriminately. Take courage from this despair" (Seneca, *Naturales quaestiones* 2.59.4–5).[3] "Certainly the great spirit and the desperate strive equally" (2.59.5).[4] The gladiator had turned his back on life; he alone of men, with his superhuman fortitude and his wretched training in pain, is able to laugh while his wounds are prodded with a knife (Aulus Gellius, *Noctes Atticae* 12.5.13).[5]

Because of his despair combined with his reckless courage, the gladiator was often thought of as a man free from restraint, a wanton, a sensualist without compunction. Augustine, in the *Enarrationes in Psalmos*,

---

[1] Quoted by Mario Praz, *The Romantic Agony* (New York, 1956), p. 28.

[2] E.g., Juvenal, *Satirae* 11.1–8, cf. 8.192–99; Tacitus, *Historia* 2.62; Propertius 4.8.23–26.

[3] "Moriendum est; animus ex ipsa desperatione sumatur."

[4] "Certe paria conantur animus magnus ac perditus."

[5] Cf. Seneca, *De constantia sapientis* 16.2.

compares the spirit of the gladiator to that of "the sinner and unjust man, already despairing of himself, and thus able to do whatever he wants, since of necessity he must be condemned" (70.1). In the *Sermones* the sinner acts "with the spirit of the gladiator: since he despairs of his life, he does whatever he can do to satisfy his desires and lusts" (20.3). "Are you not aware in what licentious cruelty the gladiator lives?" he asks (*Enarrationes*, loc. cit.).

The epithet "gladiator" was used to brand an enemy as the most degraded or vicious of voluptuaries.[6] Language drawn from the arena is adopted by Petronius to describe Encolpius's raucous and exhausting sexual encounters with Quartilla, Ascyltos's with the maid, and Giton's with the virgin (*Satyricon* 19, 21). The sexual "gangster," the "nocturne percussor," is also the "gladiator obscene" (*Satyricon* 9). (A taste for this type of "low-down and dirty" sex is ascribed by Encolpius to one of his former companions who "does the work of a woman" in the *ergastulum*, the prison or penitentiary [81.5].[7] The fierce and abandoned appetite of the gladiator makes him the "suspirium puellarum" ("the sigh of the maidens"), the "puparum dominus" ("the master of girls") in the graffiti of the gladiators Celadus and Crescens on the walls of Pompeii.[8]

The gladiators were seen as salacious libertines. Simultaneously, as I have previously demonstrated, they were the models of a severe asceticism: there were no more austerely disciplined soldiers in the Roman world than the greatest gladiators trained in the imperial *ludi*.[9] No other figure in Roman society embodied, in quite such extremes, punishment and impunity, constraint and abandon, asceticism and profligacy.

The gladiator did not resolve or close the Roman debate on desire. Rather, he stimulated and exacerbated it: he epitomized, he "represented" in his person, and in his fate, every important limit of desire; he gave form and focus to a Roman "physics of desire" that was all but

---

[6] E.g., Dio 74.2.1; Cicero, *Pro Sexto Roscio Amerino* 3.8; *In Pisonem* 12.27–28; *In Catilinam* 2.4.7, 2.5.9; Velleius Paterculus 2.91.3; *Scriptores historiae Augustae, Commodus* 18–19.

[7] Here the *ergastulum* seems to be the *cellae* of the gladiator's barracks.

[8] "Cresces puellar(i)um dominus" (*CIL* 4.8916); "Cresces retia(rius) puparum nocturnarum, mat[utin?]ar[um] aliarum . . ." (*CIL* 4.4353); "puelarum [*sic*] decus Celadus" (*CIL* 4.4289); "suspirium puellarum tr(aex) Celadus Oct. IIICIII" (*CIL* 4.4342); "puellarum decus Celadus tr(aex)" (*CIL* 4.4345); "tr(aex)/Celadus reti(arius)/Cresces/ puparru(m) domnus [*sic*]" (*CIL* 4.4356). "Tous ces graffiti, à l'exception du premier, ont été trouvés au vieux ludus de Pompéi; c'est un jeu collectif à l'égard de deux collègues dont on peut imaginer ce que l'on veut" (Ville, *La Gladiature*, p. 330n. 227). See also August Mau and Francis Kelsey, *Pompeii: Its Life and Art* (New York, 1902), p. 226.

[9] For the hardships of life in the *ludus*, see Pseudo-Quintilian, *Declamationes maiores* 9.21; Ville, *La Gladiature*, pp. 301–3.

inexpressible in its complexity. He represented and enacted the spiral of yearning to its ultimate and unendurable limits: the violence of hopelessness and the violence of hope. To desire the gladiator was to desire extravagantly, to yearn for what Emily Dickinson called a "Gay, Ghastly, Holiday": fright at liberty, the enjoyment of the unbearable.

The sharp and intolerable passions of the Romans appall. We can isolate these sentiments and condemn them. They are unacceptable; we can speedily purge ourselves of them. But perhaps, like Augustine's Alypius, we may linger just a little too long, and begin to view the events in the arena as part of a larger drama of unbearable emotions which constituted the Roman "theatre of cruelty."

The Physics of Desire

> Just as dumb creatures are snared by food, human beings
> would not be caught unless they had a nibble of hope.
> (Petronius, *Satyricon* 140)[10]

As the Romans feared disabling hope,[11] so they feared desire and its awful consequences: the flouting of social conventions, the dismantling of hierarchy, the confusion of categories, the breaking of the food chain, the unleashing of chaos, of conflagration, of the *universus interitus*. Like the winds of Aeolus, set free, the passions would carry off the sea and land and deepest heaven.[12] Petronius, writing in the age of Nero, tells the story of the "Widow of Ephesus," a prodigy of devotion, who refuses to depart from her husband's tomb or sustain her life. The widow's nurse, herself corrupted by the smell of wine, urges her prostrate mistress not to bury herself alive with her husband's corpse. A mere crust of bread eventually seduces the pious widow, renews her desire for life, and drives her thence to lust, to wantonness, and finally to the careless and brutal humiliation of her husband's corpse (*Satyricon* 111–12).[13]

---

[10] "Sicut muta animalia cibo inescantur, sic homines non caperentur nisi spei aliquid morderent."

[11] E.g., Cicero, *Epistulae ad Atticum* 7.13.1; Caesar, *Bellum civile* 1.3.2, 1.4.2–3; Seneca, *De spe* (*Poetae Latini Minores*, vol. 4, no. 25); *Thyestes* 288–96, *De ira* 2.8.2–3, 3.30.3–31; *De clementia* 1.1.7; *De brevitate vitae* 17.5; *Epistulae* 5.7–9, 70.6–7; Lucan, *Bellum civile* 1.143–46, 2.113–14. See Anton Hackl, *Die spes als negativer Charakterisierungsbegriff in Caesars Bellum civile, Ciceros Catilinariae, Lucans Pharsalia* (diss., Innsbruck, 1962).

[12] See Vergil, *Aeneis* 1.58–59.

[13] Compare Tacitus's description of the seduction of Augustus's niece Livia (*Annales* 4.3).

Cicero quotes an ancient speech of Archytas of Tarentum:

No more fatal curse has been given by nature to man than the pleasure of the body, through eagerness for which the passions [*avidae libidines*] are driven recklessly and uncontrollably to their gratification. From it come treason against the fatherland and the overthrow of states; from it spring secret conferences with public foes. In short, there is no crime and no evil deed which the lust for pleasure will not drive men to undertake. Indeed, rape, adultery, and every like offence are set in motion by the enticements of pleasure and by nothing else. (*De senectute* 12.39–40)

If the desires of the people are not carefully restrained, Cicero complains in the *De republica* (following Plato), soon not even the dumb animals will give way on the street (1.43). You have only to entertain a poor man at dinner, according to the rich man in Lucian's *Saturnalia* (8.36–38), and he will begin pawing your women and will not stop with that. Soon, the author implies, he will demand a redistribution of the land.

Passion, like violence, escalates uncontrollably, driven relentlessly by its own momentum.[14] In Petronius's "Bellum civile" (*Satyricon* 119.56ff.), this insatiable appetite escalates into bloody civil war. It is escalating desire that stimulates the "bellum plus quam civile" of Lucan's epic: after the death of Crassus the world was not enough for the two remaining triumvirs, Caesar and Pompey. "The kingdom was divided by the sword; and the fortune of the imperial people, that possessed sea and land the whole world over, was not enough for two" (*Bellum civile* 1.109–11).[15]

[14] Seneca, *Epistulae* 95.15–33; Petronius, *Satyricon* 120; Lucan, *Bellum civile* 1.158ff.

[15] Seneca: "[Cato the Younger] engaged in struggle . . . with the boundless greed for power which the division of the whole world among three could not satify" ("cum potentiae immensa cupiditate [congressus], quam totus orbis in tres divisus satiare non poterat" [*De constantia sapientis* 2.2]). "Indeed, too much happiness makes men avaricious. Nor are desires ever so temperate that they cease when they obtain their object. They ascend from much to more, and embrace the most licentious desires having gained those unhoped for" ("Facit quidem avidos nimia felicitas, nec tam temperatae cupiditates sunt umquam, ut in eo, quod contigit, desinant; gradus a magnis ad maiora fit, et spes improbissimas complectuntur insperata adsecuti" [*De clementia* 1.1.7]). Vergil: "O mind of man, ignorant of fate and the chances of our future, not knowing how to keep the measure when we are carried away by prosperity" ("nescia mens hominum fati sortisque futurae / et servare modum rebus sublata secundus!" [*Aeneis* 10.501–2]). Petronius: "The wealth that can satisfy nature administers; that which unbridled glory teaches us to pursue lacks any limit" ("Quod satiare potest dives natura ministrat; / quod docet infrenis gloria fine caret" [*Poetae Latini minores* 95]). For Vergil and Seneca, Petronius and Sallust (*Catilina* 10; *Bellum Iugurthinum* 41), getting what you want leads one inevitably to transgression, or simply to the inability to recognize limits. For the spiral of desire in the thought of Gregory the Great, see the excellent discussion in Carole Straw, *Gregory the Great: Perfection in Imperfection* (Berkeley, 1988), pp. 107–27.

"But nobody gets enough, never."
(Trimalchio in Petronius, *Satyricon* 76.3)[16]

Ovid's Erysichthon, the king for whom nothing was sacred, was cursed with an insatiable hunger that, like a fire, grew the more it was fed. In the midst of banquets he searched for a meal ("in epulis epulas quaerit" [8.832]).[17] Having sold his daughter repeatedly into slavery to feed the rapacious flame of his hunger, he is reduced, in the end, to autocannibalism.

The *avidae libidines*, once set in motion, can never be satisfied. They are always accompanied by the mocking ghost of deprivation: "Poor Tantalus amidst the waters cannot drink, nor seize the suspended fruit. His desires torment him. This is the face of the great man of wealth who, with everything before his eyes, fears starvation, and digests hunger dry-mouthed" (Petronius, *Satyricon* 82.5).[18] According to Petronius, "There was no happiness in familiar joys, or in pleasures dulled by the common man's use" (*Satyricon* 119.7–8).[19] The whole of the *imperium Romanum* had grown insatiable: "The conquering Roman now held the whole world, sea and land and the course of sun and moon. But he was not satisfied" (119.1–3).[20]

The Spectre of Satiation

Paradoxically, once within the whirlwind of lust, the thing that the Roman feared most was not the vortex of desire but the death of that desire—the nauseous *taedium vitae*, the end of wanting.[21] When the Romans' conquests exposed "the world" to them, when endless wealth made uncommon pleasures easy to obtain, and an array of cultural con-

---

[16] I could not improve on J. P. Sullivan's translation of Petronius's "nemini tamen nihil satis est." Cf. Horace, *Satirae* 1.1.61–63.

[17] *Metamorphoses* 8.738–878.

[18] Cf. Horace *Satirae* 1.1.68–70; *Epistulae* 1.2.56–57 ("semper avarus eget"); Publilius Syrus 694 ("Tam deest avaro quod habet quam quod non habet"); Seneca, *Epistulae* 108.9 ("Desunt inopiae multa, avaritiae omnia"); cf. 94.43.

[19] Non vulgo nota placebant / Gaudia, non usu plebeio trita voluptas.

[20] Orbem iam totum victor Romanus habebat, / Qua mare, qua terrae, qua sidus currit utrumque, / Nec satiatus erat.

[21] Seneca: "Some are moved by satiety of doing and seeing the same things, and they are moved to the lust for death [*libido moriendi*] not so much from hatred of life as from a cloying fastidiouness. . . . There are many who would affirm—not that life is bitter—but that it is vacuous" ("Quosdam subit eadem faciendi videndique satietas et vitae non odium sed fastidium. . . . Multi sunt qui non acerbum iudicent vivere sed supervacuum" [*Epistulae* 24.26]). Cf. Marcus Aurelius 6.46, 7.1 + 3.

tacts enlivened their idea of the possible, the Romans of the late Republic and early Empire were compelled to go to great lengths to stimulate and feed new desires and to keep one desperate step ahead of satiation. "They began to seek dishes not to remove but to stimulate the appetite" (Seneca, *Epistulae* 95.15).[22]

Seneca brilliantly describes the exquisite torments of this morbid, and ultimately exhausting, quest for novelty in his essay *De tranquillitate.* These Romans, "vexed by fickleness and boredom and by the constant change of their designs," are like those insomniacs who, restless and weary, endlessly alter their position, turning one way and then another, until they are finally worn out. They do not dare, or they simply cannot, fulfill their desires. In either case the result of timid and/or unfulfilled desires is self-loathing:

> They strive to attain their wishes by every available means, instructing and compelling themselves to dishonest and difficult acts. And when their labor is without reward, it is the fruitless disgrace that tortures them;—they are not grieved to have desired evil things but to have desired in vain. Then remorse for what they began lays hold of them, and the fear of beginning again, and thence creeps in the agitation of mind which can find no relief—because neither can they rule nor can they obey their desires. And then comes the hesitency of a life failing to clear a way for itself, and the dull wasting of a soul lying torpid amidst forsaken hopes. (2.7–8)[23]

Welcome to such as these are all opportunities for excitement and distraction. Hence the adventures, exaggerations, contortions, distinctions, atomizations, refinements, variations, and *nuances fugitives* of what we, sharing the fear of the illimitable, think of as the Roman decadence.[24]

> "Now let us head for Campania," they say. And when soft living palls, "Let us hunt out the wild passes of Bruttium and Lucania." . . . "Let us head for Tarentum with its famous harbor and its mild winter." "Let us take our turn in the City." . . . They undertake one journey after another and change spectacle for spectacle. (*De tranquillitate* 2.14)[25]

[22] "Coepit non ad tollendam sed ad irritandam famem quaeri et inventae sunt mille conditurae." Cf. Sallust, *Catilina* 13.

[23] "One does not advance when one walks toward no goal, or—which is the same thing—when his goal is infinity" (Émile Durkheim, *Suicide*, trans. Spauling and Simpson [New York, 1951], p. 248). Durkheim's discussion of anomie is highly relevant to the matter of this chapter. Cf. Seneca *De brevitate vitae* 16.1–17.5; *Epistulae* 74.11.

[24] On the characteristics ascribed to "decadence" see Richard Gilman, *Decadence: the Strange Life of an Epithet* (New York, 1975); Vladimir Jankélévitch, *L'Austerité et la vie morale* (Paris, 1956); and David Lowenthal, *The Past is a Foreign Country* (Cambridge, 1985), pp. 173–82.

[25] See Lucretius, *De rerum natura* 3.1045–86; Horace, *Epistulae* 1.11.27–30 ("strenua nos exercet inertia"); Juvenal, *Satirae* 5.84ff.

As they would see the world, so they would taste it.[26] The satisfied palate, rendered delicate, required more unusual and pungent stimulants. The biographer and connoisseur of vice Suetonius tells us that the emperor Vitellius devised a dish, which he named "Shield of Minerva, Protectress of the City," composed of pike livers, pheasant and peacock brains, flamingo tongues and lamprey spleen, "collected from every corner of the Empire, from the Parthian frontier to the Spanish Straits" (*Vitellius* 13).[27] In imitation of the early imperial gourmand Apicius, the emperor Elagabalus produced meals of camel heels, cock combs, parrot heads, mullet beards, and nightingale tongues (*Scriptores historiae Augustae, Elagabalus* 20.5–7). That a taste for surrealistic comestibles was shared by the imperial people of every status can be inferred not only from the feast of the freedman Trimalchio (devised by Nero's "Arbiter of Elegance") whose sensational variety of dishes do little to impress even the poorest of his guests but also from Seneca's description of a cookshop (*popina*) "bent on bankruptcy" creating just such an exuberant concoction (*Epistulae* 95.26).[28] These meals, offered at tremendous cost were not unlike, in their effects, those consumed by Erysichthon.[29]

The French have a word for what drove these Romans: *aboulie*. It is the negative state of being without desire. It is not contentment; it is despair.

Drawing Down the Moon[30]

Only a madman expects a fig in winter.
(Marcus Aurelius 11.33)

This endless torment of pleasure, the exhaustion of the possible, created a desire for the ultimate and the impossible. Seneca complains of these

[26] E.g., Aulus Gellius, *Noctes Atticae* 6.16, cf. 15.8; Seneca, *Thyestes* 459–62.

[27] See Petronius, *Satyricon* 119.7ff.; Seneca, *Epistulae* 95.15, 19.

[28] The Roman populace shared the aristocrats' enormous appetite for novelty in spectacles, in the theatre, and in rhetoric. Seneca the Elder, in organizing the *Controversiae*, explicitly models himself on the *editores* of gladiatorial games apportioning their novelties to maintain the suspense of the people (*Controversiae* 4 praefatio 1). The combats of dwarfs, women, or animals in the arena, the "leapers" (*desultores*) and mimic battles of the circus, the clowns, sword swallowers, tightrope walkers, jugglers, acrobats, etc. of the "medicine shows" fed the popular as well as the aristocratic "wasting" (*tabes*). See Jerome Carcopino, *Daily Life in Ancient Rome* (New Haven, Conn., 1940), p. 216.

[29] One can think of parallel instances: Caligula's loaves of bread and other foodstuffs modeled in gold (Suetonius, *Gaius* 37.1) and those of wax or mud fashioned for the Saturnalia (Petronius, *Satyricon* 69). Cf. *Scriptores historiae Augustae, Elagabalus* 25.9, 27.4–5.

[30] "Drawing down the moon" was a proverbial expression for doing the impossible and

endless attempts to break the *lex mortalitatis*, to test the barriers of one's time and place, one's age, one's size, one's sex, what Jean Brun calls "les aventures dans les possibles impossibles."[31] He complains of men wearing women's clothing, of trying by various means to stave off sexual maturity, of people "who crave roses in winter, or seek to raise a spring flower in the snow" (*Epistulae* 122.8).[32]

The tyrant, the man most capable of indulging his wishes,[33] was the man most afflicted by lunatic desire.[34] On nights when the moon was full, Suetonius's Caligula tried assiduously to coax her to his bed. At the same time, he was overheard to menace Jove with the words of Homer: "Raise me up or else . . . !" (*Gaius* 22.4) In building his palaces and villas, "there was nothing he desired to effect so much as what was considered impossible" ("nihil tam efficere concupiscebat quam quod posse effici negaretur" [37.2]).[35] Nero, likewise, appears as "the lover of the impossible" ("incredibilium cupitor" [Tacitus, *Annales* 15.42]). Such yearnings led Caligula and Nero to construct moles in deep rough water far out to sea, to drive tunnels through exceptionally hard rocks, raise flat ground to the height of mountains, and reduce mountains to the level of plains. It led Nero to build a country villa in the burned-out slums of the city.

Behold over all the land the lavish waste of the spoils of war, the wealth that rages to its ruin. They build in gold; their villas invade the starry sky. Seas

---

for sorcery. See Petronius, *Satyricon* 129 ("in hac civitate, in qua mulieres etiam lunam deducunt"); cf. Lucian, *Philopseudes* 13. The emotions associated with "drawing down the moon" are closely related to those associated with the inverse movement, falling from heaven: "If I must fall, I would prefer to fall from the sky" (Vagellius, quoted by Seneca, *Quaestiones naturales* 6.2.9). Compare the story and epitaph of Phaethon in Ovid: "Here lies Phaethon, who drove the chariot of his father; and if he failed, he fell in splendid daring" ("Hic situs est Phaethon currus auriga paterni / quem si non tenuit magnis tamen excidit ausis" [*Metamorphoses* 1.746–2.400]).

[31] Jean Brun, "Le Prestige du monstre," in *Le Mythe de la peine* (Paris, 1967), esp. p. 303.

[32] Cf. Seneca, *Naturales quaestiones* 7.31; *De ira* 1.21.1. Henry de Montherlant: "cette nostalgie de l'ubiquité, cette nostalgie de l'universalité, cette rage de n'avoir pas en soi une source inépuisable de désir, pour n'être plus hanté par le spectre de la satiété" ("Aux fontaines du désir: Syncrétisme at alternance," in *Essais* [Paris, 1963], p. 243). See also Jean Brun, "Le Prestige du monstre," pp. 304–5.

[33] Sallust: "If a man can do whatever he pleases, what is he but a despot?" ("nam impune quae lubet facere, id est regem esse" [*Bellum Iugurthinum* 31.26]). For Émile Durkheim, desires freed from all moderating influence become themselves tyrannical, and their first slave is the very subject who experiences them (*Suicide*, pp. 253–54).

[34] Cf. Suetonius, *Gaius* 31; Seneca, *Thyestes* 455–67; Juvenal, *Satirae* 6.116–32 (Messalina's nights in the brothel); Seneca, *Agamemnon* 141–44. Alexander the Great and Julius Caesar are often chided in this period as insatiable or *indomiti*: Lucan, *Bellum civile* 10.20–45, 3.304, 1.146; Seneca, *Naturales quaestiones* 3 *praefatio* 5 (Philip and Alexander compared to a flood or conflagration); *De ira* 2.23.3; 3.17.1–2; Suetonius, *Julius Caesar* 7.

[35] Suetonius, *Gaius* 37; *Nero* 42; cf. Dio 59.17.

are expelled by the land, the trees are lapped by new seas. They revolt, over-turning the order of things. The earth gapes beneath insane structures; caverns groan in hollowed hills;—and the gods of hell profess their hopes of heaven. (Petronius, *Satyricon* 120.85–93)

"Le pouvoir jusqu'au bout, l'abandon jusqu'au bout."
(Camus, *Caligula* 3.5)

As a result of this yearning for the ultimate, anticipation of the conflagration is as intense as the fear of it. Again, the tyrant was often seen as the man most afflicted by apocalyptic yearning, the man who welcomed the end of the world: "emou thanontos gaia michtheto puri," "When I am dead let the earth go up in flames!"[36] Once, in the course of general conversation, according to Suetonius, someone quoted the line "When I am dead . . ."; Nero remonstrated that the first part of the line should be altered to read, "While I yet live . . ." (*Nero* 38). Indeed, Nero himself was suspected of burning down the city of Rome to build his Golden House or to mourn his city as Priam did Troy. Seneca's Medea declares, "The only calm—if with me I see the universe overwhelmed in ruins; with me let all things pass away. It is sweet to draw the world down with you when you are perishing" (*Medea* 426).

The tyrant expressed, in the imagination of the Romans, only the concentration of a passion felt by many. Cicero states, "We feel it wicked and inhuman for men to declare . . . that they care not if, when they themselves are dead, the universal conflagration ensues" (*De finibus* 3.19.64). "If I must fall, let me fall with the world shattered" ("si cadendum est, cadam orbe concusso"), says Seneca a century later.[37] This madness, he asserts, has infected the whole people (*De ira* 3.2.2–6): they are like the Titans storming heaven—the final obstacle, the fulfillment and end of all possibilities.[38]

---

[36] "[Caligula] used to complain aloud of the state of the times, because it was not rendered remarkable by any public calamities; for while the reign of Augustus had been made memorable by the disaster of Varus, and that of Tiberius by the fall of the theatre at Fidenae, his was likely to pass into oblivion, from uninterrupted prosperity. At times he wished for some terrible slaughter of his troops, a famine, a pestilence, conflagrations, or an earthquake" (Suetonius, *Gaius* 31).

[37] *Naturales quaestiones* 6.2.9. This apocalypticism was also expressed in the cultivation of the excessively fragile. See the fascinating remarks in Pliny, *Historia naturalis* 33.2.5, 37.7.20, 37.10.29.

[38] Cf. Pliny, *Historia naturalis* 33.1.3. For the "spiral of desire," boredom, and apocalyptic thought, see Léopold Flam, "Le sacré et la désacralisation dans la pensée contemporaine," in *Le Pouvoir et le sacré* (Brussels, 1962), pp. 179–86, esp. p.181.

"Il y a de moins en moins de monde autour de moi."
(Camus, *Caligula* 3.5)

Unsatisfied yearning leads to the apocalypse, the end of the world, and yet the ability to satisfy oneself leads equally to a loss of the world, a loss of a sense of reality. When another offers us no resistance, the Other ceases to have a reality. Like Sade's "sovereign man," we live in a solipsistic universe, a world of echoes.[39] The ability of the Romans to satisfy (*and thus frustrate*) their endless appetite for spectacle and sensation entailed a profound insensibility as well as irritability.

In a world where one was alone there could be no victims, and so there could be no cruelty. The result of this phenomenon was a sense that death could be play, death could be theatre. One could become a connoisseur of suffering and death just as one was of food, or sex, or violence, or words. In the *Naturales quaestiones* Seneca describes the Roman fascination with dying mullets: the fish were removed from basins set up before the banquet couches and enclosed in glass decanters. These invisible and airless containers enabled the diners to observe the marvelous changes in color undergone by the mullets in the course of their struggle for air and life. " 'There is nothing,' you say, 'more beautiful than a dying surmullet. In the very struggle of its failing breath of life, first a red, then a pale, tint suffuses it, and its scales change hue, and between life and death there is a gradation into subtle shades' " (3.18.1).

This loss of the Other was reflected in the bloody spectacles: "The wild animal is searched out in the woods at great price, and men trouble Hammon far away in Africa to supply the beast whose tusks render him precious even unto the deaths of men; strange ravening creatures freight the fleets, and the padding tiger is wheeled in a gilded palace to drink the blood of men while the crowd applauds" (Petronius, *Satyricon* 119).[40]

The ravening creature described by Petronius's dismal poet could be the tyrant himself in his gilded cage, the supreme exemplar of the solitary creature in a world that is identical with himself, lamenting, like Camus's Caligula, that the teeming world was emptying itself.[41] His world, insu-

---

[39] See Jessica Benjamin, "Master and Slave: The Fantasy of Erotic Domination," in *The Powers of Desire*, ed. Ann Snitow et al. (New York, 1983), pp. 283–84; Georges Bataille, *Erotism* (San Francisco, 1986), pp. 154–76.

[40] "Man, a sacred thing to man, now is killed as a sport and a joke" ("Homo, sacra res homini, iam per lusum ac iocum occiditur" [Seneca, *Epistulae* 95.33]).

[41] Cicero: "The tyrant—one cannot think of an animal more loathsome, detestable, or hateful to men and gods, who, while he might have the figure of a man, surpasses the beasts in the boundlessness of his excess. Who can justly call him a man who does not want any community of law, any human society, with his fellow citizens—indeed, with the human

lated by flattering sycophants, becomes a mirrored prison, like the mirrored halls of the portico in which Domitian paced.[42]

Seneca describes the savagery (*feritas*) of the tyrants: they do not injure because they have been harmed; rather, they beat and mangle for pleasure. Why? Because their anger meets with no resistance; it is, without fail, easily exercised and satisfied. As Bataille remarks, "The man subject to no restraints of any kind falls on his victims with the devouring fury of a vicious hound."[43] Seneca observes: "Anger . . . from oft-repeated indulgence and surfeit has come to forget mercy and has expelled from the mind every conception of a human bond, and passes at last into cruelty. And so these men laugh and rejoice and experience great pleasure, and wear a countenance utterly unlike that of anger, making a diversion of ferocity [*per otium saevi*]" (*De ira* 2.5.3).

Satiation breaks the human bond ("foedus humanum"); it is surfeit and not anger that makes the tyrant cruel.[44] So the emperor Caligula whipped and tortured Roman senators and knights—not to extract information, but for amusement. "And so impatient was he of postponing his pleasure—a pleasure so great that his cruelty demanded it without delay—that he decapitated some of his victims by lamplight, as he was strolling with some ladies and senators on the terrace of his mother's gardens" (Seneca, *De ira* 3.18.3–4).[45]

The tyrant of every class and sex operated on the same model.[46] Juvenal's *domina* playfully stabbing her slave with a hairpin is only the reflected image of Domitian stabbing flies with his sharpened stylus.[47] The tyrant, meeting no resistance, becomes the master or mistress of the gratuitous act, the *acte gratuit*. By the same (equally playful, equally serious)

race?" ("tyrannus, quo neque taetrius, neque foedius nec dis hominibusque invisius animal ullum cogitari potest; qui quamquam figura est hominis, morum tamen inmanitate vastissimas vincit beluas. Quis enim hunc hominem rite dixerit, qui sibi cum suis civibus, qui denique cum omni hominum genere nullam iuris communionem, nullam humanitatis societatem velit?" [*De republica* 2.26]). Cf. Seneca, *Hercules Oetaeus* 604ff.

[42] For Domitian's mirrored hall: Suetonius, *Domitian* 14.4. For the precarious isolation of the emperor: Tacitus, *Annales* 1.72, 3.53; Pliny, *Panegyricus* 48.3–49.2.

[43] *Erotism*, p. 167. Cf. Seneca, *De ira* 3.19.2; Dio 59.13.6.

[44] Cf. *Epistulae* 47.19–20.

[45] Compare Caligula's appreciation for the sweet qualities of the voice of the actor Apelles being whipped at his command (Surtonius, *Gaius* 33).

[46] For examples of excesses of the "Little Tyrant," see Seneca, *De ira* 3.40; Dio 54.23.1–6. For similar excesses on the part of female *dominae*, see Juvenal, *Satirae* 6; Tacitus, *Annales* 3.33–34; and the Roman elegaic poets.

[47] Suetonius: "At the beginning of his reign Domitian would spend hours alone every day doing nothing but catching flies and stabbing them with a needle-sharp stylus" (*Domitian* 3.1).

indulgentia principis, one might be commanded to commit suicide or pass gas.[48]

"Now it is a pleasure to be miserable."
(Seneca, *Thyestes* 427)

A client dining with his patron, the irascible libertine Caelius, in order to protect himself from the violent temper of the more powerful man, agrees to all his patron says. Caelius, unable to endure his compliance, cries out: "*Contradict me, that there may be two of us!*" ("Dic aliquid contra, ut duo simus!" [Seneca, *De ira* 3.8.6]).

For those tyrants, little or big, male or female, surrounded by the masks of slaves and parasitical clients, the quest of suffering (one's own and another's) became a search for limits, for "reality."[49] Resistance, reaction, opposition become one's pleasure *as well as* one's frustration and suffering.[50] Insofar as one is frantic to feel, and insofar as one is progressively anesthetized by satiety, one welcomes the experience of the unendurable.[51] The unendurable becomes the only "reality," the only relief.[52] Seneca, in his discussion of the insatiably bored Roman, explains:

> Just as there are some sores which crave hands that will hurt them and rejoice to be touched, and as a foul itch of the body delights in whatever scratches, exactly so, I would say, do these minds upon which, so to speak, desires have broken out like wicked sores find pleasure in toil and vexation. For there are certain things that delight the body also while causing it a sort of pain, as

[48] Suetonius, *Claudius* 32 (the "edictum de flatu"); cf. Petronius, *Satyricon* 47; Suetonius, *Tiberius* 34.2 (Tiberius's edict on casual kissing).

[49] "We are told that Colette, in an aphoristic mood, once commented to her husband Maurice Goudeket that 'suffering is the great decadence'" (Gilman, *Decadence*, p. 29). Indeed, much of Livy's sense of the Romans, and the Romans' sense of themselves, as in decline, as impure, is a result of their sense of themselves as a people who are suffering. The *liber animus*, the untroubled spirit, was the sign of health and wholesomeness (e.g. Sallust, *Catilina* 52.21). The troubled conscience, for the Romans (as for us), signals "decadence." The Romans were like children who picked the wings off flies and lived to regret it as adults, meanwhile remembering fondly the purity and untroubled sleep of their youth. So ideas such as the "just war" or the "City of Man" were the burdens of their "decadence." Cf. Cicero, *De officiis* 1.11.35.

[50] Benjamin, "Master and Slave," pp. 282, 286, 292.

[51] "The heart rejoices to yield to the breaking of the storm" (Bataille, *Erotism*, p. 92).

[52] Compare Emily Dickinson's "I like a look of agony because I know it's true." E. M. Cioran: "We live in the false as long as we have not suffered" (*Drawn and Quartered*, trans. Richard Howard [New York, 1983], p. 172). "We exist only insofar as we suffer. A soul enlarges and perishes only by as much *insupportable* as it assumes" (E. M. Cioran, *A Short History of Decay*, trans. Richard Howard [New York, 1975 (orig. pub. 1949)], p. 28).

turning over and changing a side that is not yet tired and taking one position after another to get cool. (*De tranquillitate* 2.11–12)[53]

"She wanted both to die and to live in Paris."
(Flaubert, *Madame Bovary*)

The ability to prosecute their desires led the Romans to the love of death. Livy, in the preface to his history of Rome, laments, "Of late wealth has brought us avarice, and abundant pleasures, yearning—amidst both excess and the desire to perish and destroy all things" (*Praefatio* 12).[54]

Seneca warns against "that emotion, which has taken possession of so many, the lust for death [*libido moriendi*]" (*Epistulae* 24.25).[55] The love of death, so powerfully evident in this period, is the longing for the ultimate and for the limit at once. In this distraction, desire and the desire for death have become indistinguishable. The glutton Apicius, unable to exhaust his wealth (and thus unable to exhaust his hunger and thirst), ends by taking poison (Martial 3.22). Antony and Cleopatra's Society of Inimitable Livers evolves into the Society of Those Joined Together in Dying (Plutarch, *Antonius*). Seneca quotes Aufidius Bassus: "He never wanted to live who did not wish to die" ("Vivere noluit qui mori non vult" [*Epistulae* 30.10]).

Sympathia Malevolens

The Romans created, in their imaginations, or in their worlds (*for they ceased to be distinguishable*) the terrible suffering which was their pleasure. They were both victims and victimizers, and thus, in a sense, *neither victims nor victimizers*. Accordingly, the death-hungry young Lucan composed an epic funeral of the world (the "funus mundi"), in which Pompey dreams a victory triumph that was concurrently his funeral (*Bellum civile* 7.7–39).[56] Petronius's Trimalchio acts out, and weeps over, his own funeral before the assembled guests at his dinner party (*Satyricon* 71–72, 77–78). He is both the observer and the observed, like the condemned

[53] Cf. Martial 10.13.

[54] "Nuper divitiae avaritiam et abundantes voluptates desiderium per luxum atque libidinem pereundi perdendique omnia invexere."

[55] Cf. *Epistulae* 74.11. "Death is the solidest thing life has invented so far" (Cioran, *Drawn and Quartered*, p. 177).

[56] For *Todeslust* in Lucan, see Georg Pfligersdorffer, "Lucan als Dichter des geistigen Widerstandes," *Hermes* 87 (1959), pp. 344–77; Rutz, "*Amor Mortis* bei Lucan," pp. 462–75.

criminal acting the role of "Mucius Scaevola" who awes the poet Martial
with his performance in the arena, the actor/victim who puts his sword
hand in the altar fire and eagerly observes its burning:

> What we observe as a sport in the arena of Caesar was in the time of Brutus
> the summit of glory. See how the hand grasps the flames and enjoys the pun-
> ishment; see how the brave hand reigns over the astonished fire. He is his
> own spectator, and he applauds the noble funeral of his right hand, that hand
> which feasts on the sacrificial fire. And if this suffering had not been denied
> it against its will, the left hand, fiercer still, was ready to enter the exhausted
> flame. (8.30)

When Lucan or Seneca describe in lush detail the self-disemboweling
of the warrior or Oedipus plucking out his eyes, the mutilation of Marius
Gratidianus or the tortures inflicted by Caligula, one recognizes instantly
the pleasure, the eroticism, the self-indulgence of these descriptions, as
well as, paradoxically, the authors' profound identification with, and
sympathy for, the sufferer.[57] It is a closed and cannibalistic world.[58]

> Just as all vices become deep-rooted unless they are crushed when they spring
> up, so too, such a state of sadness and wretchedness, with its self-afflicted
> torture, feeds at last upon its very bitterness, and the grief of an unhappy
> mind becomes a morbid pleasure. (Seneca, *Consolatio ad Marciam* 1.7)

The Vaudeville of Despair[59]

This loss of a "reality" is often expressed in a Roman voice as a loss of
the category "real" as opposed to "theatrical."[60] Macrobius recalls that

---

[57] E.g., Seneca, *De ira* 3.19.1–5; *Thyestes* 760–89; *Oedipus* 952–79; *Phaedra* 1080–
1114; *Epistulae* 14.5–6; Lucan, *Bellum civile* 2.173–222, 4.540–81, 6.530–68, 8.663–91,
9.766–88.

[58] For the close and perhaps inseparable relationship between "sadism" and "masochism," see Sigmund Freud, *Three Essays on the Theory of Sexuality*, trans. James Strachey
(New York, 1975), pp. 24 and n. 2, 25 and n. 4, 33; Wilhelm Stekel, *Sadism and Masochism: The Psychology of Hatred and Cruelty* (New York, 1929), passim, esp. vol. 1, pp.
50–57.

[59] A phrase drawn from Alan Harrington, *The Immoralist* (New York, 1969), p. 46.

[60] Tacitus, *Historia* 1.32, 3.83. "In the *Republic* Plato outlined the process of degeneration. The son revolts against the father . . . and goes to the opposite extreme in ever-wid-
ening oscillations. Moreover, this insurrection of the son becomes in time rebellion for its
own sake, which is to say a purely formal act, a pose. This is the first expression of what
will later be taken to be a profound characteristic of decadence as a cultural condition: a
quality of sham passion, of theatrical gesture" (Gilman, *Decadence*, p. 45). Cf. Paul Plass,
Wit and the Writing of History: the Rhetoric of Historiography in Imperial Rome (Madison, Wis., 1988), pp. 3–5, 8, 10–11 and n. 10; Auguet, *Cruelty and Civilization*, pp. 103–
6.

the actor Pylades, appearing in the *Hercules Furens* in the time of Augustus, shot pointed arrows at the spectators.[61] He did the same in a command performance of the play at a banquet given by Augustus (*Saturnalia* 2.7.17). The slave Giton and the freedman Encolpius make histrionic gesture-suicides in Petronius's *Satyricon* (94, 108). The Romans enjoyed, as well, what one might, for want of a better word, call "snuff plays," such as the *Mucius Scaevola*, the *Prometheus*, the *Actaeon*, the *Laureolus*, and *Pasiphaë and the Bull*, where condemned criminals (and an occasional aristocrat) act out the role which will end in their death and/or mutilation.[62]

As early as 184 B.C.E., Lucius Flamininus, consul in Gaul, at the caprice of a prostitute or a youthful favorite, had a condemned man executed at a dinner party. At that time he was condemned, according to Cicero, for an act of base and abandoned lust ("flagitiosa et tam perdita libido").[63] But by the imperial period, something had changed; the use of pain and death as entertainment had ceased to scandalize. Strabo (5.4.13) and Nicolas of Damascus (Athenaeus, *Deipnosophistai* 4.153), among others, mention the frequent enjoyment of gladiatorial bouts at private dinner parties.[64] The appetites of Caligula were stimulated by having victims tortured while he ate and while he engaged in sex (Suetonius, *Caligula* 32.1).[65] The aristocrat Vedius Pollio was prepared to throw a servant into the lamprey pool as a self-indulgence ("causa luxuriae") and a novel cruelty ("novitas crudelitatis") (Seneca, *De ira* 3.40.2–3).[66] The deadly "marriage" of the female poisoner with the ass is only the second act of an elaborate and high-spirited musical comedy in Apuleius's *Metamorphoses*; the execution of the woman "damnata ad bestias" is to take place in an atmosphere reminiscent of a high-school Christmas pageant or small-town Independence Day celebration (10.23, 28–35).

The playful indifference with which the oversensitized Romans reacted to violence is epitomized, for me, by the gladiatorial bouts on the walls of Pompeii fought by Cupids, those eternal children who can feel neither pain nor sorrow, or "Amor the Incendiary," the putto condemned to the

---

[61] Compare Commodus (Dio 73.20.2).

[62] Martial, *De spectaculis* 5, 7, 8. That the aristocrat does not die is a source of regret to Juvenal (*Satirae* 8.187–88).

[63] *De senectute* 12.42; cf. Livy 39.42.7, 39.43.2; Plutarch, *Cato Maior* 17.

[64] Cf. *Scriptores historiae Augustae*, *Verus* 4.9; *Elagabalus* 25.7. Vitellius, commanding the slaughter of one of his former creditors, says that he wished "to feed his eyes" ("velle se dicans pascere oculos" [Suetonius, *Vitellius* 14.2]).

[65] Cf. Seneca, *De ira* 3.18.3–4.

[66] The freedman Encolpius, enjoying the beating received by his rival Eumolpus, remarked, "I put each eye to the chink by turns and gorged myself on the miseries of Eumolpus like a dainty dish" [*velut quodam cibo me replebam*]" (*Satyricon* 96).

beasts on a baked clay medallion from the second century C.E.,[67] or the painting of the crucified Cupid described by Ausonius as the inspiration for his awful poem "Cupido cruciatus." One can easily find in Roman late republican and imperial art what is for us a distressing conjuction of all-too-human grief with painless, playful, and frivolous eternity, cruel suffering enacted by heedless gods.[68] Many striking examples of this frolicking theatre of violence can be found in Seneca's *Apocolocyntosis*; in Petronius's *Satyricon* (especially Echion's invocation of the upcoming gladiatorial exhibition of Titus [45]);[69] in Apuleius's *Metamophoses*; and in the hortatory speeches (*suasoriae*) of the Roman schoolboy, with their pirates in chains, tyrants ordering sons to produce the heads of their fathers, etc.[70]

This paradox of apathy and erethism gave a *danse macabre* aspect to all Roman festivities: the silver skeleton and *memento mori* at Trimalchio's dinner party (Petronius, *Satyricon* 34.7–10); the lurid costumed Charons at the gladiatorial games; the slave whispering warnings in the ear of the triumphant *imperator*; the mosaics of skeletons, skulls, butterflies of transience, and wheels of necessity found in the ruins of Pompeii.

Playing with Terror

It must be understood that, for all classes, a great part of the attraction of the events in the arena, apart from their novelty and the violence directed at others, was exactly the potential for the spectators to be included in the "theatre of surprise." The audience flocked to the games given in Curio's fragile revolving amphitheatre. At greater risk than the gladiators, they nevertheless, according to Pliny, applauded their own peril (*Historia naturalis* 36.24.117–120).

[67] J. W. Salomonson, *Voluptatem spectandi non perdat sed mutet* (Amsterdam, 1979), p. 85.

[68] We tend to think of the divine as solemn and the "worldly" as trivial. To understand the meaning of the spectacle of death and suffering in the Roman world, it is important to keep in mind that the Romans, following the Greeks, were apt to think of the gods and fortune as fickle and frivolous precisely because they were not faced with suffering and death (except insofar as they were, like Achilles's horses, afflicted with compassion for mortals).

[69] Cf. 126.5–11.

[70] Cf. *Satyricon* 1–4. The endless spectacle and variety of tortures indulged in by the tyrant were often depicted as a theatrical display (see Seneca *Epistulae* 14.5–6). We know, moreover, that even children attended the bloody circus (they are active participants in the "comedy" depicted in Apuleius), that the battles were accompanied by musical instruments (particularly the water-organ), and that the Romans delighted in exotic battles such as those between trained animals, midgets, and women.

We tend to think of theatre as relaxation: we are physically safe and comfortable for a relatively short period of time, made invisible and insulated by the dark and the silence, sitting in a pattern that establishes clear boundaries between ourselves and the rest of the audience, between one's familiar order and the fantasy on stage or screen. For us, asking for or expecting participation in the theatre is exciting, scary, invigorating—and unusual. In the Roman theatre or circus, you were uncomfortable (often for long hours and even days at a stretch), visible and exposed to the weather, to your neighbors, to the authorities, *and* to the actors by the light and the shape of the theatre. Life could not and did not stop; the theatre was a busy, loud, disorderly, volatile public assembly with a hair trigger. The major and bloody battle that broke out between the Pompeian and the Nucerian spectators and their sympathizers in the amphitheatre at Pompeii in the year 59 C.E. was only an extreme version of the riotous behavior that had come to be expected at public spectacles.[71] The audience came to be seen and heard, to act and interact. Their performance was not simply a reaction, but rather a counterpoint to the one on the stage or on the sand.[72]

The Romans increasingly enjoyed the blurring of conventional boundaries between the "real" and "unreal," the permeability of the barrier between the spectators and the spectacle. Calpurnius Flaccus (*Declamatio* 52), Quintilian (*Declamationes* 9); Pseudo-Quintilian (*Declamationes minores* 302), and Lucian (*Toxaris* 58–60) imagine being suddenly thrust into the arena as a result of the vicissitudes of fortune: capture and sale by pirates, robbery and destitution. Even the exigencies of pious poverty or selfless friendship might land one on the sand. Caligula, faced with a shortage of condemned criminals to be fed to the wild animals, requisitioned spectators to be thrown to them (Dio 59.10.3). He ordered a certain Esius Proculus, on account of his striking stature and physique, to be dragged from his seat and matched with a gladiator in the arena. When he won the bout, he was compelled to face still another opponent—before being further humiliated and killed (Suetonius, *Caligula* 35).[73] Claudius drove a *nomenclator* (an attendant whose job was to remember and re-

---

[71] Tacitus, *Annales* 14.17. The battle was immortalized in a wall-painting preserved in the Museo Nazionale in Naples.

[72] E.g., Josephus, *Antiquitates Judaicae* 19.24–7; Dio 59.13; Tacitus, *Annales* 3.23; Traugott Bollinger, *Theatralis Licentia: Die Publikumsdemonstrationen an den öffentlichen Spielen im Rom der früheren Kaiserzeit und ihre Bedeutung im politischen Leben* (Winterthur, 1969); Hopkins, "Murderous Games," p. 16; Veyne, *Le Pain et le cirque*, pp. 701ff.; Foucault, *Discipline and Punish*, pp. 57–69.

[73] On the charge of having insulted his mother, Caligula forced a prominent knight into single combat in the arena (Dio 59.10.4).

peat the names of those whom his master might encounter) into the arena on a whim (Suetonius, *Claudius* 34). If a machine or any piece of work on which they had been employed should fail or displease Claudius, the carpenters and other workmen of the circus were wont to find themselves suddenly in a new role (loc. cit.).[74] Domitian dragged the author of an unfortunate witticism from his seat and threw him to the dogs (Suetonius, *Domitian* 10).[75]

The arena was merely one ring of the imperial circus. Once, according to Suetonius, when a victim was about to be offered upon the altar, the emperor, clad in the habit of the *popa* (the minister who led the victim to the altar) and holding the axe aloft for a long moment, at last surprised the spectators by slaughtering an attendant instead of the animal (*Caligula* 32).[76] In Petronius's mock epic, Trimalchio's dinner party was one continuous theatrical exhibition, in which the threat of violence, the potential for violence, was just one contingency in the endless development of all the possibilities of sensation. When a slave boy who dropped a cup was ordered to kill himself by his master Trimalchio, the attendant guests are required to entreat his pardon (52.4).[77] Encolpius remarks, in an aside, that they would have gladly seen the suppliant's skull cracked but they did not want to ruin the dinner party—Trimalchio certainly would

---

[74] At the time I am writing there is a fashion in live comedy for the comedian to engage in vicious verbal attacks on random individuals in the audience. The audience is invited to engage in this vituperative repartee. The "spectators" for this type of comedy seem to welcome and even relish the danger of being singled out for what, to the uninitiated, seems brutal humiliation.

[75] Cf. Hopkins, "Murderous Games," p. 10.

[76] The popular theme of "sudden changes in fortune" was often enacted in the arena. This theme is exemplified by the career of Vitellius's favorite Asiaticus. Slave and beloved companion of the future emperor, Asiaticus ran away and attempted to make a living selling cheap wine drinks from a stall; captured and chained, he was nonetheless restored to his former influential position at the side of Vitellius. A falling-out with his master resulted in his being sold into the arena, but the repentant Vitellius rescued him from a dangerous bout and made him a knight (Suetonius, *Vitellius* 12; Tacitus, *Historia* 2.57, 95.). For other exemplary tales of sudden changes in fortune, see Cicero, 2 *Philippic* 27.65ff.; Ovid, *Metamorphoses*, passim; Seneca, *De tranquillitate* 11.10–12 (Pompeius, Sejanus, Croesus, Jugurtha, Ptolemy, Mithridates); *Thyestes* 617–22; *Epistulae* 4.6–9 (Pompeius Magnus, Crassus, Lepidus, Caligula); Petronius, *Satyricon* 54, 115, 120.79–95; Tacitus, *Annales* 1.74, 3.18; Plutarch, *Aemilius Paullus* 32–36, esp. 34.8–36; Apuleius, *Metamorphoses*, passim, esp. 1.6–7.

[77] While the incident seems improbable to us precisely because it appears in Petronius, we have similar stories of theatrical displays of summary justice visited upon slaves. When a slave was caught stealing some plate at a public banquet in Rome, Caligula had his hands amputated and caused him to be led around before the guests with his hands tied by a cord around his neck and a placard on his breast (Suetonius, *Caligula* 32).

have made them display their grief and lament his death just as they were asked to do when the great man enacted his own funeral! (54.1; cf. 71.4).

The Forbidden

The Roman flirtation with the ultimate and the fearful was expressed, as well, in the attraction to the prohibited.[78] As the dangers and penalties of indulging in adulterous relations with a slave or another married person increased, so did the allure of such relations for many who simply did not fear (and perhaps even craved) unhappiness. Horace, Propertius, Ovid, and many others confessed to being excited by them.[79] Petronius's maidservant Chrysis is coolly indifferent to the charms of the slave who would seduce her mistress:

> There are women who are hot for the dregs, whose desire is aroused only by the sight of a slave or attendant girded for work. There are those who are inflamed by a gladiator, or a muleteer mired in dirt, or an actor disgraced by his exposure on the stage. My mistress is one of this brand; she leaps clear over the first fourteen rows of the orchestra to look for what she wants up where the rabble sit. . . . I've never gone down for a slave. Heaven forbid I should throw away my embraces on the cross! Let matrons kiss the tracks of the whip; for my part, though I am a servant, I never sit anywhere except in the seats reserved for the knights. (*Satyricon* 126)

Affect-hungry men and women were willing to encounter danger and disgrace in order to have relations with the *damnati*, the *perditi*, the *obscaeni*. Eppia, the otherwise diffident Roman matron, became dauntless when with her gladiator (Juvenal, *Satirae* 6.82–113).[81] Seneca sees this *nostalgie de la boue* as the culmination of the spiral of decadence. The *vir mollis*, the soft man, with his refined and delicate disposition, caught in

---

[78] Paula Webster, "The Forbidden: Eroticism and Taboo," in *Pleasure and Danger*, ed. Carole S. Vance (Boston, 1984), pp. 385–98.

[79] E.g., Ovid, *Amores* 2.7–8; Juvenal, *Satirae* 6.73–81, 116–32, 149–52; Martial 12.58; Suetonius, *Tiberius* 35.2; *Domitian* 3.

[80] "Quaedam enim feminae sordibus calent, nec libidinem concitant nisi aut servos viderint aut statores altius cinctos. Arena alias accendit aut perfusus pulvere mulio aut histrio scaenae ostentatione traductus. Ex hac nota domina est mea: usque ab orchestra quattuordecim transilit et in extrema plebe quaerit quod diligat. Ego adhuc servo numquam succubui nec hoc dii sinant ut amplexus meos in crucem mittam. Viderint matronae quae flagellorum vestigia osculantur. Ego etiam si ancilla sum numquam tamen nisi in equestribus sedeo."

[81] See Gillian Armstrong's penetrating film portrait of *Mrs. Soffal* (1986), the wife of the prison warden who is prepared to endure hardship and even death as the price of her elopement with a condemned criminal.

the spiral of desire, ended by risking death in the arena just to be on intimate terms with the gladiators (Seneca, *Quaestiones naturales* 7.31.1–3).

The Shards of the Mirror

It is important to emphasize that the employment of gladiators in private
entertainments for erotic excitement did not exclude an obsessive identification with them. The emperors, under whose aegis tens of thousands
of men encountered death in the arena, did not *only* disdain their victims.
Pliny breathes a sigh of relief when Domitian is dead that now one is not
compelled to root for the emperor's favorites in the arena: "That man
was demented, blind to the true sense of honor, who collected charges of
treason in the arena, who felt himself despised and scorned unless we
venerated his gladiators, considering any criticism of them to be of himself and a violation of his godhead—while deeming himself the equal of
the gods he deemed his gladiators equal to himself" (*Panegyricus* 33.4).
According to Suetonius, Caligula let himself be ruled by the charioteers
and gladiators and was the slave of actors and others connected with the
stage (*Caligula* 54–55).[82] The former slave "Trimalchio tyrannus—ipsis-
simus" felt no shame at covering his cups with depictions of the fights
between the gladiators Hermeros and Petraites (52.3),[83] his walls with
paintings of the games of Laenas (29–30), or his tomb with representations of gladiators—as did the Pompeian aristocrat Umbricius Scaurus.[84]
Indeed, a catamite found especial favor in Trimalchio's eyes for having
bought himself the panoply of a "Thracian" gladiator from his daily al-
lowance (75.4). Emperors emulated as well as sacrificed the gladiator:
Caligula, Titus, Hadrian, Lucius Verus, Commodus, Didius Julianus,
Caracalla, and Geta were also known to have "played" gladiator in and
out of the arena.[85]

This "gladiator madness" was shared by all social classes and both
sexes. Women as well as men played at being gladiators and *venatores*
(wild-beast hunters), both in and out of the arena.[86] Encolpius, former
gladiator, still possessed his gladiator's panoply, and wore it in a moment

[82] Seneca speaks of the "nobilissimi iuvenes" enslaved to the pantomimists (*Epistulae*
47.17).

[83] Henry T. Rowell, "The Gladiator Petraites and the Date of the *Satyricon*," *Transactions of the American Philological Association* 89 (1958), pp. 14–24.

[84] Mau and Kelsey, *Pompeii*, pp. 418–20; Ville, *La Gladiature*, pp. 201–2.

[85] See Hopkins, "Murderous Games," p. 20 and n. 29.

[86] E.g., Juvenal, *Satirae* 1.22–23, 6.246–67, 265–67; Petronius, *Satyricon* 45.7; Statius,
Silvae 1.6.51–56; Tacitus, *Annales* 15.32; Dio 62.3.1, 67.8.4, 76.16.1; Suetonius, *Domitian*
4.2; Ville, *La Gladiature*, p. 263; Robert, *Les Gladiateurs*, no. 184.

of desperate, suicidal love-sickness (81.2–82.1). Both Giton and Encolpius take the gladiator's oath (117.5), and like the Christian Perpetua, used the gladiator's gesture of baring the throat (97, 101.1).[87]

Erethism and Insensibility

The Roman trivialization of violence was not incompatible with a Vergilian supersensitivity to it. Our impression of Roman indifference to suffering is the result, in part, of the constant, unrelieved intensity of our literary sources. For example, the aphoristic and lapidary style of Seneca's tragedies has often been branded, paradoxically, "rhetorical" or "bombastic." Indeed, it is the insistent and excruciating emotional pitch of the plays of Seneca, the *eintöniger Donner*, that, like the music of Arnold Schoenberg or the virtuoso keyboard playing of a Wanda Landowska or a Maurizio Pollini, can anesthetize or "petrify" the listener and create an impression of cold detachment. We are wearied in Seneca, as in Lucan and Petronius, by the absence of catharsis.[88]

Toward animals, for instance, the Romans are both indifferent and empathetic. A Roman who might tolerate the slaughter of animals by the thousands in the circus might lament the death of one animal. Macrobius reports that Lucius Crassus, a man of censorial rank, was distracted by grief for the death of an eel:

> [Crassus], whose reputation as a man of gravity and seriousness Cicero himself attests, although he was regarded as preeminently eloquent and a leading figure among the most distinguished citizens, neverthless put on mourning when a lamprey died in a fishpond at his house and grieved for it as though for a daughter. The matter was not a secret, for when his colleague Domitius reproached him with it in the senate, as a disgraceful blot on his character, Crassus was not ashamed to admit what he had done and actually . . . gloried in it and avowed it to be an act of dutiful affection. (*Saturnalia* 3.15.3–5)[89]

If Caligula threatened to make his horse Incitatus a senator as still another vicious insult to the Roman aristocracy, he nevertheless, like James I of England, built his horse a palace and often slept in the stables with it

[87] *Passio Perpetuae* 21.9 (ed. Musarillo).

[88] See Regenbogen, "Schmerz und Tod in den Tragödien Senecas," pp. 167–218; Guido Bonelli, "Autenticità o retorica nella tragedia di Seneca," *Latomus* 39 (1980), pp. 612–38.

[89] Ovid laments a dead parrot (*Amores* 2.6); the orator Hortensius was believed to have wept for his beloved moray (Pliny, *Historia naturalis* 9.81.172); the Romans gave a public funeral for a talking raven (ibid. 10.60.122–23); Lucius Arruntius Stella wrote a poem on the death of a dove (Statius, *Silvae* 1.2.101–2).

(Suetonius, *Caligula* 55.3). Statius immortalized the lion lamented by Domitian and the Roman people as they would a great gladiator (*Silvae* 2.5).

The people who witnessed the wanton slaughter of wild animals in numbers that confound the imagination were the origin of, and/or audience for, many excessively tender animal stories, such as the hunt and slaughter of the tame stag of Vergil's Almo (*Aeneid* 7.475ff.), or Apion's tales of the dolphin who fell in love with the Neapolitan youth Hyacinthus, and, dying for grief when the boy died, was buried with him (Aulus Gellius, *Noctes Atticae* 6.8), or (greatest of all) the unforgettable story of Androcles and the lion (ibid. 5.14). Along with each and every fight of the gladiator Petraites, Trimalchio would have his tomb decorated with a portrait of his little lap dog.[90] One is reminded of the sparrow of Lesbia in Catullus, of the splendid and lavishly detailed paintings, mosaics, and sculptures of wild and, especially, of domestic animals in Pompeii, and of the Roman penchant for vegetarianism in this period. (Ovid brands meateating as a form of cannibalism in *Metamorphoses* 15.141–42.) The Romans were fascinated, as well, with the question of animal intelligence and language, with teaching animals to speak and procuring talking animals.[91]

The Romans of the "decadence" could form attachments to and indulge animals (and slaves and women—and for the same reasons) in a way that confounded their traditional hierarchy of values. At the same time the Romans also played the roles and even the deaths of animals for sexual titillation. Suetonius informs us that Nero would, in sexual play, bind his victims (male and female) and attack them in the guise of a wild animal in the circus (*Nero* 29); and Dio tells us the story of a prostitute sporting in the role of a leopard with a senator (76.8.2). The rich and noble matron of Apuleius is as excited to have sexual relations with the ass as Pasiphaë was with the bull (*Metamorphoses* 10.19–22).[92] Roman "bestiality" formed part of the extended repertoire of pleasures which included the enjoyment of the available array of monsters, freaks, fools, exotic persons, animals, and food. Indeed, all of these elements—erotic miscegenation, spectacular fantasy, variety and invention, violence and death—are combined in the anticipated execution of the female poisoner in Apuleius's *Metamorphoses* (10.28–35).

[90] For depictions of pets on funeral monuments, see E. Saglio, "Deliciae," in *D-S*, vol. 2.1, pp. 60–61.

[91] Pliny, *Historia naturalis* 10, esp. 10.58–60.117–124; *Anacharsis* 8; Plutarch, *Bruta animalia ratione uti, Moralia* 959–85; Aulus Gellius, *Noctes Atticae* 10.12.7; Petronius, *Satyricon* 28.9; Ovid, *Amores* 2.6. Steven Callahan, in the account of the withering ordeal that followed his shipwreck, depicts in wonderful detail the powerful sympathy that he developed for the species of fish on whose death his waking life was focused and upon whose death his life depended (*Adrift* [Boston, 1986]).

[92] Pasiphaë and the bull and Leda and the swan were two of the principal visual themes in the art of this period.

The Reflection of Divine Indifference

J'ai simplement compris qu'il n'y a qu'une façon de s'égaler
aux dieux: il suffit d'être aussi cruel qu'eux.
(Camus, *Caligula* 3.2)

The gods were often seen as the First Cause of the spiral of desire, the abettors of this devolution, this *mutatio in peius*. Even the "Stoics" in this period were wont to have somewhat "Epicurean" gods—if they were good, they might be indifferent. Seneca imagined Jove contemplating his own thoughts while the world perished (*Epistulae* 9.16).[93] If there were gods that were not indifferent, and not evil, they had none the less left this world in the hands of powers that had usurped their names and prerogatives: it is Trimalchio, holding the wand of Mercury, that Minerva conducts into Rome (*Satyricon* 15.29). Most often, these new and human gods simply imitated the old, wearing their beastly and incomprehensible faces. These human masters encouraged the desires of their subjects in order to demoralize and enslave them or in order to reproduce themselves.[94] The reign of the tyrant did not end the insatiable squandering by the gods and nature; it echoed and reproduced it. His regime did not end chaos and civil war; it *was* chaos and civil war (*De clementia* 1.26.2–5, 1.5.2).[95]

His subjects, in turn, gladly modeled themselves on the Powers That Be. The poet of *Priapea* 29 used the shamelessness of the god Priapus to justify his own, as the author of the *Elegiae ad Maecenatem* used the model of Hercules, totally abandoning himself to Queen Omphale and acting the role of a woman and slave, to justify his hero Maecenas's luxurious and "unmanly" behavior. Ovid's affair with the maidservant Cypassis was justified by the precedent of kings (*Amores* 2.8), and the Roman matron Paula masked and excused her adulteries with the deliberate (but plausible) lie "Caesar has ordered me to come in the morning to his Alban villa; Caesar has sent for me to Circeii" (Martial 11.7).

[93] Cf. Quintilian, *Institutiones oratoriae* 6 *praefatio* 4.

[94] According to Pliny, the princes (prior to the reigning Trajan) were cheered by the vices of their subjects more than by their virtues; first, because they enjoyed seeing their own character reproduced in others, and second, because they judged that those who were unworthy to be anything but slaves would suffer slavery more docilely (*Panegyricus* 45.1). Cf. Sallust, *Catilina* 11, 14; *Epistulae ad Caesarem* 2.1; Tacitus, *Annales* 1.10.1.

[95] "Our desire to consume, to annihilate, to make a bonfire of our resources, and the joy we find in the burning, the fire and the ruin are what seem to us divine, sacred" (Bataille, *Erotism*, p. 185). Seneca's Oedipus, like his Medea, Deiianira, Atreus, and Clytaemnestra yearn for the extremity of crime even against their own people (e.g. *Thyestes* 180–91; *Phoenissae* 350–58; *Agamemnon* 114–24). See Elizabeth Keitel's excellent article "Principate and Civil War in the *Annals* of Tacitus," *American Journal of Philology* 105 (1984), pp. 306–25.

The Disorder of Lost Beings

Sometimes there is no corrective or end to the spiral of desire. Seneca says in the *De ira*, "More crimes have been committed than could ever be rectified" (2.9.1).[96] Once wrath has taken over, a headlong plummet ("ir-revocabilis praecipitatio") cuts off all reconsideration and remedy (*De ira* 1.7.4). Things are so bad that once engaged in resistance or correction, one would be swept into the evil and soon go mad (*De ira* 2.9). "Gone are good customs, right doing, honor, piety, faith, and modesty, which, once gone, know no return," Clytaemnestra says to herself in the *Agamemnon* (111–12), one of Seneca's many allegories of civil war (along with the *Thyestes*, the *Hercules Furens*, the *Phoenissae*, the *Troades*). There is no kernel of goodness or innocence left to be preserved. There is now a necessity of erring, "necessitas errandi" (*De ira* 2.10.1).

In this topsy-turvy universe nature's laws are reversed. "What was virtue has become evil," according to Seneca.[97] In this case desire and its avatar hope had become evils, and one could only give oneself over to the moment, to "the fat hog of Epicurus"—as Petronius did. In the world of the *Satyricon* every quarrel is a civil war,[98] every tiff a tumult (e.g., 95). Yet, at the same time, there is little nostalgia for order and community in Petronius, little *Weltschmerz*. The desire to live, to experience, conquers. Petronius, like the modern nihilist E. M. Cioran, is a hero of flux. The beings in Petronius's fantasy adapt themselves to everything, endure everything. As for Cioran, so for Petronius: there is no other world than this—and there is not even this. When, in the *Philosophy of History*, Hegel calls the comic frame of mind "a hale condition of soul which, fully aware of itself, can suffer the dissolution of its aims and realizations," he might have been speaking of Petronius.

Rejuvenated Desire

Sometimes, though, through the application of austerity, asceticism, it was possible to create a positive hope, a positive desire, an order *that has ceased to be divine, automatic, or "natural."* Vladimir Jankélévitch, in his brilliant book, *L'Austerité et la vie morale* (p. 9), remarks on the relationship between asceticism and license: "L'école de la rigueur n'est-elle pas

---

[96] Cf. *Phaedra* 978–89; Tacitus, *Annales* 1.4.1.

[97] *Phoenissae* 477–79; *Anthologia Latina* 72.19; cf. 72.36, 73.9, 20; *Agamemnon* 813–84; Petronius, *Satyricon* 120.84–93.

[98] E.g., 59.2: "Semper in hac re qui vincitur vincit."

comme la rançon du libertinage érotique?"[99] One can compare Epictetus's "On Training": "I am inclined to pleasure: in order to train myself I will incline beyond measure in the opposite direction" (*Arrian, Epicteti dissertationes* 3.12.7). Jankélévitch explains: "If all is permitted, all is equal and indifferent: there is nothing here below save *isostheneia* and *adiaphora*: driven to despair by such easy terms, the *decadent* spirit proceeds to create imaginary difficulties and to invent artificial obstacles in order to restore, by veto, that wholesome resistance that alone is capable of protecting life against ennui and atrophy; lacking real problems, the spirit takes refuge in charades, enigmas and rebuses" (p. 32).[100] The self-imposition of limits will allow one to desire without despair, to be restored, rejuvenated.[101]

The Romans ransomed their desires. They threw up in order to eat (Suetonius, *Vitellius* 13). They fasted while they drank in order to feel the alcohol more powerfully (Seneca, *Epistulae* 122.6).[102] They built "poor men's huts" inside their palaces in order that, when the fancy struck them, they might experience poverty: "You need not suppose that I mean meals like Timon's or 'paupers's huts,' or any other device which luxuri-

---

[99] "De là ce jeu du renoncer pour regagner, qui a nom ascétisme" (Huguette Fugier, *Recherches sur l'expression du sacré dans la langue latine* [Paris, 1963], p. 28). See also the chapter "Nature du sacrifice: ascétisme et offrande," in Roger Caillois, *L'Homme et le sacré* (Paris, 1950).

[100] Pomponius: "There are those who have fled so far into the shadows that they believe to be in obscurity whatever is in light" ("quidam adeo in latebras refugerunt ut putent in turbido esse, quicquid in luce est" [quoted by Seneca, *Epistulae* 3.6]). I am reminded of the poem "Diagnosis" by Marcia Lee Anderson:

> We multiply diseases for delight,
> Invent a horrid want, a shameful doubt,
> Luxuriate in license, feed on night,
> Make inward bedlam—and will not come out.
> Why should we? Stripped of subtle complications,
> Who could regard the sun except with fear?
> This is our shelter against contemplation,
> Our only refuge from the plain and clear.
> Who would crawl out from under the obscure,
> To stand defenseless in the sunny air?
> No terror of obliquity so sure,
> As the most shining terror of despair
> To know how simple is our deepest need,
> How sharp, and how impossible to feed.

(Quoted by Ernest Becker in *The Denial of Death* [New York, 1973], p. 66, from Harold F. Searles, "Schizophrenia and the Inevitability of Death," *Psychiatric Quarterly* 35 [1961], pp. 633–34).

[101] Cf. Straw, *Gregory the Great*, pp. 128–46.

[102] Encolpius's undertakes an ascetic regime to cure his impotence; the aim of the regime is pleasure (Petronius, *Satyricon* 130).

ous millionaires use to beguile the tedium of their lives" (Epicurus frag. 158 [Usener]).[103] According to Lucian, the wealthy get bored of rich food and eat vegetables and thyme as a diversion (*Saturnalia* 28).[104] Pliny the Younger is tired by the lewd dancers and buffoons of the dinner party (it's always the same old thing!) and longs for the novelty of serious conversation (*Epistulae* 9.17).[105] Fasting, eating gruel, and sleeping on a board, like danger and even death, became additional forms of playful self-indulgence, like the risky and rigorous mountain-climbing expeditions of the modern bourgeois or the painful tattoos of the Japanese gangster. The extreme example of this juxtaposition of self-indulgence and abstemiousness (as he was of simultaneous desire and deprivation) was the miser: the man who lived midst great abundance with sunken, emaciated cheeks.[106]

The Temptation of Castration

You are more libidinous than any eunuch.

Libidinosior es quam ullus spado.

(a Roman proverb[107])

Self-denial becomes the culmination of the spiral of desire.[108] Seneca imagines the climax of unchecked self-indulgence in men to take the form

---

[103] Martial thinks it a fine irony that Olus, having built himself a "pauper's hut," is compelled by bankruptcy to actually live in it! (3.48). Seneca also uses the phrase *pauperis cella* metaphorically of the rhetorical device that an excess of luxury adds to speech that is not content with simple charms (*Epistulae* 100.6).

[104] Cicero, speaking of the "magnificentia et sumptus epularum": "Who does not see that need is the spice of all such things?" ("quis non videt, desideriis omnia ista condiri?" [*Tusculanae disputationes* 5.34.97]). "Those who are hottest in the pursuit of pleasure are furthest from catching it . . . the pleasantness of food lies in appetite and not in repletion" ("qui voluptatem maxime sequantur, eos minime consequi, iucunditatemque victus esse in desiderio, non in satietate" [ibid. 5.34.100]). "Intemperance is the plague of sensual pleasure; and temperance is not its scourge, it is its seasoning" (Montaigne, "On Experience").

[105] Cf. Marcus Aurelius 6.46.

[106] E.g., Apuleius, *Metamorphoses* 1.21ff.; Horace, *Epistulae* 1.2.56, 1.16.63–65; *Satirae* 1.1.

[107] Quoted by Quintilian, *Institutiones oratoriae* 6.3.64.

[108] Oliver Sacks, in his fascinating and moving book *Awakenings* (New York, 1973) offers many vivid illustrations of this apparent paradox. The stimulation, by the administration of dopomines, of men and women paralyzed by viral encephalitis awakened desires for excitement, for food, for sex, etc. that were the more intense for their having been so long and violently suppressed. Their desires became so fierce and so tormenting, their sense of loss and deprivation so severe, that several of the patients chose to return to the state of

of a self-inflicted insult to their own virility (*Naturales quaestiones* 7.31.3)[109]—Tertullian's "exitus furoris" (*Apologeticus* 23.2).[110] The search for endless diversion ends with men either cutting off their genitals, like the *galli*, the devotees of Cybele, or entering the brothels of the *ludi* to serve the lusts of the gladiators.

A Roman *tintinnabulum* from Pompeii depicts a gladiator/*bestiarius* whose enormous penis is a ravening wild animal. This penis, a dog with gaping jaws, is a part of the gladiator's own body turned furiously against him. He is about to slay the beast which is threatening him; in so doing he will castrate himself.[111] There is no more apt icon for the Roman cosmology of desire and the place of the gladiator in it. Emasculation is, then, the ultimate price a man pays for lust, and he pays it voluntarily. Petronius's Eumolpus depicts the Roman spiral of vice and its result: "The Roman youth despised their own strength" ("Ipsa suas vires odit Romana iuventus" [*Satyricon* 120.84]).[112] As a result, self-castration, what we would think of as an extreme act of asceticism or self-sacrifice,[113] is often categorized as a form of self-indulgence by the Romans, and the castrated as extreme libertines.[114]

Concomitantly, the culmination of the escalation of lust for women was the assumption of the male role: the women began keeping the late hours of men, drinking as much, being as sexually active. "They desire the most improbable varieties of unchastity, and in the company of men they play the part of men" (Seneca, *Epistulae* 95.20–21). One can think of Fulvia or Julia or Agrippina, or Petronius's Domatilla and Tryphaena.[115]

---

paralysis (or to die) rather than to cater to their ravening needs. (See especially the cases of Rose R., Maria G., and Leonard L.) For notorious examples of the spiral of desire leading to the point of self-destruction, see Myra Friedman, *Buried Alive* (New York, 1973); Jerry Hopkins and Danny Sugerman, *No One Here Gets Out Alive* (New York, 1980); Albert Goldman, *Elvis* (New York, 1981).

[109] Cf. *Naturales quaestiones* 1.17.10; Lucan, *Bellum civile* 1.164–65; Sallust, *Catilina* 13.3.

[110] See Seneca Rhetor, *Controversiae* 10.4.17; Seneca, *Epistulae* 122.7; *De ira* 1.21.3; Quintilian, *Institutiones oratoriae* 5.12.17. The "inexplebiles populi fauces" result in "fastidiosae mollesque mentes" (Cicero, *De re publica* 1.43).

[111] Catherine Johns, *Sex or Symbol: Erotic Images of Greece and Rome* (Austin, Tex., 1982), p. 68.

[112] Cf. Seneca Rhetor: "ipsos pudet viros esse" (*Controversiae* 10.4.17).

[113] E.g., Georges Bataille, "Sacrificial Mutilation and the Severed Ear of Vincent Van Gogh," in *Visions of Excess*, trans. Allan Stoekl (Minneapolis, 1985), pp. 66–68; Aline Rouselle, *Porneia*, pp. 162–65.

[114] See Juvenal, *Satirae* 8.171–76; Martial 3.81; Apuleius, *Metamorphoses* 8.25–30, 9.8–10.

[115] Sallust, *Catilina* 13.3.

1. Bronze *tintinnabulum* from Pompeii depicting a gladiator/bestiarius attacking a wild beast that is also his own penis (Naples Museum).

Infinite Regressions

Asceticism comes to Rome, then, as the companion of novelty and the symptom of desire.[116] The ubiquity of the figure of the "hypocrite" and the frequency of the conjunction of vice with austerity reveals how conscious the Romans are of this connection.[117] The equation "severity" = "self-indulgence" is so common in Roman thought that the Romans had only to perceive asceticism to conceive excess as its motivation.[118] (Hence the consistent attribution of orgies of self-indulgence to the Cynics, to the followers of Ceres and Cybele, to the Jews, the Christians, the Gnostics, etc. Tertullian laments that the Romans think *Christianus* one more vice to be charged against, *or commended in*, the "mulier lasciva et festiva" and the "iuvenis lascivus et amasius.")[119] Petronius has his sybarite Trimalchio decry the Romans' insatiable consumption of the products of empire (*Satyricon 55*), and Tacitus has the greedy and self-indulgent Piso lecture on the evils of luxury (*Annales 2.57*), while his arch-hypocrite Tiberius addresses a lengthy letter to the Senate decrying the hypocrisy of the Roman aristocracy (who demand sumptuary legislation and then rebel against it [*Annales 3.52–54*]).

Roman "conservatism"—the admiration for order, simplicity, gravity, and discipline (such as appears in Cicero, Juvenal, Tacitus, Lucan, and Seneca)—coincides at this time and in these authors with an appetite for novelty. (One thinks of Cicero's endless gyrations from villa to villa or of his vying with the mime Roscius to express the same idea in the greatest

[116] Stoic, Cynic, and Sceptic *ataraxia* and *anaisthesia*, freedom from disturbance, were other versions of desire taken to its logical conclusion. They were forms of emotional self-castration, and just as castration did not lead to the remission of desire, neither did passivity and indifference lead to a lessening of sadistic cruelty. Plutarch's cold-hearted apathy did not prevent him from viciously beating his slave; it only freed him from feeling compassion (Aulus Gellius, *Noctes Atticae* 1.26). The methods of asceticism and eroticism often resembled one another: flagellation, scarification, etc. (see Lucian, *Nigrinus* 27), either inflicted or suffered at another's hands. The same affect-hungry persons were drawn to both. As John Findlay points out, asceticism gives the flesh central importance (*Philosophy of Hegel* [New York, 1958], pp. 99–100). See Freud, "On the Universal Tendency to Debasement in the Sphere of Love" (1912), in *The Standard Edition of the Complete Psychological Works of Sigmund Freud*, trans. James Strachey, vol. 11 (London, 1957), pp. 187–88.

[117] E.g., Cicero, *Pro Murena* 19.46; Tacitus, *Annales* 1.7, 1.10.1; Pseudo-Sallust, *In Ciceronem* 2 (cf. Aulus Gellius, *Noctes Atticae* 12.12); Pseudo-Cicero, *In Sallustium*; Juvenal, *Satirae* 2.1–3, 8–9, 23–35; Martial, *Epigrams* 7.58, 11.2. Jasper Griffin, in "Propertius and Anthony," *Journal of Roman Studies* 67 (1977), pp. 17–26 treats of the stereotype of "the man of action who lives a life of luxury." See also Amy Richlin, *The Garden of Priapus: Sexuality and Aggression in Roman Humor* (New Haven, 1983), p. 22n. 52, pp. 88, 91.

[118] E.g., Tacitus, *Historia* 5.4.

[119] Tertullian himself feels called upon to argue that Christianity is not simply another vice but the antidote and emendation of vice (e.g., *Apologeticus* 3.3).

variety of ways [Macrobius, *Saturnalia* 3.14.12]). These trends amplify and intensify one another. Annaeus Serenus, like Seneca himself, attempts to be an ascetic in luxury (cf. Seneca, *De tranquillitate* 1.4–9). It is not surprising that Seneca imagines his severe and celibate Hippolytus dying in an orgy of erotic violence, or that Augustus condemned his daughter Julia, and his granddaughter Julia, profligates both, to die slow deaths of destitution. Vergil's frantic Dido and long-suffering Aeneas are alternatives; they are also mirrored images of one other.[120] The Seneca who wrote the emotionally frenzied plays is the same who writes the monotonously restrained *Moral Epistles*; the dour Lucan wrote a *Saturnalia*. It does not surprise anyone familiar with the emotional patterns of this period that Seneca, at the very end of a long essay on tranquillity and restraint, erupts in a dithyrambic rapture on intoxication.[121]

Necessary Lies

Art and ritual, like asceticism, were given compensatory and regulatory roles. There are arts and artifices that undermine the established order of the world, and there are arts and artifices that forge an order. The more effective the first, the more necessary the second. Nietzsche needs the Apollinian to give form and majesty to the otherwise chaotic and sordid horror of the Dionysian. But according to Josephus (answering the charge that the Jews had not produced great artists), the Jewish people's fierce and constant adherence to tradition, made them value art less; they do not make innovations, so they do not need innovations to correct them (*Contra Apionem* 2.19–21). In the Rome of the late Republic and early Empire, we are in a world that more closely resembles Nietzsche's than it does Josephus's, a world in which there must be "noble fictions."

I should point out here that asceticism itself was (and is) a form of "fiction" or play-acting, a version of the "necessary lie": one "plays" at being poor or in pain or endangered (like going to a horror movie, where one plays at being frightened). Little Marcus Aurelius plays "sleeping on a board" in the palace. Austerity becomes a sort of festival from the state of disorder—like the Saturnalia that Seneca proclaims in the *Apocolocyntosis* as the release from the reign of "the most Saturnalian of princes" ("saturnalicius princeps"). In fiction, at least, austerity is the return to cosmic order.[122]

---

[120] It is characteristic of Roman epic poetry to combine a fierce discipline and a phantasmagorical imagination. This is true of Vergil, Ovid, Lucan, and Statius.

[121] *De tranquillitate* 17.10–11.

[122] Brian Moeran, "The Beauty of Violence: *Jidaigeki, Yakuza* and 'Eroduction' Films in

When we think of the gladiatorial games as unbearably sordid, it is in part because we are unaware of, or are not moved by, the art and artifice, the "fictions," that framed and ordered them, the pomp and circumstance with which they were ennobled.[123] A great deal of bright pagentry (to us superficial or peripheral, to the Romans central and necessary) framed the bloody battles in the arena, as they did the execution of the poisoner in Apuleius's *Metamorphoses* 10. The effects on those who experienced them of the ritual parade (the *pompa*), the ceremonial meal (the *cena libera*), the music, the costumes, and the etiquette surrounding the gladiatorial games is lost to us, as is the importance of the gladiator as a theme of artistic creation.[124]

Unfortunately, the effectiveness of austerity as a remedy to desire was vitiated in this world by the presence of unequal power relations. Self-restraint might simply be, as it was for the client and mimic of Caelius, a form of collusion with, or provocation of, the excesses of the powerful. The proximity of the tyrant *requires* one to exercise deliberate and theatrical self-control. Marcia, the daughter of the martyr for free speech Cremutius Cordus, is compelled to choke back her sobs (Seneca, *Consolatio ad Marciam* 1.2). Pastor must calmly celebrate with the imperial monster the slaughter of his first son . . . because he has another (*De Ira* 2.33.3–6).[125]

As a result, the expression of passion, of emotion, of anger, of suffering could be seen as liberation from the constraint of rejoicing—and thus from the arbitrary and tyrannical license of the more powerful. There is exuberance (as well as pain) in just describing the crimes of those who have compelled us to smile; one feels this compound of emotions in Seneca's *Apocolocyntosis*, in Lucan's *Bellum civile*, in Petronius's *Satyricon*, in Tacitus's *Annales* and *Historia*, in Pliny's *Panegyricus*—just as one does in Nikita Khrushchev's "Feasts and Holidays with Stalin."[126] The abandonment to passion becomes a form of resistance to tyranny.

Japanese Cinema," in *The Anthropology of Violence*, ed. David Riches (Oxford, 1986), pp. 103–17, esp. p. 114 and n. 10. (See the extensive discussion of the "Saturnalia from the Saturnalia" in the chapter "Striking the Monster.")

[123] Cf. Ville, *La Gladiature*, pp. 366 and n. 47, 386–430, 455; Clavel-Lévêque, *L'Empire en jeux*.

[124] Horace's servant Davus, for instance, is depicted as admiring the representations of the gladiators Fulvius, Rutuba, and Pacideianus (*Satirae* 2.7).

[125] Cf. Tacitus, *Annales* 1.7.1. Lucan's Roman matron, faced with the imminent invasion of Caesar's forces, urges her fellows to weep: they should weep while they can, for under the tyrant they will perforce rejoice (*Bellum civile* 2.38–42; cf. 7.40–42 and Dio 74.23.2).

[126] In Nikita Khrushchev, *Khrushchev Remembers*, trans. Strobe Talbott (Boston, 1970), pp. 296–306. One senses this in the memoirs of Ilya Ehrenburg, Evgenia Ginzburg, and Nadezhda Mandelstam, and a work like the *Gulag Archipelago* of Alexander Solzhenitsyn.

Violence as Austerity

It is a weak spirit that can not endure wealth!
Infirmi animi est pati non posse divitias.

(Seneca, *Epistulae* 5.6)

The problem remained for the Romans, as it does for us: when does austerity create balance, security, and order, and when does it stimulate explosive violence or incite the transgressions it was designed to curb? Here it is important to note that *any act* could be, and was, categorized now as licentious, now as ascetic. Seneca categorizes the eating of gruel and sleeping on a board (or in a "pauper's hut") both as acts of discipline *or* as vices, and as both in *Epistulae* 18.[127] Wine drinking could be an *exercitatio* in resisting the effects of wine (Aulus Gellius, *Noctes Atticae* 15.2.6–8).[128] In just such a way, living luxuriously could be an exercise in inuring oneself to the allure of luxury (Macrobius, *Saturnalia* 2.8.7).[129] Thievery and marriage could both be forms of ascetic discipline (Aulus Gellius, *Noctes Atticae* 11.18.17) and celibacy a vice (ibid. 2.15). Violence could likewise be either:[130] There is a violence that breaks the code and a violence that restores it, a violence that destroys and a violence that remedies.[131] Petronius's Eumolpus remarks on the Roman civil wars: "In despair they turn to violence, and bloodshed restores the good things lost by luxury" (*Satyricon* 119.56). As Jankélévitch explains: "Shapeless violence is the hypocritical substitute and successor of austerity. . . . Violence is the means available to the players of being austere: waging war, or waging war on themselves."[132]

Stifling one's desires could, just like indulging them, cause one to turn upon oneself, to eat up oneself and others:

[127] Cf. Martial 3.48; Seneca, *Epistulae* 100.6.

[128] Cf. Macrobius, *Saturnalia* 2.8.7.

[129] Cf. Horace, *Epistulae* 1.17.

[130] Tacitus distinguishes the violence that is pollution and the violence that is expiation (*Annales* 1.43–44).

[131] Tacitus's Germanicus finds it hard to distinguish the violence that cures from the violence that kills: "This is destruction rather than remedy" (*Annales* 1.49). See Moeran, "The Beauty of Violence," p. 115 and n. 12; René Girard, *Violence and the Sacred*, trans. Patrick Gregory (Baltimore, 1977), esp. p. 115.

[132] *L'Austerité*, p. 9. Margarethe von Trotta's movie *Marianne and Julianne* (1982) is about the effects of the horrors of the Nazi period on the development of two German sisters after the war. The austere and "disciplined" sister, who did not want and could not bear the guilt and impurity, joins, as an adult, the Baader-Meinhof terrorist group. The "rebellious" sister, who even as a girl indulged her desires, is more tolerant and flexible, but at the price of having to live in a body and a world in which violence is "incorporated."

Desires, pent up within narrow bounds from which there is no escape, strangle one another. Thence comes mourning and melancholy and the thousand waverings of an unsettled mind, whose hopes, being unsatisfied, hold it in suspense and, being lamented as lost, render it melancholy. . . . Thence too the bitterest jealousy of the advancement of others. For their unhappy sloth fosters envy, and, because they could not succeed themselves, they wish everyone else to be ruined. (Seneca, *De tranquillitate* 2.10–11)

The hopes, both *incoatae* and *deploratae*, both incipient and mourned, do not go away; rather, they are aggravated.[133]

Food strangles the voracious, abstinence the austere . . . there is shipwreck everywhere. (Petronius, *Satyricon* 115.16)[134]

Conclusions

> What joy and what torture!
> I cannot leave this vision.
> How strangely that one scarlet thread,
> no thicker than the blade of a knife
> decorates her lovely neck.
> (Goethe, *Faust*, part 1)[135]

These are the lines that Faust speaks when he beholds the fascinating Medusa in whose deadly face every man sees his own beloved, the fatal reflection of his own inordinate desire.[136] Faust cannot see the horror that Mephistopheles sees. But the point of contact in their visions is that thin red line adorning the phantom's throat, the thin red line signaling violent death and enhancing the beauty of the wraith.

The Romans made their own Medusas, in the image of their fiercest desires. The gladiator was to the Romans what the Uffizi *Medusa* was to

---

[133] When the camp-prefect Aufidienus Rufus tried to restore "the old severe discipline" to the idle and luxurious camp in Pannonia under Tiberius, the result was mutiny. Similarly, Tiberius, according to Tacitus, did not yet dare to curb the *theatralis licentia* that had been indulgently treated for so many years (*Annales* 1.54). The Roman aristocracy reacted with furious obstinacy and indignation—or with approval—to the austerities imposed by Augustus (cf. Tacitus, *Annales* 3.28). The defence of wealth and ostentation could be provoked by attempts to limit it (ibid. 2.33). That the Romans themselves were highly aware of the uncertain effects of control is evident from their debates on the usefulness of sumptuary legislation (ibid. 3.52.1–54.5).

[134] "Cibus avidum strangulavit, abstinentem frugalitas . . . ubique naufragium est."

[135] MacIntyre translation.

[136] See the chapter "The Beauty of the Medusa" in Mario Praz, *The Romantic Agony*, pp. 25–50. See also Michael Lieris, *Manhood*, trans. Richard Howard (New York, 1963).

the Romantics, what Guido Reni's *Saint Sebastion* was for Yukio Mishima.

According to the elder Seneca, "[the rich] throw into the gladiatorial schools all the best-looking, the most fit for combat."[137] The finest, the most valuable gladiators were "the beautiful ones." An inscription from the second century lists the classes of gladiators, starting with the "promiscuous multitude," and proceeding through the "common sort" and the "better," to the "best," and finally arriving at the "beautiful" ("promiscua multitudo, gregarii, meliores, summi, formonsi [*sic*]").[138]

"In sacrifice," according to Georges Bataille, "the victim is chosen so that its perfection shall give point to the full brutality of death" (*Erotism*, p. 144). "Beauty has a cardinal importance, for ugliness cannot be spoiled, and to despoil is the essence of eroticism . . . the greater the beauty, the more it is befouled" (ibid., p. 145).[139] This yearning to destroy the fine, the strong, and the most fit is not just the conceit of modern Romantics. Nicolas of Damascus transmits the story of a will by which a man designated certain of his slaves, remarkable for their beauty, to fight to the death at his funeral.[140]

For Bataille eroticism is the hunger for life up to the point of death, a burning to the point of incineration. It is, for him, the product of paradox. We tend to think of eroticism as the opposite and inversion of asceticism, but Bataille explains that it is not the whore that is erotic, nor the madonna, but the juxtaposition of these images. Eroticism results from the concentration of extremes: continuity and discontinuity, attraction and horror, etherealness and carnality, asceticism and license. It is not Margarete nor Medusa but the juxtaposition that makes Goethe's phantom, like the gladiator, so high-charged, so "erotic," so "cruel."

The contradictory and inflammatory desires that infused every aspect of Roman society were, in the arena, focused in a circle of intense heat. I

[137] "Non curatis quod iuvenum miserorum simplicitatem circumeunt et speciosissimum quemque ac maxime idoneum castris in ludum coniciunt" (*Controversiae* 10.4.18, cf. 5.33); see also Nicolas of Damascus in Athenaeus, *Deipnosophistai* 4.39.

[138] *CIL* 2.6278. For the appreciation of the beauty of the gladiator see also Lucilius 4.28 ("formosus puello"); Lucian, *Toxaris* 58 (the procession of noble and fair young men into the arena); Arrian, *Epicteti dissertationes* 2.24.23; Robert, *Les Gladiateurs*, p. 63 and no. 139; Ville, *La Gladiature*, pp. 301, 330.

[139] I would add that the reverse is also true for the gladiator, as it is for the bullfighter or the soldier: the closeness of the blade, the closeness to death and violation, rendered the gladiator beautiful. Eppia's Sergius is quite hideous, according to Juvenal, disfigured and infected. "But he was a gladiator!—it is this that makes all these fellows into Hyacinthuses! . . . It is the sword that the women love" (*sed gladiator erat; facit hoc illos Hyacinthos / . . . ferrum est quod amant*" [Juvenal, *Satirae* 6.110 + 112]). For the erotic appeal of the gladiator, see Martial 5.24.10: "cura laborque ludiarum."

[140] Athenaeus, *Deipnosophistai* 4.39. The people opposed the execution of his will.

have tried to show that the gladiator did not, by any means, monopolize the conflicting emotions he epitomized. Rather, I assert that he concentrated the extremes of beauty and violation, power and powerlessness, control and abandon to be found in the late Republic and early Empire. The "gladiator madness" of the Romans was simply a distillation of the parching liquors of despair and desire that had, elsewhere within that culture, reached a point of saturation.

The skeletons of seventeen men who perished in the Vesuvian holocaust have been recovered from the ashes of the gladiatorial barracks of Pompeii. They were trapped in a cell in which weapons were stored. Several had had no possibility of escape; their legs were still bound in stocks. With them was found the skeleton of a woman richly adorned with gold jewelry—a necklace of emeralds, two armbands, rings, and other ornaments—and carrying a cameo in a small casket. A lady, we will never know what brought her to the barracks. She can only tease our imaginations. Was she a *ludia*, one of the "groupies" who attended the "families" of gladiators?[141] Was she like Eppia, mocked by Juvenal, the senator's wife who fled to Alexandria with her scarred "Sergiolus" and his family of fellow gladiators (6.82–83)? Was she like those men and women whom Tertullian disdained for giving their bodies and souls to the gladiators, the actors and the charioteers?[142] Was she like those scorned by Petronius for being "inflamed by the arena, or by a muleteer mired in dirt, or an actor disgraced by his exposure on the stage?" Did she kiss the tracks of the whips?

> SCIPIO: Il [Caligula] m'a appris à tout exiger.
> CHEREA: Non, Scipio, il t'a désespéré.
>
> (Camus, *Caligula* 4.1)

[141] For the *ludia*, see Ville, *La Gladiature*, p. 330 and n. 226; Martial 5.24.10; Juvenal 6.104–5 (Eppia as *ludia*).
[142] *De spectaculis* 22.

THE MONSTER

THREE

FASCINATION

A VAIN, BARREN, EXQUISITE WASTING

The monster terrifies and attracts. He is, simultaneously,
hideous and seductive; you flee him even while he
fascinates you.
(Jean Brun, "Le Prestige du monstre")[1]

I was fascinated—fascination being, after all, only the
extreme of detachment.
(Roland Barthes, *A Lover's Discourse*)

LIKE THE GARGOYLE of the Gothic cathedral, the monster charms and repels within a paradoxical system of homeopathic magic. The monster fascinates; the monster cures the fascination. The monster fixates; the monster frees.[2]

The Romans of the late Republic and early Empire were entranced by the horrific, the miraculous, and the untoward, hypnotized by violence and cruelty and death,—as if a type of *paralysis agitans* afflicted the whole of the people. One of the signals of this emotional state is the proliferation of monsters. The *anceps*, the two-headed, the ambiguous, always important to Roman culture, was also dangerous and constricted by taboo. But in this period the filtering systems, the systems of discrimination within the culture, appear to be undergoing a transformation allowing the barriers to be breached and the grotesque and the miraculous to spill over into every aspect of Roman life.

The Curious Ones

To the degree that our speech is twisted and bent, according to Quintilian, we admire it as exquisite. The first-century teacher of rhetoric proceeds

[1] *Le Mythe de la peine*, p. 301.

[2] "Gargoyles and demons, which fall into the same class as drolleries, are intended to ward off demons. . . . But they also represent the demonic forces themselves" (Geoffrey Galt Harpham, *On the Grotesque: Strategies of Contradiction in Art and Literature* [Princeton, 1982], p. 37).

to compare the Roman admiration for the improper, obscure, swollen, base, foul, lewd, and effeminate ("impropria, obscura, tumida, humilia, sordida, lasciva, effeminata") in speech to the placing of a higher value in the slave market on the bodies of the distorted than on those of the fair.[3] There are those at Rome—the *curiosi*—who, according to Plutarch, pass by the handsome boys and girls for sale and proceed to the "monster market," the *teraton agora*, and search out those who have three eyes or ostrich heads or weasel arms.[4] Indeed, the value placed on the *distorti* is so high, according to Longinus, that children are deliberately deformed by being bound and confined in boxes (*De sublimitate* 44.5).[5]

In the late Republic and the early Empire the exaggerated and the astonishing permeated life in a manner and to a degree unprecedented in Roman history. The dwarf and the giant, the hunchback and the living skeleton ceased being prodigies and became pets; they ceased being destroyed and expiated and became objects of the attention and cultivation of every class. A pinhead in red livery stood beside the emperor Domitian.[6] Wealthy men and women surrounded themselves with freaks and "naturals" (not to mention Greek philosophers and Maltese lapdogs),[7] with miniature paintings and colossal statues. Pliny recalls, in his catalogue of human wonders, the giant Gabbara brought to Rome in the age of Claudius and the ten-foot-high titans of the Augustan city. He recalls the dwarf Cinopas among the pets of Julia, Augustus's granddaughter, as well as the tiny freedwoman of the elder Julia.[8] Calpurnius Siculus's Corydon, like tens of thousands of his fellows, stared in amazement at the *monstra* of the arena (which we can identify as the giraffe, the polar bear, the seal, and the hippopotamus—creatures for whom the Romans had no names [*Eclogae* 7.64]). Horace tells us that the white elephant or the "diversum confusa genus panthera camelo" gave the Roman playwright tough competition (*Epistulae* 2.1.195–96), and he had to compete as well with the street-corner mime and its cast of distorted figures. Little

---

[3] *Institutiones oratoriae* 2.5.10–12.

[4] *De curiositate* 10 *Moralia* 520c.

[5] Cf. the cynical use of the deliberately deformed as described by Seneca the Elder, *Controversiae* 10.4 + 8.

[6] Suetonius, *Domitianus* 4.

[7] "A la fin de la République et sous l'Empire, il n'y avait pas une riche Romaine qui, outre ses oiseaux de l'Inde, ses paons de Médie et son bichon de Malte, n'eût aussi son nain" (O. Navarre, "Nanus," in *D-S*, vol. 4.1, p. 1). E. g., Seneca, *Epistulae* 15.9, 50.2; *Apocolocyntosis* 3; Pliny the Elder, *Historia naturalis* 7.74–75; Martial 3.82, 6.39, 7.38, 14.210, 212; Juvenal, *Satirae* 8.32–38; Suetonius, *Tiberius* 61; See W. A. Becker, *Gallus: Roman Scenes of the Time of Augustus* (New York, 1903), pp. 210–11; Friedländer, *Sittengeschichte*, vol. 2, p. 372; Enid Welsford, *The Fool* (New York, 1961 [orig. publ. 1935]), pp. 58–59.

[8] *Historia naturalis* 7.74–75.

"Hellenistic" or "Alexandrian" grotesques made of clay or bronze prolif-
erated: *ridiculi* and *obscaeni* presided over the tradesman's shop and the
baker's oven and "anatomical whimsies" combining human, animal, veg-
etable, and architectural forms sprouted from the walls of Nero's Golden
House.[9]

In English the adjective *curious* categorizes both the one who looks and
the strange or unusual object which attracts that look. This reciprocal
mirror of ideas is at the heart of the Roman concept of fascination. The
"monstrous" was in the eye of the beholder; to see the Roman monster,
we must look into the gaze of the Roman spectator.

Horace tells us that it is the abnormal and unusual—the *curious*—that
captures and transfixes the eyes (*Epistulae* 1.6).[10] It is the extraordinary
that we desire.[11] And so the heralds of the emperor Claudius, to draw the
people to his Secular Games, cried through the streets that the games
would be unlike those anyone had seen before or would see again: "ludos
quos nec spectasset quisquam nec spectaturus esset" (Suetonius *Claudius*
21.1).[12] It was the exceptionally large penises of Martial's smooth-
skinned attendants at the baths that attracted the *curiosus* Philomusus.[13]
It was the exposure of Ascyltos's outsized genitals that fixed the attention
of the applauding crowd of bathers in Petronius's *Satyricon* (92). Finally,
it was the preposterousness of the nuptials of the seven-year-old Panny-
chis with the teenaged Giton that stupefied Encolpius (*Satyricon* 25).[14]

The prodigy was often, but not necessarily, hideous. The inexpressible
beauty of Apuleius's Psyche made her a freak marveled at by multitudes
of natives and pilgrims "admiratione stupidi" (*Metamorphoses* 4.28).[15]

---

[9] It is from sixteenth-century descriptions of the underground excavations of the Golden
House and the Baths of Titus that we derive the word "grotesque." For histories of the
concept, see Frances K. Barasch, *The Grotesque: A Study in Meanings* (The Hague, 1971),
pp. 17–31; Mikhail Bakhtin, *Rabelais and His World*, trans. Helene Iswolsky (Cambridge,
Mass., 1968), pp. 31ff.; Harpham, *On the Grotesque*, pp. 23–47.

[10] The amazing thing was the *miraculum*. "La rencontre, fréquente, des deux termes de
'prodige' et de 'miracle', à propos des mêmes objets, souligne, en outre, qu'on ne saurait
assigner à chacun un sens complètement distinct" (Jean Céard, *La Nature et les prodiges*
[Geneva, 1977], p. 20). For examples of *miracula*: Pliny, *Historia naturalis* 7.32, 8.20; Livy
1.45.4, 1.59.3; Martial 1.21; Tertullian, *Apologeticus* 23.

[11] "Concupiscuntur enim etiam parva, si notabilia sunt, si rara" (Seneca, *Epistulae* 105.3
[Madvig]).

[12] Cf. Cicero, *In Pisonem* 65.

[13] Martial 11.63. There are those *curiosi* who, like Hostius Quadra (Seneca, *Naturales
quaestiones* 1.16.3), go to the baths to look for just such objects of interest.

[14] Martial is struck, for example, by the hideous giant owned by Severus: "So huge and
ugly are you, Polyphemus, that even the Cyclops himself might wonder at you" ("Tantus es
et talis nostri Polypheme Severi/ Ut te mirari possit et ipse Cyclops" [7.38]).

[15] Compare Livy's Sabine cow (1.45.4–5). Compare, as well, Johannes Chrysostomus's
description of the fascination exercised by the gorgeous, bejewelled mime with her devil's

The exotic animals, but above all, the sheer magnificence of Nero's games awed Corydon:

> The splendor of the scene struck me from every side. I stood transfixed and admired it all with mouth agape, without yet being able to absorb any single marvel, when an old man who happened to be at my left remarked: "Do you wonder, peasant, that you are spellbound by such magnificence—you who know nothing of gold but only your squalid houses and huts—for even I, a white-haired and palsied old man, grown old here in the city, am stupefied by all this."[16]

Beautiful or ugly, it is the *monstrum*, the *miraculum*, the *ostentum* that fills us with awe. Encolpius's magically enhanced virility fills Eumolpus with horror as well as wonder (*Satyricon* 140).

The "monster market" was frequented by the *curiosi*. In modern Western culture curiosity is a neutral or even positive emotion. But for the Romans it was a sad and exasperated emotion, identified with envy and malice. "No one is curious who is not also malevolent [*Nam curiosus nemo est quin sit malevolus*" (Plautus, *Stichus* 208)].[17] It is because they envy that Catullus, frantically kissing Lesbia, fears the *curiosi* (7).[18] This equation (curiosity = envy = malice) rendered the *curiosus*, the "Peeping Tom," a dreaded type in ancient Rome. Among them were numbered the

---

song (*Homilia* 37, in *Patrologia Graeca* (hereafter *PG*), vol. 57, cols. 425–26; *Homilia* 18, in *PG*, vol. 59, col. 120; *Homilia* 69, in *PG*, vol. 58, cols. 644–45); cf. Hermann Reich, *Der Mimus* (Berlin, 1903), p. 118. Medusa, the enchantress par excellence, was ugly *or* beautiful. So the extraordinary qualities of the beloved (often invisible save to the beloved) render the beloved fascinating.

16   sic undique fulgor
percussit. Stabam defixus et ore patenti
cunctaque mirabar necdum bona singula noram,
cum mihi iam senior, lateri qui forte sinistro
iunctus erat, "quid te stupefactum, rustice," dixit
"ad tantas miraris opes, qui nescius auri
sordida tecta, casas et sola mapalia nosti?
an ego iam tremulus iam vertice canus et ista
factus in urbe senex stupeo tamen omnia: certe
vilia sunt nobis, quaecumque prioribus annis
vidimus, et sordet quicquid spectavimus olim"
          (*Eclogae* 7.35ff.).

[17] See Plautus, *Stichus* 198ff.; Catullus 5; Martial 11.63; Plutarch, *De curiositate* 1 *Moralia* 515d. Compare the remark of Francis Bacon in his essay "Of Envy": "A man that is Busy, and Inquisitive, is commonly Envious" (*The Essayes*, pp. 27–28).

[18] The curious and envious "Peeping Tom" need not be human. A prying lamp might act the spy (Apuleius, *Metamorphoses* 5.23; Minucius Felix, *Octavius* 9.6–7; cf. Martial 11.104).

skulking informers (*delatores*) and peering spies (*speculatores, percontores*).[19] Such *curiosi* were the emperor's brother and informer Lucius Vitellius, driven by "aemulatio prava," emulation twisted by envy,[20] and the misshapen and acid-tongued Vatinius, buffoon and *delator* of Nero.[21]

Curiosity was a product of envy, and envy of desire—"the covetous irritation of unattainable desire."[22] The *curiosus* was driven by frustrated longings. He or she could not resist those things in heaven and earth prohibited by the Powers That Be.[23] The secret was the rare; the secrets of the gods the rarest and most forbidden—and therefore the most desired. Like Eve or Pandora, Ovid's Aglauros cannot resist uncovering the secret of the god. Not surprisingly, given the Romans' "physics of envy," she reappears in Ovid's meandering tale filled with bile and envy for her sister Herse's magnificent match with Mercury (*Metamorphoses* 2.552–61, 637ff.). Like Aglauros, the sisters of Apuleius's gorgeous Psyche are paradigms of the *curiosi*. Out of poisonous envy of Psyche's good fortune, they instigate her to expose the fatal secret of the god.[24] The curious, the *polupragmones* ("busybodies"), according to Plutarch, pass over the stories and subjects of common speech and pick out "ta kruptomena" and "lanthanonta," the hidden scandals of every household (*De curiositate* 3 *Moralia* 516d–f). The secret and sexual offenses of the women, in partic-

---

[19] "Chez Sénèque le père, puis Suétone (ici comme synonyme de *speculator*), *curiosus* substantivé puisse désigner les délateurs et les espions" (André Labhardt, "*Curiositas*: Notes sur l'histoire d'un mot et d'une notion," *Museum Helveticum* 17 (1960), p. 208. The connection between the spy and the curious is clarified by the mime Publilius Syrus: "Envy tells what she sees" ("Invidia id loquitur quod videt" [302]). Ovid, while admitting he beheld a fatal secret, insists on his absolute discretion (*Tristia* 2.103, 3.5.47–50, 3.6.9–12). Compare Cicero's wonderful line: "I'm not dissimulating when I declare that I am ignorant of those things which, even if I knew, I would dissimulate ignorance of—lest I seem to others an annoyance or to you even a *curiosus*" ("Non dissimulo me nescire ea, quae etiam si scirem, dissimularem, ne aliis molestus, vobis etiam curiosus viderer" [*De domo sua* 46.121]). For the anxiety inspired by these inquisitive ones, see Suetonius, *Augustus* 27.3; Cicero, *Epistulae ad familiares* 9.16 (Cicero seems to suggest that the men who would inform Caesar of his [rebellious] witticisms were motivated by envy); Horace *Epistulae* 1.18.69–71. Philip Corbett (*The Scurra* [Edinburgh, 1986], pp. 23, 28–31, 38, 62) discusses the *curiosus* as he appears in Plautus's comedies and the backbiting *scurra* as a type of *curiosus* (e.g., Horace, *Satirae* 1.4.65ff.).

[20] Tacitus, *Historia* 3.38. See Tacitus's description of the *delator* Caepio Crispinus under Tiberius: "egens, ignotus, inquies" (*Annales* 1.74); Juvenal, *Satirae* 1.26–30.

[21] For Vatinius, see Tacitus, *Annales* 15.34; Gilbert Charles-Picard, *Augustus and Nero*, trans. Len Ortzen (New York, 1968), p. 90.

[22] F. T. Elworthy, "Evil Eye," in *Hastings Encyclopaedia of Religion and Ethics*, vol. 5, p. 608.

[23] Labhardt, "*Curiositas*," p. 206: "Saint Augustin affirme dans le *De utilitate credendi* (9.22) que *curiosus* implique toujours un blâme, car, au contraire du *studiosus*, le *curiosus* désire savoir ce qui ne le regarde pas (*ea requirit quae nihil ad se adtinent*)."

[24] *Metamorphoses* 4.28–6.24, esp. 5.8–27.

ular, charm the scopophiliac, the "philopeuthes."[25] The "marriage" of the prepubescent maid beckons Domatilla and Encolpius (already deeply in trouble for having witnessed the secrets of the god Priapus) to a chink in the door (*Satyricon* 25).[26] The nocturnal metamorphosis of the naked witch of Thessaly lures Apuleius's Lucius, another indefatigable *curiosus*, to spy through another crack (*Metamorphoses* 3.22).

Curiosity was a hunger.[27] The curious (and resentful) eye was often linked in Roman thought with metaphors of eating and cannibalism. The malicious Vitellius feasted his eyes on the spectacle of his enemy's death ("se pavisse oculos spectata inimici morte iactavit" [Tacitus, *Historia* 3.39]),[28] as Encolpius feasted his on the sight of his rival being beaten (*Satyricon* 96).[29] The appetite of the *curiosus* metamorphosed into the *torvus oculus*, the devouring stare. Seneca's Hostius Quadra (*Naturales quaestiones* 1.16.3) and Martial's Philomusus (11.63) fed their empty eyes by staring—at the baths and before mirrors. "We put our meddlesomeness into our malice, like an eye," according to Plutarch (*De curiositate* 2 *Moralia* 516a). The interfering Aglauros, who could not restrain her desire to uncover Minerva's secret, looks at her sister's lover "with the same eye" (*Metamorphoses* 7.748).[30]

The Trojan Horse[31]

Looking at the secret, the prodigious, and the miraculous is hard to resist, but the price of admiration is high. Horace admonishes us "Nil admi-

[25] See Plutarch, *De curiositate* 6 *Moralia* 517f–518a,c; *De curiositate* 8 *Moralia* 519b–c. Silia, a woman of note and a senator's wife, who knew from personal experience all of Nero's ingenious sensualities, aroused Nero's wrath and was exiled when Nero received the doomed Petronius's account of these obscenities (Tacitus, *Annales* 16.20). Petronius's affidavit and Silia's suspected indiscretion typify them as *curiosi*.

[26] So the young legacy-hunter watches his sister's sexual encounters with Eumolpus through a keyhole (*Satyricon* 140).

[27] "[The curiosity of the Andalusians] gnaws like a hunger, and looking is a nourishment" (David D. Gilmore, *Aggression and Community: Paradoxes of Andalusian Culture* [New Haven, 1987] pp. 156–66). For the link between insatiability and the evil eye, see Apuleius, *Metamorphoses* 2.5 and 8.24. For related metaphors of envy, see chapter 4, "*Envy*: Embracing the Monster."

[28] Cf. *Historia* 3.44.

[29] Compare Cicero, *Actio in Verrem* 5.65–67: "cum eius cruciatu atque supplicio pascere oculos animumque exsaturire vellent."

[30] For more on the *curiosus*, see Martial 1.34, 1.96; Apuleius, *Metamorphoses* 1.2, 12; 2.1, 6; 3.14, 21; 4.16; 6.19–21; 9.12–13, 30; N. M. Kay, *Martial Book XI: A Commentary* (London 1985), p. 209; George M. Foster, "The Anatomy of Envy: A Study in Symbolic Behavior," *Current Anthropology* 13 (1972), p. 183.

[31] Cf. Vergil, *Aeneis* 2.31–32. The Trojans are fatally tempted by the wondrousness of the gift of the Achaeans.

rari!"—admire nothing, lest you grow still and numb. "His eyes trans-fixed, he grows torpid in body and mind" ("defixis oculis animoque et corpore torpet" [*Epistulae* 1.6.1 + 14]). The fascinated one is stupefied (*stupefactus*). His admiration, his *stupor*, renders him the *stupidus*, the vulnerable one. Livy's Romulus was able to lure his curious Sabine neighbors to Rome with an invitation to view the new city and its festive Consualia. While the Sabines' greedy eyes were fixed on the spectacle, Romulus ambushed them and carried off their women (Livy 1.9.1–10).[32] Encolpius nearly fell and broke a leg while gazing at the wonders of Trimalchio's entryway (Petronius, *Satyricon* 29); and the philosopher Thales fell into a well while rapt in contemplation of the sky—the symbol, for Tertullian, of those who exercise "stupidam curiositatem" (*Ad nationes* 2.4.14).[33] Through his fatal fascination Apuleius's curious Lucius loses everything, even his human form, and becomes himself a monster, a human ass.[34]

The Paradox of the Eye

By despair fire has entered into something that cannot burn.
(Soren Kierkegaard, *The Sickness unto Death*)[35]

The charm, the *venenum*, worked through the senses, particularly the eyes.[36] "It is sight, according to Plutarch, which stimulates love, the great-

---

[32] Cf. 2.37.5–6.

[33] Cf. Augustine, *Sermones* 241.3.3; Labhardt, "*Curiositas*," pp. 216–17. By the time of Seneca a line from Ennius's lost *Iphigenia* had become proverbial: "No one looks at what is before their feet; instead they gaze at the quarters [or "snares": *plagas*] of the sky" ("Quod est ante pedes nemo spectat, caeli scrutantur plagas" [*Remains of Old Latin*, Loeb Classical Library, vol. 1 (London, 1967), p. 310; Seneca, *Apocolocyntosis* 8]).

[34] So, for Horace, the fascination of the Roman people with monsters turns the people themselves into a spectacle: "If he were on earth, Democritus would laugh: "Whether a hybrid species, a camelopard, or a white elephant should draw the attention of the mob, he would gaze at the people more intently than the games—as offering far more of a spectacle" ("Diversum confusa genus panthera camelo/sive elephas albus volgi converteret ora;/spectaret populum ludis attentius ipsis,/ut sibi praebentem nimio spectacula plura" [*Epistulae* 2.1.194–98]). Cf. Tacitus, *Historia* 3.83. The voyeur is easily transformed into the exhibitionist, the spectator into the wonder. According to many modern psychologists, including Freud, Fenichel, Bergler, Saul, and Allen, the two phenomena are mirrors. See R. Spencer Smith, "Voyeurism: A Review of the Literature," *Archives of Sexual Behavior*, vol. 5 (1976), pp. 597–98.

[35] Trans. Walter Lowrie (Princeton, 1941), p. 152.

[36] For *venenum* (potion, medicine, poison) as *anceps*, see Aulus Gellius, *Noctes Atticae* 12.9.2. For its relationship to the similarly complex and ambiguous notion of the *pharmakon*, see Marcel Mauss, *The Gift*, trans. Ian Cunnison (New York, 1967 [orig. publ. 1925]), p. 127 n. 101, and Jacques Derrida, *Dissemination*, trans. Barbara Johnson (Chicago, 1981

est and most powerful suffering [or experience: *pathema*] of the soul, and causes the lover to melt and be dissolved when he looks at those who are beautiful, as if he were pouring forth his whole being into them" (*Quaestiones conviviales 5.7 Moralia* 681a–b). The fascinated one, deprived of strength, grows torpid and wastes away, literally exhausted by the object of his or her desires. Narcissus and Eutelidas, arrested by their own eyes, fascinate themselves and melt away.[37] In the case of lovers, according to Plutarch's Mestrius Florus, the exchange of glances destroys them—in pleasure and pain (*Quaestiones conviviales 5.7 Moralia* 681b).

According to Varro, care (*cura*) burns the heart, and the *curiosus* is afflicted with this burning care beyond measure (*De lingua latina* 6.46). Narcissus, "the numb one,"[38] simultaneously burns and hungers: "What he sees he does not know, but what he sees he burns for, and the same illusion incites the eyes that it deceives" ("Quid videat, nescit; sed quod videt, uritur illo / atque oculos idem, qui decipit, incitat error" [*Metamorphoses* 3.430–31]).[39]

The eye is the "sense" of wanting. To admire is to desire. The eye is Narcissus, the body turned against itself, taking away everything it gives. The more it seems to be a window, the more it offends as a wall. Does it hold out before you a world, a self, a salvation that can never be possessed? Does it seem to pierce all barriers that can never be breached? Like Derrida's *pharmakon*, "We watch it infinitely promise itself and endlessly vanish through concealed doorways that shine like mirrors and

---

[orig. publ. 1972]), esp. pp. 131–32. The whole of Derrida's brilliant essay on "Plato's Pharmacy" is highly relevant to the physics of compensation discussed in this chapter—indeed, to the whole of this book.

[37] The story of Eutelidas is told by Plutarch, in *Quaestiones conviviales 5.7 Moralia* 682b and 682e–f. The first passage = Euphorion frag. 175, in John U. Powell, *Collectanea Alexandrina* (Oxford, 1970 [orig. publ. 1925]). Like Narcissus, Eutelidas of the fair tresses saw himself in a whirling stream and cast upon himself both the evil eye ("hauton baskainen"), and a shameful disease ("nousos aeikes"). The more familiar story of Narcissus is most wonderfully told by Ovid in the *Metamorphoses* 3.344ff. (Compare Theocritus's Damoetas, who spits on his own breast to immunize himself from the effects of gazing at himself in the sea [*Bucolici* 6.34–40].) For autofascination, see S. Seligmann, *Der böse Blick und Verwandtes*, 2 vols. (Berlin, 1910), vol. 1, pp. 142, 157, 178; Elworthy, "Evil Eye," p. 611; Marilyn Disalvo, "The Myth of Narcissus," *Semiotica* 30 (1980), pp. 15–25; Eugene S. McCartney, "Praise and Dispraise in Folklore," in *The Evil Eye: A Folklore Casebook*, ed. Alan Dundes, p. 18–19 (New York, 1981); Tobin Siebers, *The Mirror of Medusa* (Berkeley, 1983), pp. 57–86. Seneca's Hostius Quadra was another victim of autofascination (*Naturales quaestiones* 1.16ff.).

[38] "Narcissus" derives from *narke*, numbness, deadness; the stingray or torpedo. Cf. Plato, *Meno* 80a–b; Derrida, *Dissemination*, pp. 118–19; Siebers, *The Mirror of Medusa*, p. 59. The *narke* wields an electric charge that benumbs and stupefies its target.

[39] For the relationship between fire and hunger, see Francis Huxley, *Affable Savages* (New York, 1957), pp. 14–15.

open onto a labyrinth."[40] "The evil eye," *invidia*, was, for the ancient Romans, the eye of seduction and deprivation. It struck the most vulnerable, and the most vulnerable parts.

The eye realized the polarization that magnetized Roman culture during this period: the operation, concurrently, of the extremes of power and powerlessness.

From one perspective, the eye was aggressive. The most active stream of emanations emitted by the body passed through the eye: "For vision, being of an enormous swiftness and carried by a breath [*pneuma*] that gives off a fiery brilliance, diffuses a wondrous power [*thaumaste dunamis*], and so man both suffers [*paschein*] and commits [*poiein*] many things through his eyes" (Plutarch, *Quaestiones conviviales* 5.7 *Moralia* 681a).

There were strange peoples from beyond the edge of the world who could kill with just a glance.[41] And Isis was able to kill the child of king Malcandros with only a look.[42] "We know of those who seriously hurt children by looking at them, influencing and impairing their susceptible, vulnerable constitutions, but who are less able to affect in this way the firm and established health of older persons" (*Quaestiones conviviales* 5.7 *Moralia* 680d, cf. 680f.). Why are children particularly vulnerable to the evil eye? Because they are fragile . . . and because they are desired. The one who casts the evil eye is the one who looks at them with longing.[43]

The eye was very powerful, but, from another perspective, the eye was excruciatingly vulnerable. There were twenty thousand gladiators in the *ludus* of Caligula, according to Pliny, and of these there were only two that could resist blinking when threatened with steel. (These two were, consequently, invincible [*Historia naturalis* 11.54§144]). "In every battle," according to Tacitus, "the eye is conquered first" (*Germania* 43.4).[44] The eye made one vulnerable because it exposed the soul. "No other part

[40] *Dissemination*, p. 128.

[41] Plutarch mentions the legendary Thibeis (= Thebaeans) of the Black Sea. Ovid mentions the Telchines (*Metamorphoses* 7.635); cf. Pliny, *Historia naturalis* 7.16 (quoting Alexander of Aphrodisias 2.53). For the evil eye as a characteristic of exotic, barbarian, or distant peoples, see George Lafaye, "Fascinum," in *D-S*, vol. 2.2, p. 984; Elworthy, "Evil Eye," p. 610. Notice Cicero's special advice to the foreigner and resident alien in Rome: "Mind only your own business and minimize your curiosity in the affairs of the republic in which you have no part" ("nihil praeter suum negotium agere, nihil de alio anquirere minimeque esse in aliena re publica curiosum" [*De officiis* 1.34.125]).

[42] Plutarch, *De Iside et Osiride* 17 *Moralia* 357d.

[43] For the special vulnerability of children to the evil eye, see Foster, "The Anatomy of Envy," pp. 166, 173–76; McCartney, "Praise and Dispraise."

[44] The eye was a particular object of attack in Roman culture according to H. C. Nutting, "Oculos Effodere," *Classical Philology* 17 (1922), pp. 313–18.

of the body reveals more of the spirit of every animal—but particularly of men."[45]

All the body shared, to some degree, in the ambiguity of the eye, especially the breath, the voice, and the sense of hearing. The breath of Ovid's Invidia wasted the countryside (*Metamorphosis* 2.791–94). The Thebaeans could kill with a glance, with their breath, or with their speech (*Quaestiones conviviales* 5.7 *Moralia* 680d–e). Evil speech was often interchangeable, or conjoined in its effects, with the evil eye. So, Pliny the Younger feared the sinister talk ("sinistres sermones") that attended the active life in Rome (*Epistulae* 1.9.5), and Catullus sought to protect himself and his darling Lesbia from the *curiosi*, who might "fascinate with an evil tongue" ("mala fascinare lingua" [7]).[46]

But it was the paradox of heightened power and heightened vulnerability that made the eye especially fascinating: it injured and was injured simultaneously.[47] (In contrast the ear was inflamed by the mouth.)[48] Plutarch tells the wonderful story of the plover the sight of whom cures jaundice. It draws the affliction from the patient, which passes like a stream through the sufferer's eyes. "Consequently, plovers cannot bear to face people who are afflicted with jaundice, but turn away and keep their eyes closed, not because they begrudge the effect of their healing power, as some think, but because they are wounded thereby, as if by a blow" (*Quaestiones conviviales* 5.7 *Moralia* 681c–d).[49]

The notion of the *evil* eye is, in many cultures, built around the dialectic of the *extremes* of desire and deprivation, power and vulnerability. It is a compensatory system: the visual assaults of the *curiosi* rebounded.[50] The stare that needy Aglauros casts on Mercury is parried by the "torvi lu-

[45] "Neque ulla ex parte maiora animi indicia cunctis animalibus, sed homini maxime" (Pliny, *Historia naturalis* 11.54 145). See Quintilian, *Institutiones oratoriae* 11.3.75: "oculi, per quos maxime animus eminet."

[46] *Kakologion* (evil-speaking) was a necessary attribute of the *curiosi*, the "polupragmones" (Plutarch, *De curiositate* 9 *Moralia* 519c). For "nocere mala lingua," see Vergil, *Eclogae* 7.28.

[47] For the combination of vulnerability and aggressive power of the eyes, see Plutarch, *Quaestiones conviviales* 5.7 *Moralia* 681b–d; Seneca, *Epistulae* 105.3; Otto Fenichel, "The Scopophilic Instinct and Identification," *International Journal of Psycho-Analysis* 18 (1937), pp. 6–34; Garfield Tourney and Dean J. Plazak, "Evil Eye in Myth and Schizophrenia," *Psychiatric Quarterly* 28 (1954), pp. 489, 491; G. Coss "Reflections on the Evil Eye," in Dundes, *The Evil Eye*, ed. Alan Dundes (New York, 1981) pp. 181–91.

[48] For the special quality of sight compared with the other senses, see Publilius Syrus: "The ears bear insult more easily than the eyes" ("Iniuriam aures facilius quam oculi ferunt" [303]); Plutarch, *Quaestiones conviviales* 5.7 *Moralia* 681b–c (speaking of lovers who fascinate one another): "Neither by touch nor by hearing do they suffer so deep a wound as by seeing and by being seen."

[49] McCartney, "Praise and Dispraise," p. 34 n. 10.

[50] For the reflexive nature of the malice of the *curiosus*, see Plutarch, *De curiositate* 4 *Moralia* 517a–b.

minis orbis," the glare of Minerva, who remembers that Aglauros had violated her secret (Ovid, *Metamorphoses* 2.752). The prying eye elicited a hostile response: "The wind which most disgusts us," according to Ariston, "is the one that lifts our gown."[51]

"It is with peril that the inferior inquires into what his superior hides," the mime Publilius Syrus warns.[52] As Actaeon perished as a result of beholding Diana unclothed (Ovid, *Tristia* 2.105–7), so sharing Augustus's secrets had had fatal consequences for poor Fulvius and his wife (Plutarch, *De Garrulitate* 11 *Moralia* 508a–b) and for miserable Ovid (*Tristia* 2.103ff., 3.5.49–50, 3.6.9–12, 25–38).

The envious induce their own suffering. Ovid's walleyed Invidia is her own torment ("supplicium suum est"); she devours and is devoured (*Metamorphoses* 2.781–2).[53] "The malevolent," according to Publilius Syrus, "feed on themselves"(378).[54] They are held fast by the affliction of *epichairekakia* (joy at another's misfortune), the mirror of *phthonos* and *baskania* (pain at another's good fortune), the evil eye.[55]

Wherever she traveled Envy wasted the countryside, polluting with her breath peoples and cities and homes.[56] The envious created a miasma in which even their own children were infected.[57] The frustrated desires of Seneca's (and Euripides') Medea, her loss of status, her humiliation, envy, and hatred, bring her at last to slay, not only her rival, but her own children. Envy is a monster; envy is civil war.

The Paradox of the Phallus

Because of a similar emotional complexity and function, there is among the ancient Romans an insistent connection, and even identification, of

---

[51] Von Arnim, *Stoicorum veterum fragmenta*, vol. 1, pp. 89–90, fragment 401; quoted by Plutarch, *De curiositate* 3 *Moralia* 516f.

[52] "Cum periculo inferior quaerit quod superior occulit" (140). Horace warns the client not to pry into his patron's secrets, or to disclose them if they are revealed in confidence (*Epistulae* 1.18.37–38). Petronius, like his protagonist Encolpius, was endangered by knowing forbidden secrets, as Publius Clodius was by "overseeing" the Bona Dea festival, and Euripides' Pentheus by witnessing other women's rites.

[53] For envy as self-injuring, see Helmut Schoeck, *Envy*, trans. Michael Glenny and Betty Ross (New York, 1966), esp. pp. 22, 43.

[54] "Malivolus semper sua natura vescitur."

[55] Plutarch, *De curiositate* 6 *Moralia* 518c. Ovid's monster Invidia is pleased only by another's troubles (*Metamorphoses* 2.777); cf. Tacitus, *Historia* 3.38–39.

[56] Ovid, *Metamorphoses* 2.791–94.

[57] See Plutarch, *Quaestiones conviviales* 5.7 *Moralia* 682c–d. Heliodorus, the fourth-century bishop of Triccia in Thessaly, remarks: "When any one looks at what is excellent with an evil quality he transmits his own envenomed exhalations into whatever is nearest to him" (*Aethiopica* 3.7.2–5).

the genitalia with the the aggressive and prophylactic eye, and with the *fascinum*, the object that caught and deflected the eye.[58] Indeed, this association seems all but universal. The word *fascinum* is used as a synonym for phallus.[59] The eye could also be linked with the female, and depictions of the apotropaic eye and the female genitalia are often indistinguishable. Exposure of the pudenda could drive away the eye and break the fascination.[60]

The source of the identification of the eye with the genitals (especially the phallus)[61] was that the genitals shared with the eyes the excruciating paradox of exceptional vulnerability and power.[62] Fascination, therefore, is associated with immoderate rigidity and flaccidity, with sexual potency both fantastically augmented and (thus) utterly destroyed. As Fenichel observed, "To be turned into rigid stone symbolizes not only erection but also castration" ("The Scopophilic Instinct," p. 26).

Fascination was that final castration that Seneca saw as the ultimate expression of ardent and impossible desires.[63] Just so, the admiration of unnatural speech and prodigious bodies were linked, for Quintilian, with "effeminacy" and loss of "normal" sexual characteristics—with men depilating their bodies, curling their hair with irons, and using cosmet-

[58] For the relationship of the male genitalia to the evil eye and *invidia* see A. Michaelis, "Serapis Standing on a Xanthian Marble in the British Museum," *Journal of Hellenic Studies* 6 (1885), pp. 315–16; Albrecht Dieterich, *Pulcinella: Pompejanische Wandbilder und römische Satyrspiele* (Leipzig, 1897), p. 38 (on the obscene sense attached to the squint eyes of Mylos in Doric farce); Tourney and Plazak, "Evil Eye," p. 484; Percival Turnbull, "The Phallus in the Art of Roman Britain," *Bulletin of the Institute of Archaeology* 15 (1968) pp. 199–206, esp. pp. 199, 204; George Ryley Scott, *Phallic Worship* (London, 1966 [original n.d.]), esp. pp. 107–8 and n. 1; Johns, *Sex or Symbol*, pp. 63–70, figs. 52, 53, 77; Larissa Bonfante, "Nudity as a Costume in Classical Art," *American Journal of Archaeology* 93 (1989), pp. 549–50 and n. 38.

[59] E.g., "Habebat enim inguinum pondus tam grande, ut ipsum hominem laciniam fascini crederes" (Petronius, *Satyricon* 92; cf. 138). "Aeque pro virili parte posuit quoniam praefascinandis rebus haec membri difformitas adponi solet" (Porphyrio, *Commentum in Horatium Flaccum*, ed. Alfred Holder [Hildesheim, 1967], ad epodos 8.18).

[60] For apotropaic qualities attached to the female pudenda: Paul Graindor, *Terres cuites de l'Egypte gréco-romaine* (Antwerp, 1939), p. 131n. 4; p. 150n. 1; W. Weber, *Die aegyptish-griechischen Terrakotten* (Berlin, 1914), p. 100, no. 131 (plate 12); Bonfante, "Nudity," p. 559 and n. 91, p. 568.

[61] The female genitals operated in a manner similar to the eye, closely resembling it in its paradoxical blend of power and vulnerability, but not to the same *extremes* as the phallus. As a result the female genitalia appear less frequently as equivalents or substitutes for the eye.

[62] " 'The most noble organ' and 'the vulnerable organ' probably suffice to explain the phallic nature of the eye" (Fenichel, "The Scopophilic Instinct," p. 25). For the vulnerability and aggressiveness of nakedness, see Bonfante, "Nudity," pp. 547 and n. 23, 553n. 61, 556, 560, 562–63 and nn. 111–13, 568–69.

[63] See chapter 2, "Desire: Wine without Water."

ics.[64] Plutarch, similarly, parallels the taste for discordant and "modern" music with the loss of masculinity.[65]

In Apuleius's *Metamorphoses*, the witches threaten the peeking *curiosus* with castration (1.12–13). It is no coincidence that modern psychologists frequently associate fear of the evil eye and fear of fascination with fear of castration,[66] and the evil eye itself with the genitalia.[67] A wonderful example of this genital "physics" comes from the *Miles Gloriosus*. When Plautus's swaggering, lusty Pyrgopolynices is caught trying to bed the "wife" of his elderly neighbor, the old man's cook, brandishing a sharp knife, threatens to castrate the transgressor and to make the genitals of the adulterer into an *apotropaion* to hang around a young boy's neck.[68]

It is important to understand, however, that in the "physics of envy," the terror of castration is also experienced as a *temptation*. To the fascinated man, castration and mutilation lose their fearful quality, and like Martial's "Mucius Scaevola," he may voluntarily give to the god that which he fears to lose most: "He amputates his manly parts; he cuts off his strength. Why should he fear the malice of the gods who in so doing

---

[64] *Institutiones oratoriae* 2.5.10–12. Quintilian compares the man who crafted flaccid and extravagant rhetoric to charm the ear (rather than defeat his enemies in forensic warfare) with the dealer who castrates his slaves to fetch a higher price for them (5.12.17–23). Only, in this case, the orator is guilty of self-castration: like the Galli, he willingly makes of himself what would be a *monstrum* if it appeared in nature. For the monstrous in Roman speech, see Edward Norden, *Die Antike Kunstprosa*, 2 vols. (Darmstadt, 1958), vol. 1, pp. 277–80. For the spellbinding quality of "untamed" and ambiguous speech, see Derrida, *Dissemination*, pp. 115–18, esp. p. 116, and the language of "anti-structure" described by Victor Turner in "Metaphors of Anti-Structure in Religious Culture," in *Dramas, Fields, and Metaphors* (Ithaca, N.Y., 1974), pp. 272–99.

[65] *Quaestiones Conviviales* 7.8 *Moralia* 711c.

[66] See Karl Abraham, "Restrictions and Transformations of Scopophilia in Psycho-Neurotics; with Remarks on Analogous Phenomena in Folk-Psychology" [1913], in *Selected Papers of Karl Abraham*, trans. D. Bryan and A. Strachey (New York, 1968); Sigmund Freud, "Medusa's Head" [1922], in *Collected Papers*, ed. James Strachey (New York, 1959), vol. 5, pp. 105–6; Tourney and Plazak, "Evil Eye in Myth and Schizophrenia," pp. 485–92. See also Gilmore, *Aggression and Community*, p. 161.

[67] E.g., Abraham, "Restrictions and Transformations," esp. p. 179 and n. 5; Freud, "Medusa's Head"; and Sandor Ferenczi, "On Eye Symbolism," in *Sex in Psycho-analysis* (New York, 1956), pp. 228–33; Ferenczi, "On the Symbolism of the Head of Medusa" [1923], in *Further Contributions to the Theory and Technique of Psychoanalysis*, ed. J. Rickman, trans. J. I. Suttie (London, 1926), p. 360. Both Freud and Ferenczi interpret Medusa's head as embodying the active force of female and male genitalia, *and* sexual castration. For the eye as a sexual organ, see Freud, *Three Essays on the Theory of Sexuality*, pp. 35, 75.

[68] "Quin iamdudum gestit moecho hoc abdomen adimere ut faciam quasi puero in collo pendeant crepundia" (*Miles Gloriosus*, 1398–99). Compare the horns of the cuckold and the horns of the devil, both phallic symbols (Julian Pitt-Rivers, "Honour and Social Status," in *Honour and Shame*, ed. J. G. Peristiany (Chicago, 1966), p. 116.

deserves their grace?" (Seneca, quoted by Augustine, *De civitate dei* 6.10).[69]

Anguish and Indifference

Rousseau speaks in his *Confessions* about the "devouring but barren flame by which ever since my childhood I had felt my heart to be consumed in vain."[70] Rousseau, like Kierkegaard, connects despair with a vain, barren, and exquisite wasting, a frustration and longing that cannot be overcome.[71]

Fascination is both the desire that devours and its consummation. To be fascinated is to be petrified—*and* dissolved. Aglauros, obsessed by her sister's splendid marriage (which Envy has wickedly made still more resplendent), "is eaten up in secret misery . . . she groans and is liquefied with slow and wretched wasting, like ice touched by the tentative sunshine . . . just as a fire is set under a pile of weeds, which gives out no flames and wastes away with no consumption."[72] In the end she is turned into a black stone.[73]

Both rigidification and liquefication are images of death in Roman thought. The constant juxtaposition of both of these metaphors with the effects of *invidia* captures the peculiar intensity and indescribability of the experience. In both cases, fascination is a crushing alienation from everything, including oneself and one's consciousness. It is the development of a heightened but alienated self-consciousness through a crippling excess of limitations *and* the unnerving dissolution of all limitations. Narcissus, the beautiful and unself-conscious, failing to recognize other human beings, is condemned "to know himself," and that knowing is accomplished through the rapturous stimulation—and brutal frustration—of all desires. His knowing himself, his extreme self-consciousness, attends the utter loss of self. In a similar fashion, the fascinated Lucius comes to ex-

[69] "Ille viriles partes amputat, ille lacertos secat. Ubi iratos deos timent qui sic propitios merentur?" For the lure of emasculation in this period, see my "All Things Beseem the Victor" (in preparation).

[70] Jean-Jacques Rousseau, *Confessions*, trans. J. M. Cohen (Baltimore, Md., 1954), p. 397.

[71] But perhaps their formulation of this unbearable frustration is a kind of redemptive paradox—like that of James B. Pritchard's Sumerian "Job," who declares "My food is hunger" (*The Ancient Near East*, vol. 2 [Princeton, 1975], p. 138).

[72] Ovid, *Metamorphoses* 2.805–11. The evil eyes of the envious or malevolent were the *oculi urentes, flagrantes* (e.g., Suetonius, *Augustus* 27.3, *Galba* 16.1).

[73] Compare Ovid's Echo, whose bones are turned to stone even as she wastes away (*Metamorphoses* 3.396–99).

treme self-consciousness only as the monstrous ass.[74] "The moment of self-recognition therefore is not a recognition at all," according to Tobin Siebers. "It is the moment of the greatest blindness" (*The Mirror of Medusa*, p. 84).

Both sensitized and benumbed, the fascinated endures the queer emotional state described by Lucius on seeing the metamorphosis of the naked witch into a bird: "And she, by her magic arts, was transformed at will, but I, although not bewitched by any spell, was so fixated and stupefied by the act that I seemed something else than Lucius, so vanquished of sense, and astonished to the point of madness, that although awake [*vigilans*] I slept" (Apuleius, *Metamorphoses* 3.22).[75] It is the same narcosis of pain Ovid experienced on the night of his exile: "I was as stupefied as one who, struck by the lightning of Jove, lives and yet knows not that he lives."[76]

For the fascinated, all categories dissolve, including those by which he or she defines the self. The victim of fascination enters a world beyond (or lost to) symbolic representation and systematic categorization, a world which can only be hinted at through paradox, where satisfaction cannot be distinguished from hunger, presence from absence, self from other, beauty from hideousness, the pious from the obscene. For the stupefied, speech is also silence, and there is no way to distinguish excruciating excitement from dull torpor, activity from passivity, gaiety from bereavement, frustration from satiation.[77] To be fascinated is to enter a secret world which, like Foucault's Gothic cathedral, loses its meaning from an excess of signification.[78] It is the expression of an insatiable yearning that mystifies everything, that eliminates everything.[79] "Because I wanted to understand everything, everything is a mystery," wrote Gustave Flaubert in a letter to Alfred Le Poitterin on a September day in 1845.[80]

[74] Dostoevsky's "Underground Man" is a splendid paradigm of the hyperconscious and self-alienated autointoxicant.

[75] "Et illa quidem magicis suis artibus volens reformatur, at ego, nullo decantatus carmine, praesentis tantum facti stupore defixus quidvis aliud magis videbar esse quam Lucius, sic exterminatus animi, attonitus in amentiam vigilans somniabar."

[76] "Non aliter stupui, quam qui Iovis ignibus ictus/ vivit et est vitae nescius ipse suae" (*Tristia* 1.3.11–12). This stupefaction is also experienced by the poet as a mutilation.

[77] See Brun, "Le Prestige du monstre," pp. 309–15.

[78] Michel Foucault, *Madness and Civilization*, trans. Richard Howard (New York, 1973), p. 18.

[79] The yearning to know everything results in fascination; the yearning to say everything results in *aporia*.

[80] For the relationship between fascination and mysticism, see the chapter "The Element of Fascination," in Rudolf Otto's *The Idea of the Holy*, trans. John W. Harvey (New York, 1958 [orig. publ. 1917]), pp. 31–40. Unfortunately, Otto apprehends only the curative aspects of fascination.

The Song of the Siren

He is his own spectator and applauds the funeral
of his own right hand.
(Martial 8.30)

Martial observed with wonder the condemned criminal who, in turn, observed with rapture the burning of his own right hand. This "Mucius Scaevola" of the arena, the man condemned and exalted, was a hero for his time: he was fascinated and fascinating.[81]

To be fascinated is the process of ending the tension between the self and the fleeing object of desire.[82] It is to reject the endless deprivation and dissatisfaction that come with reflection and symbolization. As it was for Martial's "Mucius Scaevola," fascination is both the experience of, and escape from, the pain of mutilation and deformation that is mirrored in everything one sees, that we reflect in infinite regression onto a world. And yet it is that very mutilation of oneself, that mirroring and alienation of oneself in the world, that is fascinating. As Plutarch explained, the *curiosi* are like those who stare into the sun or who cannot resist a taste of poisonous aconite.[83]

In the indifference of fascination Stoic and Sceptic *ataraxia* meet. The apathy of the wise man was a kind of autointoxication or autofascination, which, according to Plutarch (*Questiones conviviales* 7.8 *Moralia* 711b), rendered him proof against enchantment ("akeletos"). The Stoic was immunized by insensibility against the malice of another. What was the wise man's method of autofascination? "Think nothing but your own soul to be admirable."[84] The Cato who did not react when spat upon was

---

[81] Martial 8.30 (quoted in chapter 2). Martial was so struck with this event that he wrote three poems on the same theme. For a detailed analysis of the meaning of this event, see my "Savage Miracles: The Redemption of Lost Honor in Roman Society and the Sacrament of the Gladiator and the Martyr" (in preparation). Although Damiens is not so willing or so silent as "Mucius Scaevola," he shows the same fascination with his own mutilation (Foucault, *Discipline and Punish*, p. 4). One can compare John Keats's fascination with his own death, as expressed in some of his most famous poems (e.g., "When I have Fears" and "Ode to a Nightingale").

[82] Foucault describes the saint's gradual fascination with the monsters in Flaubert's *Temptation of St. Anthony*: "These things that haunted the imagination of the hermit from inside can now become the object of enraptured contemplation, and where he had pushed them aside in fear, they now attract and invite him to a dormant identification: 'to descend to the very depths of matter, to become matter' " ("Fantasia of the Library," in *Language, Counter-Memory, Practice*, ed. Donald F. Bouchard, pp. 87–109 [Ithaca, N.Y., 1977], p. 100).

[83] They are as imperiled as those who share the secrets of a king (*De curiositate* 4 *Moralia* 517a–c).

[84] Cf. Seneca, *Epistulae* 8.5: "Cogitate nihil praeter animum esse mirabile, cui magno nihil magnum est."

like the person who spat on his or her own breast. Being at once nothing and god, the wise man fixated on paradox. Plutarch cannot tell, in the end, whether it was the elder Brutus's extreme virtue that made him incapable of suffering or his extreme suffering that made him insensible. All others turned their eyes away, but Brutus gazed unflinchingly at the beheading of his sons. "In either case his act was not a trivial one or a human one, but either that of a god or a beast" (Plutarch, *Publicola* 6.3–4). It is not surprising that men like Lucan, Seneca, and Marcus Aurelius, often attracted to Stoic thought, were men of exacerbated sensitivities and given to frustration, men in whom feelings of heightened power and powerlessness coincided.

It was a great temptation to be fascinated. It was hard to resist, impossible to defeat, because it was born of longing and frustration and loss. The unsightly, the unspeakable—the *obscaenus, deformis,* the *turpis, teater, foedus, immundus*—were things which confounded one. They should be hidden; their sighting should be expiated. At the same time they were *monstra* (like *monstro,* "to indicate, show," from *moneo,* "to warn"), things which spoke a mysterious language calling for decipherment.[85] They carried a message, however unclear.[86] The ambiguous, the paradoxical, the puzzling, the obscure and difficult to categorize—in short, the monster—was the great and fatal temptation.[87]

As Plutarch's Mestrius Florus points out in the *Quaestiones conviviales,* "the man who demands to see the logic of each and every thing destroys the wonder in all things" ("ho zeton en hekasto to eulogov ek panton anairei to thaumasion" [5.7 *Moralia* 680C]).[88] Fascination, he

[85] "When we use the word 'grotesque' we record, among other things, the sense that though our attention has been arrested, our understanding is unsatisfied" (Harpham, *On the Grotesque,* p. 3; cf. pp. 19–21). See also Clifford Geertz, "Religion as a Cultural System," in *The Interpretation of Cultures* (New York, 1973), p. 101.

[86] "Transcategorical hybrids . . . offer endless compelling temptations to interpretation. Confused, unresolved, unstable, and apparently filled with great but uncertain significance, such images seem to demand that we rescue them from absurdity, that we make them complete, as Martin Luther 'completed' the 'Mönchskalb,' a terribly deformed man [sic] in whom he read allegorical witness of the 'sign of the times' " (Harpham, *On the Grotesque,* p. 21).

[87] "La contemplation des réalités mineures trouve son symbole dans l'appel des Sirènes, retentissant pour la perte des curieux qui ne savent résister et qui, faute de respecter la hiérarchie des valeurs, se détournent de l'essentiel et viennent se briser sur l'écueil de la *polymathia*" (Labhardt, "*Curiositas,*" p. 211).

[88] Michel Foucault was a modern thinker who was both subject to, and aware of, the intellectual process of fascination. He himself was prone to fascination by such subjects as sex or madness or death. Foucault's fascination was both the experience of endless differentiation and the embrace of it so as to dissolve all distinctions. "The historical sense can evade metaphysics and become a privileged instrument of genealogy if it refuses the certainty of absolutes. Given this, it corresponds to the acuity of a glance that distinguishes, separates, and disperses, that is capable of liberating divergence and marginal elements— the kind of dissociating view that is capable of decomposing itself, capable of shattering the

realizes, is not compatible with "the logic of things" ("ho tes aitias logos" [5.7.680C]).[89] To subject something which is uncommon, anomalous, monstrous, to a *sensus communis*, to subject it to a physics, to "naturalize" the "unnatural," to give the absurd a species—in short, to interpret— is to wrest control of, to break the spell and fascination of, the monsters. This is what Florus's dinner guests would do in Plutarch and what Cicero would do in his discussions with his brother Quintus on the subject of divination.[90]

Envy and the Absolute

Nothing almost sees miracles but misery.
(Shakespeare, *King Lear* 2.2.161–62)

Fascination did not make the emperors or the gods, but it made the emperors and gods that the Romans saw. No one would yearn for or tolerate a god, or a king or a soul, that was both immanent and transcendent, manifest and hidden, all and nothing, unless she or he had felt profoundly this hypnotic loss of self, this melting and fixing. Envy creates the splendor; curiosity creates the secret. The immoderate reverence and hatred directed at the generals and emperors and gods of this period can be ex-

---

unity of man's being through which it was thought that he could extend his sovereignty to the events of the past" (Michel Foucault, "Nietzsche, Genealogy, History," in *Language, Counter-Memory, Practice*, pp. 152–53). For the "anatomic gaze," see Angèle Kremer-Maretti, *Foucault et l'archéologie du savoir*, and J. G. Merquior, *Foucault* (Berkeley, 1985), p. 140.

[89] Wonder gives rise to philosophy (Plato, *Theatetus* 155d; Aristotle, *Metaphysics* 982 B12. Cf. Turner, "Passages, Margins, and Poverty: Religious Symbols of Communitas," in *Drama, Fields and Metaphors*, pp. 256–57). But, simultaneously, philosophy is a method of dispelling that wonder—it is the antidote to the wonder that elicited it!

[90] Cicero, *De divinatione*. Teratology (the study and classification of monsters) is a way of fighting fascination. As Victor Turner remarks, "To name an inauspicious condition is halfway to removing that condition. . . . This is not so very far removed from the practice of the modern psychoanalyst. When something is grasped by the mind, made capable of being thought about, it can be dealt with, mastered" (*The Ritual Process: Structure and Anti-Structure* [Ithaca, N.Y., 1969], p. 25). For teratology and its significance, see Céard, *La Nature et les prodiges*; Harpham, *On the Grotesque*, p. 16; Mary Douglas, *Purity and Danger* (London, 1966), p. 39; E. E. Evans-Pritchard, *Nuer Religion* (Oxford, 1956), p. 84. For an example of the process of naming the monster, see Paul Ricoeur, *The Symbolism of Evil*, trans. Emerson Buchanan (Boston, 1967), pp. 171–74. The thing that cannot be classified is the sacred, the taboo: see Douglas, *Purity and Danger*, especially her discussion of the Hebrew system of classifying animals (pp. 41–57), and Harpham, *On the Grotesque*, p. 4. Are Plutarch's Florus and Cicero's Quintus, in interpreting the *prodigium* or the evil eye, acting differently from those who assert there are no *prodigia*, no evil eye? Is there a distinction to be drawn between the reductionists and the interpreters? How is "breaking" the code related to asserting that there is no code?

plained, in part, by the Romans' tendency to fascination. The envious one fears and despises those he envies—and simultaneously exalts them. In the "physics" of envy, the fascinated one yearns to be separated from himself and exalts a god/self with no needs, no envy: the totally wondrous, unseeable, unknowable. Like the Stoic soul, it is both one's most essential self and the absolute. As Melanie Klein explains in her *Envy and Gratitude*, "destructive impulses, envy and persecutory anxiety are very strong and . . . idealization serves mainly as a defence against these emotions."[91] "Idealization not only serves as a defence against persecution but also against envy. . . . Strongly exalting the object and its gifts is an attempt to diminish envy." "However," Klein points out, "if envy is very strong, it is likely, sooner or later, to turn against the primal idealized object, and against other people who, in the course of development, come to stand for it."[92] Freud, who intimated many of the ideas later developed by Klein, believed that the elevation was motivated, in part, by the desire to render the exalted more "sacrificeable," a better scapegoat, by making him or her the source of all evil and persecution.[93] As Foucault observed, "The condemned man represents the symmetrical, inverted figure of the king" (*Discipline and Punish*, p. 29).[94]

Fascination and Civil War

Fascination is the product of unsatisfied desire, of envy and curiosity working through the medium of the *oculus malignus*, the evil eye. It arises from an irreconcilable juxtaposition of power and vulnerability. The monsters were the cause, but even more the product, of simultaneous abundance and deprivation, the power of conquest and the powerlessness of being conquered that the Romans of the civil war period and the establishment of the monarchy experienced simultaneously.

[91] Melanie Klein, *Envy and Gratitude* (New York, 1957), p. 25. Cf. p. 73: "Excessive idealization denotes that persecution is the main driving force. As I discovered many years ago in my work with young children, idealization is a corollary of persecutory anxiety—a defence against it—and the ideal breast is a counterpart to the devouring breast."

[92] Ibid., p. 62.

[93] Sigmund Freud, *Totem and Taboo* [1913], trans. A. A. Brill (New York, 1938 [orig. pub. 1913]), pp. 59–68. See the example of Valerius in Livy 2.7.5.

[94] "We can conceive of eternity only by eliminating all the perishable, all that *counts* for us. Eternity is absence, being that fills none of the functions of being; it is privation erected into . . . something or other . . ." (Cioran, *Drawn and Quartered*, p. 152). Ernest Becker, like Etty Hillesum, like Simone Weil, and like Augustine of Hippo, raises a transcendent god from a hell of unsatisfied desire. "Ultimately, narcissism relies on the kind of accusatory thought that creates gods to be idolized or despised" (Siebers, *The Mirror of Medusa*, p. 85.) Siebers's excellent discussion of narcissism (pp. 57–86) is very relevant here. "Narcissism" is a reproach leveled by the rejected or unrecognized; the unembraceable is exiled (to heaven or hell)—even while this exile is made into a self-exile.

The shock of civil war is described by Lucan in terms of the emotional paralysis it engendered in both the community and the individual:

> When the Romans understood by what horrible disasters the faith [*fides*] of the gods would be confirmed, a paralysis [*ferale iustitium*] prevailed throughout the city. Honor hid itself in plebeian dress, and no purple attended the fasces. At that moment the people suppressed their lamentations, and a great sadness without a voice spread everywhere. Just so, households are stunned and silent at the moment of death, before the body is laid out and lamented, and before the mother with her hair unbound bids the arms of her maids to beat their harsh laments, as at the moment when she presses to her the limbs stiffening with departing life, and the inanimate face, and the eyes still menacing in death. She feels no fear—nor yet grief: in distraction she broods over the corpse, and marvels at her loss.[95]

Likewise, when Horace confronts his fellow citizens with the enormity and unfathomability of the civil wars, the Romans are speechless: "A white pallor bleaches their faces, and their stricken minds are stupefied" ("tacent, et albus ora pallor inficit mentes perculsae stupent" [Horace, *Epodi* 7.16]).[96]

By far the most telling, and most terrible, illustration of the psychology of fascination and its relation to the unendurable contradictions of civil war comes in Tacitus's account of the street fighting in Rome in the war between Vitellius and Vespasian during the Saturnalia of 69 C.E. (*Historia* 3.83). There the Roman people, even while actively cheering and supporting one side or the other, preserved the sangfroid of the spectator: "The people of Rome attended the fighting like an audience at a show, favoring with their cheers and applause now this side or that—as if this

---

[95]
> *Ergo, ubi concipiunt, quantis sit cladibus orbi*
> *Constatura fides superum, ferale per urbem*
> *Iustitium; latuit plebeio tectus amictu*
> *Omnis honos, nullos comitata est purpura fasces.*
> *Tum questus tenuere suos, magnusque per omnes*
> *Erravit sine voce dolor. Sic funere primo*
> *Attonitae tacuere domus, cum corpora nondum*
> *Conclamata iacent, nec mater crine soluto*
> *Exigit ad saevos famularum bracchia planctus,*
> *Sed cum membra premit fugiente rigentia vita*
> *Voltusque exanimes oculosque in morte minaces;*
> *Necdum est ille dolor, nec iam metus: incubat amens*
> *Miraturque malum.*
>   (*Bellum civile* 2.16–28)

Like all forms of fascination, this paralyzed state is a hair's breadth from hysteria and frantic activity. Lucan goes on to describe the panic following the *ferale iustitium*.

[96] The apocalyptic visions of the period are also a metaphor for shock and frustration; e.g., Seneca, *Thyestes* 991.

were a mock battle in the arena."⁹⁷ Caught somewhere between celebration and violation, the people reveled in the mayhem of festival while suffering the ravages of a conquered city:

> The face of the whole city was savage and disfigured. On the one side were battles and wounds, on the other baths and cookshops; beside the gore and the heaps of the dead stood the prostitutes and their like; there was all the wantonness of a city luxuriating in idleness, all the crime of a city enduring a pitiless sack. You would think that the same city was both in a furor and frolicking free from care.⁹⁸

The city had become a monstrosity, filled with citizens rejoicing in their own destruction ("malis publicis laeti"). The result of so much contradiction, added to the unbearable tension of civil strife was, for Tacitus, a kind of shocking voyeurism, a seeming emotional and moral paralysis, what he calls an "inhumana securitas," an absence of care that moves them beyond the realm of human emotions.

Voyeurism is alienation carried to the point of inversion. The excess of care (*cura*) manifested by the *curiosus* finally ends in the total absence of care of the *securus* (*sine cura*). The *cura* that is care becomes the *cura* that is cure.⁹⁹ In the topsy-turvy universe of the war of all against all, even while each person is compelled to experience himself or herself as part of the fractured group, he or she is alone and distracted, like the American housewife of the fifties watching the exaggerated passions of her favorite soap opera in curious isolation.

Thralldom

In what a fragile position stand the proud!

[*Quam fragili loco starent superbi*]

(Seneca, *Troades* 5–6)¹⁰⁰

To be fascinated is to be transfixed, to be lost to oneself, like Ovid's Narcissus before the image in the pool.¹⁰¹ To be fascinated is to *cease to reflect*

⁹⁷ "Aderat pugnantibus spectator populus, utque in ludicro certamine hos rursus illos clamore et plausu fovebat."

⁹⁸ "Saeva et deformis urbe tota facies: alibi proelia et vulnera, alibi balineae popinaeque; simul cruor et strues corporum, iuxta scorta et scortis similes; quantum in luxurioso otio libidinum, quidquid in acerbissima captivitate scelerum, prorsus et eandem civitatem et furere crederes et lascivere."

⁹⁹ In Latin *cura* can mean both "anxiety" and "alleviation."

¹⁰⁰ "Whatever exceeds due measure hangs suspended in an unsteady place" ("quidquid excessit modum / pendet instabili loco" [Seneca, *Oedipus* 909–10]). Cf. *Thyestes* 391–92.

¹⁰¹ Disalvo, "The Myth of Narcissus," p. 22.

a terrible loss, to cease to discriminate or make comparisons, to cease to be unequal to the world. Seneca's Oedipus is prepared to look the monstrous portents "in the eye," because if they are sufficiently horrible he will feel relief: "The worst of ills make men calm" ("solent suprema facere securos mala" [*Oedipus* 386]).[102]

The proud and preeminently powerful Romans of the last century of the Republic and the first century of the Empire, were in a kind of collective state of shock. They were enthralled by deformity, disgrace, dishonor (the *dehonestamentum*), particularly their own; tirelessly rehearsing their own debasement and degeneration. The Romans were enthralled because they were thralls. They were enthralled in order to set themselves free.

The despairing Ovid with his baneful secret, driven in a storm-tossed bark toward the frigid wastes of exile, fixates on his poetry. Whether to call it stupor or insanity he does not know. He only knows that his stupor alleviates his stupefaction. It is the pain that cures pain, the care that eases care.[103]

---

[102] "Light cares speak, the weighty are struck dumb" ("curae leves loquuntur, ingentes stupent" [Seneca, *Phaedra* 607]).

[103] "Seu stupor huic studio sive est insania nomen, / omnis ab hac cura cura levata mea est" (*Tristia* 1.11.11–12).

FOUR

ENVY (PART ONE)

EMBRACING THE MONSTER

The highest temptation is the longing to be another, to be all
others; it is to renew identification.
(Michel Foucault, "Fantasia of the Library")[1]

The constitution of the monster implies that taboos have been
transgressed to promote adventures into the realm of
impossible possibilities. . . . It is an evasion at once liberating
and intoxicating, lifting from life all the barriers confining the
species. And so, the monstrous is exalting.
(Jean Brun, "Le Prestige du monstre")[2]

EQUALITY has been lost! is a characteristic lament of the late Republic and early Empire. To many it seemed as if the balance between difference and identity had ceased functioning. Undue discriminations were monstrous aberrations, reifications of envy, and among these monsters of envy was the *derisor*, the mocking mimic who embodied and demanded an identity otherwise unmet.

The Derisor

According to Tacitus, the deformed and low-born Vatinius was a monster ("ostentum") and author of "scurrilous witticisms" ("facetiae scurriles").[3] Like the parasite of Horace's first epistle (1.18.10–14), Vatinius played the emperor's *derisor lecti*, the scoffer who sat at the foot of his master's couch, in the seat reserved for children.[4] Augustus, like Claudius, appears to have kept a stable of these *derisores*, including a certain Sar-

---

[1] *Language, Counter-Memory, Practice*, p. 101.

[2] P. 303.

[3] *Annales* 14.34.2; cf. *Historia* 3.56.2. The other function that Tacitus attributes to Vatinius—to be the butt of abuse (the *stupidus*)—will be discussed in chapter 5.

[4] See Suetonius, *Claudius* 32. Gaius and Lucius sometimes occupied this seat under Augustus (Suetonius, *Augustus* 64.3). It implied honor and dishonor, a relationship of familiarity *and* subservience.

mentus and the great Gabba.[5] Indeed, the tongue of the scoffer was sharpened at many an imperial table: we hear from Suetonius that Tiberius
allowed himself to be mocked by a dwarf standing near the dining table
among the buffoons ("copreae" [*Tiberius* 61.6]),[6] and Claudius liked to
pass his leisure in the conversation of *scurrae* such as Julius Paelignus,
despised, according to Tacitus, for both the worthlessness of his spirit and
his deformed body ("ignavia animi et deridiculo corporis iuxta despicien-
dus" [*Annales* 12.49.1]). Suetonius paints Vespasian soliciting bold ridicule from "quidam urbanorum"—and receiving it (*Vespasianus* 20). And
among the pets kept by Trajan was the brilliant *derisor* Capitolinus.[7]

The guests of monarchs and grandees were lavishly provided with ridicule. But the *derisor* found a welcome at humbler tables as well. According to Horace, there was always someone at the dinner party who would
take upon himself the abuse of the other guests (and eventually, with a
bit of wine under his belt, the host as well)—and be thought inoffensively
clever and urbane (*Satirae* 1.4.86–91). In another satire of Horace
(1.5.51ff.), as a part of the celebration of dinner, an exchange takes place
between the Oscan Messius Cicirrus and the *scurra* and former slave Sarmentus.[8] Sarmentus attacks the *deformitas* of the gentleman in strong
words. In turn, Messius addresses the low birth of the freedman. And yet
Horace gives no indication that offense was taken by either.[9]

How and why did a culture so sensitive to "face" accommodate the
mockery of the buffoon and the *scurra*? What did the Romans see in the
mirror of deformity?[10]

[5] See Plutarch, *Antonius* 59.8; Juvenal, *Satirae* 5.1ff. Cf. Martial 1.41, 10.101.

[6] The *copreae* put slippers on the dozing Claudius at a dinner party and then roused him
suddenly so that, to the glee of his companions, the emperor rubbed his eyes with his shoes
(Suetonius, *Claudius* 8).

[7] Martial 10.101.

[8] See Corbett, *The Scurra*, pp. 66–68.

[9] Compare the *scurra* Varus's mockery of Acilius Buta at a dinner party (Seneca, *Epistulae*
122.10–13). For other examples of the contest of ridicule see Vergil, *Eclogae* 3 (modeled on
Theocritus 5) and Martial 1.41.14–20, 10.101. In the banquet described in the *Lapithae*,
the second-century Greek satirist Lucian has taken great pains to paint a group of philosophers obsessed with their personal dignity. Indeed, they all but came to blows over their
positions at the banquet table. Nevertheless, the harsh (but evenly apportioned) derision by
the ridiculous dwarf buffoon is not only accepted but appreciated by those very philosophers who constitute the target of his wit.

[10] Before proceeding, it is important to note that the *derisor* was not alone; equally prominent in this period was his mate and inversion, the *stupidus*. But because the conceptions
and functions of the two are distinct and relatively complex, I have elected, for heuristic
purposes, to disentangle their roles, with the intention of reintegrating them at a later point.
In this chapter I am telling only half of the story.

Saturn in Chains

At the banquet license befits the humble and gaiety all.

Nam in convictibus . . . lasciva humilibus, hilaria
omnibus convenient.

(Quintilian, *Institutiones oratoriae* 6.3.28)

The dinner party in ancient Rome was a miniature or more circumscribed "Saturnalia" in which there was generous display. It was a form of spectacle in which musicians, dancers, and buffoons (and occasionally gladiators) participated, to the credit of the host.[11] Simultaneously, the banquet called for a temporary and ritualized relaxation of status considerations for the guests.[12] In the words of John D'Arms, "the convivial milieu is associated above all with congeniality, with the loosening of conventions and the lowering of barriers, with the fostering of friendship."[13] It was, according to Jean-Noel Robert, "un véritable moment de détente," in which the toga was cast aside and the absence of any form of cincture or knot was the rule.[14]

The sharing of food and hospitality was, for the living, the dead, and the immortal, the chief mechanism for alleviating the envy occasioned by status distinctions. But a persistent complaint is heard in the period of the late Republic and early Empire that the equality of the banquet is not being observed.[15] Martial protests the unequal treatment received at the dinner parties of Caecilianus, Ponticus, and Sextus: "Am I invited to dine, Sextus, or to envy?" ("ut cenem invitor, Sexte, an ut invideam?" [4.68]).[16] "Do you wonder," he asks, "that in our day there is no Pylades, that there

---

[11] See John D'Arms, "Control, Companionship, and *Clientela*: Some Social Functions of the Roman Communal Meal," *Échos du Monde Classique* 28 (1984), p. 340.

[12] "Demokratikon esti to deipnon" (Plutarch, *Quaestiones conviviales* 1.2.3 *Moralia* 616f.).

[13] D'Arms, "Control," p. 345.

[14] Jean-Noel Robert, *Les Plaisirs à Rome* (Paris, 1986), pp. 99, 105. According to Ovid, the "laws" of the banquet were carefully detailed (*Tristia* 2.488). See Aulus Gellius, *Noctes Atticae* 13.11ff.; Cicero, *De officiis* 1.40.144; Propertius 4.8; Pliny, *Epistulae* 9.17.1–3; Petronius, *Satyricon*; Plutarch, *Sulla* 2; Robert, *Les Plaisirs*, pp. 99–100, 114, 120–26; Becker, *Gallus*, pp. 110–33, esp. p. 111 and n. 4; John D'Arms, "The Roman *Convivium* and the Idea of Equality" (forthcoming), ms. p. 317.

[15] D'Arms has done an excellent job of revealing the tensions between *patrocinium* and *amicitia*, hierarchy and equality, at the Roman dinner party. In this chapter I will be dealing with only one aspect of the contradictory and/or complementary functions of the *convivium* that D'Arms discusses. The other aspect will be tackled in chapter 5.

[16] Cf. 1.20, 3.60. For the envy of the client, see Douglas, *Purity and Danger*, p. 104.

is no Orestes? Pylades, Marcus, drank the same wine as Orestes, and no better bread or gamebirds were given to Orestes; but equal and the same were the dinner of the two" (6.11). The fifth satire of Juvenal is dedicated in its entirety to a bitter expostulation against the distinctions made at the board of the Roman patron. Juvenal's contemporary, the younger Pliny, harshly rebukes the host who preserved hierarchy at a banquet:

> "I serve the same meal for everyone, for when I invite guests it is not to humiliate them [*ad cenam enim, non ad notam invito*]: I have brought them as equals to the same table, so I give them the same treatment in everything." "Even the freedmen?" "Of course, for then they are my fellow diners, not freedmen." (*Epistulae* 2.6.2–4)

Pliny, in the *Natural History*, recalls that Cato the Elder, sailing to Spain against the Celtiberians in the early second century B.C.E. "drank no other wine than what was drunk by the whole crew of his galley, so little did he resemble those who give even their guests other wines than are served to themselves" (14.14.91).[17] In a long letter Seneca decries the progressive limitation of function imposed on the Roman slave and the petrifaction of the barrier between servant and master. In the old days, according to the philosopher, even the slave was allowed to speak at the dinner party, and therefore felt less frustration and dangerous malice toward his master (47.4).[18] All these plaints belong to the sour litanies of the client insufficiently compensated for his *obsequia*, the subordinate enslaved, reduced to flatterer and parasite.[19]

---

[17] Plutarch, *Cato Maior* 25.2–3. The young poet who penned the *Laus Pisonis* claims that his prospective patron, Piso, unlike other Roman grandees, treats his clients uniformly as friends, regardless of their wealth and status: "unus amicitiae summos tenor ambit et imos" (117). According to Richard Saller, the patron often had recourse to the equalizing language of *amicitia* to alleviate the onus of clientage when speaking of or addressing his subordinates. See "Patronage and Friendship in Early Imperial Rome: Drawing the Distinction," in *Patronage in Ancient Society*, ed. Andrew Wallace-Hadrill (London/New York, 1989), pp. 49–62; D'Arms, "The Roman *Convivium*," ms. pp. 313–14.

[18] Cf. 47.14.

[19] The host who insists on making his guests aware of their relative status calls down upon himself Martial's curse: "May you eat such mushrooms as Claudius ate!" (1.20); compare his curse on the envious (9.97.12). See also Martial 3.60, 3.82; Quintilian, *Institutiones oratoriae* 6.3.52 (Fabius Maximus complains of the meagerness of the *congiaria*, the gifts to clients, of Augustus). According to Robert C. Elliott (*The Power of Satire: Magic, Ritual, Art* [Princeton, 1960], esp. pp. 38–39), the giving of poor food and hospitality were the two offenses that drew the bitterest fire of the ancient Irish poet/shaman, who was also a client. For other descriptions of the often galling lot of the client, see Cicero, *De officiis* 2.20.69 ("Truly [to some men] it is the image of death to resort to patronage or to be called a client" ["patrocinio vero se usos aut clientes appellari mortis instar putant"]); Horace, *Epistulae* 1.18; the *Laus Pisonis* 110–37, esp. 126–31; Juvenal, *Satirae* 5.84ff.; Lucian's painfully funny *De mercede conductis potentium familiaribus* (esp. 8, 26) and his *Saturnalia* 22, 32; Saller, "Patronage and Friendship."

Surprisingly, the impulse to assert these distinctions did not always come from the top of the social hierarchy: Suetonius remarks that Julius Caesar once put his baker in irons for giving him bread of a different quality than that served his guests (*Julius Caesar* 48), and Hadrian had to take special precautions to counteract the propensity of his caterers to distribute food according to status.[20]

The "laws" of the Saturnalia, like those of the dinner party, demanded indiscrimination.[21] But the poor man complains, in Lucian, that these laws are not being kept.[22] The rich fear that any concession to equality is too great and bound to stimulate the poor, first to sexual outrage, and then to—who knows what? redistribution of the land?[23] Indeed, there is some evidence that Romans began to shun the Saturnalia and other situations in which status distinctions were not stringently demarcated. Martial's Charisianus insists on wearing the formal toga rather than the traditional light *synthesis* on the Saturnalia (6.24). Ovid's daughters of Minyas profane the holy day and stay within at the festival of the Bacchanalia, weaving and feeling self-righteous;[24] they are not unlike Pliny the Younger, who retires to his study to await patiently the end of the Saturnalia with its noisy reveling.[25] Those who fail to keep the laws of the Saturnalia are like the prurient "Catones," the *tristes et superciliosi censores,* the sclerotic "sourpusses" who look askant at all celebration,[26] or

[20] *Scriptores historiae Augustae, Hadrianus* 17.4. Hadrian, like Domitian in Statius's *Silvae* 1.6, insists on all the guests being served alike. Compare the story of King Arthur's institution of the Round Table in *Layamon's Brut*, trans. Donald G. Bzdyl (Binghamton, N.Y., 1989), p. 214.

[21] *Saturnalia* 7, 13, 17–20, 32; Seneca, *Epistulae* 47.14.

[22] *Saturnalia* 22, 32. Moreover the spirit of the Saturnalia could be corrupted by the gearing of the traditional gifts to rank. Might not sumptuary laws express a longing for relative equality? Jack Goody suggests that "even if such laws are construed as attempts to preserve the structure of existing inequality, their very introduction implies a threat to hierarchy" (*Cooking, Cuisine, and Class* [Cambridge, 1982], p. 103). See D'Arms, "Control," p. 337.

[23] Cf. Cicero, *De republica* 1.42–43 (following Plato, *Republic* 563e–566b). Compare the arguments of the haughty slave-owners whom Seneca chides (47.18).

[24] "Spernit deum, festumque profanit" (*Metamorphoses* 4.390, cf. 4.1–415); cf. Lucian, *Saturnalia* 32 (on the rich man dining alone).

[25] *Epistulae* 2.17; cf. Cicero, *De officiis* 39.103. Pliny, like many of the municipal or provincial gentry, the *domi nobiles* who have adopted the Roman heritage, is most upset by the failure of so many of the Romans to respect those distinctions he himself so coveted; see *Epistulae* 1.23; 2.7.

[26] Cf. Martial 1.35, 11.2; Petronius, *Satyricon* 132.15; Juvenal, *Satirae* 2.38–40. Seneca, in defending the attitudes of the criticized prudes, repeats the complaints against them (*Epistulae* 123.10–11). There is a famous story told of Cato the Younger that his presence at the Floralia of 55 B.C.E. inhibited the nude dancing of the female mimes until he voluntarily withdrew (Valerius Maximus 2.10.8; cf. Martial 1 *praefatio*; Reich, *Der Mimus*, pp. 53–54). Similarly, the presence of Brutus makes Lucretia blush to read Martial. (But let

the ascetic athletes and philosophers who flee from a banquet at the word "sex" or the sound of a flute.[27]

Sour Grapes

Righteousness was often interpreted as aggressive envy. "Most readers impute to malevolence and envy," according to Sallust, "whatever charges you level against crime."[28] It is the envious who accuse the impetuous, the *simplicior* (as Horace would present himself to his patron Maecenas), of being troublesome and lacking in common sense (*Satirae* 1.3.60–66). The *livor*, the spiteful indignation, of Martial's rival, arises from his envy: the "circumcised" poet who rails at and belittles Martial's poems also plagiarizes them (11.94). It is *malus livor* that hypocritically accuses Martial of writing verses dyed with spite; the envious accuse him of being envious and of writing with a poisoned pen (10.33). Elsewhere Martial complains about the small-minded provincial, the envy that passes for judgment, and the "municipalium robigo dentium," the rusty, rotten teeth of the provincial (12 *praefatio*).[29] If envy was an unsatisfied hunger, righteous indignation was its teeth.[30]

Brutus retire and she will read! [Martial 11.16].) "[Titus Labienus] adfectabat enim censorium supercilium, cum alius animo esset" (Seneca Rhetor, *Controversiae* 10 *praefatio* 4).

[27] Plutarch, *Quaestiones conviviales* 7.7 *Moralia* 710d–e. Compare Martial's "wife" at 11.104.

[28] "Plerique quae delicta reprehenderis malevolentia et invidia dicta putant" (*Catilina* 3.2). Cf. Juvenal, *Satirae* 2, esp. 36–46. "Elle [l'envie] tourne ordinairement à la réprobation morale, en vertu de notre tendance à condamner moralement ce qui nous fait souffrir ou nous met mal à l'aise" (Veyne, *Le Pain et le cirque*, p. 309); cf. David Epstein, *Personal Enmity in Roman Politics 218–43 B.C.* (London, 1989), p. 128 and nn. 128, 136. "Moral indignation, like complimenting, may also on occasion represent a socially sanctioned way of expressing envy. . . . To appeal to conventional norms by exhibiting shocked outrage not only reassures the threatened person of the moral unassailability of his position, but to him also justifies the repressive action which he feels is essential to the solution of the problem. Whether moral indignation is interpreted as a way of expressing envy of others or of responding to the fear of envy of others, its consequence—repressive action—is the same" (Foster, "The Anatomy of Envy," p. 174). One can compare the complaints lodged against the "Catones" to those leveled against the authorities that attempted to suppress the clerical Feast of Fools in the cathedral towns of France in the early modern period. The latter were burlesqued as Hypocrisy, Pretense, and False Semblance. See Welsford, *The Fool*, p. 203.

[29] The monster Manducus (the "Chewer") was a manifestation of the voracious hunger ascribed to the envious. The *manduci* were *edaces* (Nonius, ed. Wallace M. Lindsay [Hildesheim, 1964], p. 24).

[30] "The malevolent mind has hidden teeth" ("Malivolus animus abditos dentes habet" [Publilius Syrus 382, cf. 378]). "Truly there is no happiness so modest that it can escape the teeth of spite" ("Verum nulla tam modesta felicitas est quae malignitatis dentes vitare pos-

Making the Play Serious

In 67 B.C.E. the law of Roscius Otho was passed, which reserved the first fourteen rows of the *cavea*, the auditorium, for the knights (Livy, *Epitome* 99).[31] Prior to that time, according to Plutarch (*Cicero* 13.2), the knights had sat promiscuously with the people, in whatever order they happened to arrive. Roscius Otho was the first to separate, to distinguish ("diakrinein") them from one another to the honor ("epi time") of the equites.[32] The elevation of the equestrians was, however, taken as an insult by the people ("touto pros atimias ho demos elabe"). The people were, as the elder Pliny notes, "marked" by the separation of their seats ("notatas se discrimine sedis" [*Historia naturalis* 7.30.117]). When Roscius appeared in the theatre in 63 B.C.E., the knights cheered him, but the people jeered. It was only the mysterious charm of Cicero's oratory that prevented the hostility between the equites and the people from erupting into a donnybrook.[33] Augustus not only reinforced the privileges of the senators but further elaborated seating distinctions, separating men and

---

sit" [Valerius Maximus 7.7 ext.2]). These gruesome metaphors for envy are closely related to Horace's "morsu venenare" (*Epistulae* 1.14.38, cf. 1.18.82, 2.1.150–51; *Satirae* 2.1.76–78), to Ovid's hypostatized Invidia chomping on poisonous snakes, her mouth dripping with gore, or to Martial's own "livor edax." For envy depicted as hunger, see chapter 3, p. 90 and n. 27.

[31] Suetonius, *Nero* 11.1: "circensibus loca equiti secreta a ceteris tribuit [63 C.E.]." Cf. Tacitus, *Annales* 15.32.2; Dio 36.42.1; Calpurnius Siculus, *Eclogae* 7.25ff. (The country-folk climb up to where the multitude in their dingy grey robes and the women sit; the knights or tribunes in snowy white thronged the area under the open sky.) On the development of seating arrangements in the theatre, see Ugo Scamuzzi, "Studio sulla *Lex Roscia Theatralis*," *Rivista di Studi Classici* 17 (1969), pp. 133–65, 259–319; 18 (1970), pp. 5–57, 374–447; Monique Clavel-Lévêque, "L'Espace des jeux à Rome: champs de lutte et lieux d'obtention du consentement," in *Mélanges offerts à la mémoire de Roland Fietier* (Paris, 1984), pp. 197–226, esp. 206–7; Elizabeth Rawson, "*Discrimina Ordinum*: The *Lex Julia Theatralis*," *Papers of the British School at Rome* 55 (1987), pp. 83–114; Jean-Marie André, "Die Zuschauerschaft als sozial-politischer Mikrokosmos zur Zeit des Hochprinzipats," in Jürgen Blänsdorf, *Theater und Gesellschaft im Imperium Romanum* (Tübingen, 1990), pp. 165–73. Velleius (2.32.3), following Cicero (*Pro Murena* 19.40), seems to regard the rights granted by the *lex Roscia* as a restoration. See Scamuzzi, pp. 270–91; Rawson, p. 102n. 110. The senate had been segregated as early as 194 B.C.E. (Livy 34.54.4).

[32] That is, those with a census status of four hundred thousand sesterces, and perhaps additional qualifications such as membership on a jury or a minor magistracy. For a Roman account of the gradual solidifying of the order of equestrians in the late Republic and early Empire see Pliny, *Historia naturalis* 33.7–9.

[33] Unfortunately, apart from the slightest hint preserved by the fourth-century grammatician Arusianus Messius we do not know what he said. See Plutarch, *Cicero* 13.3–4; Pliny, *Historia naturalis* 7.30.117; Arusianus, *Grammatici Latini*, ed. Keil, vol. 7, p. 490.23.

women and giving special seats to soldiers, to the married among the plebs, and to young men wearing the purple-bordered robe (*praetexta*) and accompanied by their tutors.[34]

The superordination of the equestrians was attended by the even greater superordination of the emperor: in the circus the prince occupied the *pulvinar*, a kind of royal box, located on a *podium* or *suggestum*, a raised platform above the racecourse; in the theatre or amphitheatre he sat on the elevated *tribunal*.[35]

Resentment and resistance to the *lex Roscia* did not end, as Cicero supposed, with his address to the plebs.[36] Octavian's insistence on the maintenance of status distinctions in the theatre nearly resulted in his own destruction. In 41 B.C.E. the young general arrested a soldier who dared to sit in the first fourteen rows of the theatre. This aroused such mutinous indignation among the soldiers that they surrounded the departing Octavian, demanding their comrade. According to Suetonius, Octavian was in danger of losing his life (*Augustus* 14; cf. Appian, *Bellum civile* 5.15). The law was continually thwarted.[37] The relevant passages in Suetonius (*Augustus* 44; *Claudius* 21.3; *Nero* 11.1; *Domitianus* 8.3), Tacitus (*Annales* 15.32), and Dio (60.7.4) suggest that the tendency of the classes to mingle indiscriminately at the spectacles reasserted itself over the discrimination implemented by Augustus, Claudius, Nero, and Domitian.[38]

Monstrous Refinements

"*Urbanitas* signifies what is proper to Rome . . . the style, the language, the taste, the sense of humor."[39] Edwin S. Ramage emphasizes that *ur-*

---

[34] Suetonius, *Augustus* 44; Rawson, "*Discrimina ordinum*"; Clavel-Lévêque, "L'Espace des jeux," pp. 207–8.

[35] E.g., Suetonius, *Julius* 76.1; *Nero* 12.1; *Augustus* 45.1 ("Ipse [Augustus] circenses ex amicorum fere libertorumque cenaculis [upper story, garret, attic] spectabat, interdum ex pulvinari et quidem cum coniuge ac liberis sedens"); *Claudius* 21.1 (Claudius inaugurates the games to celebrate the rededication of the theatre of Pompey from a raised seat in the orchestra ["e tribunali posito in orchestra"]).

[36] E.g., Juvenal, *Satirae* 3.152–59. See Scamuzzi, "*Lex Roscia*," pp. 292–306.

[37] See Martial 3.95, 5.14, 5.23, 5.25, 5.38; Suetonius, *Domitian* 8.3; Meyer Reinhold, "Usurpation of Status and Status Symbols in the Roman Empire," *Historia* 20 (1971), pp. 281–82.

[38] For the segregation of the classes by Augustus: Dio 55.22.4. By Claudius: Dio 60.7.4. By Nero: Tacitus, *Annales* 15.32; Suetonius, *Nero* 11.1; Pliny, *Historia naturalis* 8.7.21. By Domitian: Suetonius, *Domitianus* 8.3; Martial 5.8.

[39] Jean-Michel David, "Les Orateurs des municipes à Rome: intégration, réticences et snobismes," in *Les 'Bourgeoisies' municipales italiennes aux IIe et Ier siècles av. J.-C.* (Paris/Naples, 1983), p. 315.

banitas (particularly in the Republic) implied restraint and decorum, *pudor* and modesty, aloofness and a strong devotion to "common sense."[40] It seems that the restraints of Roman decorum grew ever more subtle and elaborate in the period of the civil wars and after. In the age of Cicero, according to Ramage, "the refined Roman was more outspoken than ever before in his refusal to accept those who did not exhibit or maintain the standards of urbanity."[41] Walking, sitting, reclining, facial expressions and gestures, and, above all, speech—its tone and tenor, rhythm and accent—were subject to regulation according to a set of increasingly refined stylistic models.[42] Every aspect of the individual's appearance and behavior was scrutinized and subject to strictures, ignorance of which invited ridicule and exclusion. "It is evident that no one, not even those on extended sojourn in Rome, could sufficiently assimilate all the idioms, all the nuances of intonation of Roman Latin. And to commit an error was to reveal oneself as a foreigner. . . . This nuance, or rather, this fault—for it was insurmountable—became decisive in the promotion and social integration of the *domi nobiles*."[43] The esoteric, exclusive, highly scripted politesse of the Romans rigidly segregated them. To enter the society of the elite from outside required total immersion in the fastidious etiquette that distinguished it.[44] The severity of the behavioral demands placed on men and women and slaves can be gleaned from the *De officiis*

[40] Edwin S. Ramage, *Urbanitas; Ancient Sophistication and Refinement* (Norman, Okla., 1973). See Otto Lutsch, "Die Urbanitas nach Cicero," in *Festgabe für Wilhelm Crecelius* (Elberfeld, 1881), pp. 80–95; Mary Grant, *The Ancient Rhetorical Theories of the Laughable*, University of Wisconsin Studies in Language and Literature, no. 4 (Madison, 1924), pp. 119–24. Following Lutsch, Grant asserts that "*urbanitas* partakes in some degree of *gravitas* in that Crassus, who is called (*De oratore* 2.228) *gravissimus*, is also called *urbanissimus* (cf. *Brutus* 38.143). The Socratic philosophers, too, whose *genus iocandi* is called *urbanum* (*De officiis* 1.104), were men of earnest purpose. So Demosthenes, to whom Cicero attributes *urbanitas*, but denies *dicacitas* (*De oratore* 90), was undeniably *severus*" (p. 119).

[41] *Urbanitas*, p. 65.

[42] "Il faut donc croire qu'il existait une façon de prononcer spécifiquement romaine, faite de nuances insensibles et inaccessibles à qui n'avait pas passé sa petite enfance à Rome même. C'est ce qu'indique cette notion si imprécise d'*urbanitatis color*" (David, "Les Orateurs," p. 315). See Cicero, *De oratore* 3.161, 1.17; *Ad Quintum fratrem* 2.10; Ramage, *Urbanitas*, pp. 35, 63, 90–91, 129; Grant, "Theories of the Laughable," p. 120.

[43] David, "Les Orateurs," p. 315.

[44] For resistance to the excessive formalization of the dinner party, see Horace's "We have no silly rules here" (*Satirae* 2.6.67–70). It is interesting that here the revolt is against having to drink equal amounts of wine in a set of prescribed toasts. (See Robert, *Les Plaisirs*, p. 114.) Horace wants a more informal, casual meal at which one is free to consume the type and amount of wine one wishes.

(1.27.96ff., esp. 1.40.144) of Cicero, the *Ars amatoria* of Ovid, and Epistle 47 of Seneca.[45] The wearing of incorrect attire was no less a crime in the second century C.E., in the time of Aulus Gellius, than when Mark Antony wore Gallic sandals and a cloak.[46] And not even the preeminence of Hadrian could save him from being mocked in the senate for his Spanish accent (*Scriptores historiae Augustae, Hadrianus* 3.1).[47]

Evidence of the elaboration and crystallization of the Roman social hierarchy could be multiplied: the finer and finer differentiation in the function and status of slaves that attended the general lowering of their station and the strengthening of measures of control;[48] the regulation, and separation, of the classes by laws limiting marriage and severely punishing adultery;[49] the increased "rationalization" and "bureaucratization" of the Roman imperial administration, with its articulation of different competing *cursus honorum*,[50] the multiplication of fictive offices and honors,[51]—all helped to create an impression of a people divided against itself according to competitive and hierarchical principles. The Roman historian and sociologist Keith Hopkins speaks of "the institutionalization of spheres of conduct which had previously been relatively undifferentiated."[52]

---

[45] See Ramage, *Urbanitas*, pp. 35, 63, 88, 90–91, 129.

[46] Cf. Cicero, *Philippicae* 2.30.76. For the *chirodotae*, see Aulus Gellius, *Noctes Atticae* 6.12.1–2. Cicero recalls with indignation the animal-skin loincloth that Antony, while consul, wore at the Lupercal (*Philippicae* 2.34.85). See Bonfante, "Nudity as a Costume in Classical Art," p. 563. For the regulation of dress on public occasions, particularly at the public spectacles, see Rawson, "Discrimina Ordinum," p. 112.

[47] For the Roman fanaticism concerning the subtleties of pronunciation and oral expression, see Ramage, *Urbanitas*, pp. 47, 59–62, 68–69, 72–75, 106–10, 115–17, 126, 129, 149.

[48] See Seneca, *Epistulae* 47.

[49] On Augustus's legislation concerning adultery, see Paul Jörs, "Die Ehegesetze des Augustus," in *Festschrift Theodor Mommsen*, ed. Jörs, Schwartz et al. (Marburg, 1893), pp. 1–65; H. A. Last, "The Social Policy of Augustus," in *Cambridge Ancient History*, vol. 10 (1952), pp. 425–64; Leo Ferrero Raditsa, "Augustus' Legislation Concerning Marriage, Procreation, Love Affairs and Adultery," in *Aufstieg und Niedergang der römischen Welt*, vol. 2.13 (Berlin, 1980), pp. 278–339. For the resentment and resistance that this caused see, for example, Propertius 2.7.

[50] For this phenomenon in Roman life, see especially Keith Hopkins, "Elite Mobility in the Roman Empire," *Past and Present* 32 (1965), pp. 12–26, and P.R.C. Weaver, "Social Mobility in the Early Roman Empire: The Evidence of the Imperial Freedmen and Slaves," *Past and Present* 37 (1967), pp. 3–20.

[51] Reinhold, "Usurpation," p. 287.

[52] Keith Hopkins, "Structural Differentiation in Rome (200–31 B.C.E.)," in *History and Social Anthropology*, ed. I. M. Lewis (London, 1968), p. 71. See A. N. Sherwin-White, *The*

The Fount of Inequality

The divine right of kings, papal infallibility and the modern
totalitarian state all flowered after the
Feast of Fools disappeared.
(Harvey Cox, *The Feast of Fools*)[53]

The increasing singularity and domination of the prince, the *immanis maximitas* of a single man,[54] a single patron, aggravated the Roman sensitivity to relative status. Formerly collective prizes became prerogatives: after 19 B.C.E. no general who was not a member of the imperial family could triumph, but a Nero could triumph as citharode in the chariot of Augustus.[55] Moreover, many honors, such as the "public horse," membership on the jury panels, a position in the equestrian *cursus honorum*, and entry into the senate, became perquisites to be disbursed by the emperor to the obsequious.[56] These prizes ceased to signal personal victory in a competition between relative equals and became, more and more, expressions of inequality and subordination.

Accordingly, a status-hungry Cicero expressed the opinion that a man in private life (*privatus*) ought to live on equal and fair terms with his fellow citizens, neither subordinate and abject nor domineering: "aequo et pari cum civilibus iure neque summissum et abiectum neque se efferentem" (*De officiis* 1.34.124).[57] The equally status-conscious Tacitus laments lost equality: the growth of the Roman empire had fed an instinctive lust for power until it overwhelmed the primitive equality of the Romans and became an uncontrollable force leading to civil war, and finally, to the domination of the emperors (*Historia* 2.38.1). Already under Augustus, "the state of the city being overturned, nothing remained of the ancient and uncorrupted traditions; stripped of equality, all waited on the bidding of the prince" ("Igitur verso civitatis statu nihil usquam prisci et integri moris: omnes exuta aequalitate iussa principis aspectare"

Letters of Pliny: A Historical and Social Commentary (Oxford, 1966), pp. 484–85, on the development of the categories *honestiores* et *humiliores* (with bibliography).

[53] Harvey Cox, *The Feast of Fools* (Cambridge, Mass., 1969), p. 5; cf. p. 155.

[54] This phrase, indicating size beyond measure, is from Lucretius (*De rerum natura* 2.498).

[55] Suetonius, *Nero* 25.1.

[56] See Fergus Millar, *The Emperor in the Roman World* (London, 1977), p. 11; Richard P. Saller, *Personal Patronage Under the Early Empire* (Cambridge, 1982), pp. 32–33.

[57] Cicero is defining the distinct duties of magistrates, citizens, foreigners. Elsewhere Cicero is not so democratic. See, for example, *Ad familiares* 7.16.2, 9.26.

[Tacitus, *Annales* 1.4.1]).[58] To many it seemed as if there could be no balancing the power of the prince, no Saturnalia at the table of the king. Tiberius, according to Suetonius, would not interrupt his executions for sacred days—not even for New Year's! (Suetonius, *Tiberius* 61; cf. Tacitus, *Annales* 6.19).

The Barmecidal Feast

As a result of radically unequal power relationships, all food was hunger. Plutarch asserts that even the needy flatterer feels plundered at the table of an immodest man, be he king or satrap. He quotes Menander's parasite: "This feasting makes me thin!" (Plutarch, *De se ipsum citra invidiam laudando* 22 *Moralia* 547d–e).

The eminence of Caesar turned courtesy to compulsion: "Power, should it invite, should it even supplicate, compels" (Macrobius, *Saturnalia* 2.7.2).[59] As a result, the gratuities of the powerful often met with little grace.[60] "No one," asserts Seneca, "is obligated by accepting what he cannot refuse" (*De Beneficiis* 2.18.7).[61] "It is," he says, "a terrible torment to be in debt to someone to whom one does not wish to be" (ibid. 2.18.3; cf. 2.18.8).[62] "To accept a benefit," according to Publilius Syrus, "is to sell your freedom" (60).[63] Livy's Sergius preferred to be conquered by the enemy than to gain victory with the assistance of the arrogant Virginius (5.8). The humiliation of defeat could be borne more easily than the benefit that manifested the donor's superiority.[64]

---

[58] According to Elizabeth Keitel, "The phrase '*exuta aequalitate*' recurs only at 3.26.2, where the casting off of equality facilitates the rise of *vis* and *ambitio* and the establishment of *dominationes*" ("Principate and Civil Wars in the *Annals* of Tacitus," p. 315).

[59] "Sed potestas, non solum si invitet, sed etiam si supplicet, cogit." Cf. Florus on the death of Caesar: "Envy of Caesar prevailed over Caesar's clemency, for his very power to confer benefits was oppressive to free men" ("Quippe clementiam principis vicit invidia, gravisque erat liberis ipsa beneficiorum potentia" [2.13.92]).

[60] Even giving hospitality could be a form of humiliation when rendered under compulsion. As the haughty younger Cato reminds his reluctant hosts, "Romans need little excuse for taking by force what they fail to get by consent" (Plutarch's *Cato Minor* 12). Martial associates both being entertained and entertaining with humiliation (12.48, 12.60).

[61] "Nemo id accipiendo obligatur quod illi repudiare non licuit."

[62] "Grave tamen tormentum est debere cui nolis."

[63] "Beneficium accipere libertatem est vendere."

[64] For the superiority established by the donor, see Mauss, *The Gift*, esp. p. 72; D'Arms, "Control," p. 339. This superiority was greeted with the malice of the recipient. For the horrors of gratitude, see Schoeck, *Envy*, esp. pp. 21–22, 51, and Ruth Benedict, *The Chrysanthemum and the Sword* (New York, 1946), esp. pp. 98–113 ("The *on* [incurred obligation] is a festering sore"). Seneca speaks of the pain of being beholden: "Just because you have saved me does not mean you are my savior" ("si servasti me, non ideo servator es" [*De beneficiis* 2.18.8]).

The enormous inequality of their powers rendered it impossible for the knight Laberius (106–43 B.C.E.), a man of acute and desperate freedom ("Laberius asperae libertatis eques Romanus" [Macrobius *Saturnalia* 2.7.2]), to refuse Julius Caesar's "request" to degrade himself and perform as a mime at Caesar's public shows. In lines from a preserved prologue, Laberius the mime, *ignominiatus*, expresses clearly both his grief at this loss of status and his association of this loss with the advancement of Caesar: "How could I, a mere man, say 'no' to him whom the gods themselves could deny nothing? . . . I left my household gods today a Roman knight; I shall return a mime. In very truth, today I have lived a day too long."[65]

The anguish of Laberius was shared by those who felt compelled to witness his ordeals. Cicero complains in a letter (46 B.C.E.) of having to sit through Caesar's shows: "Indeed, I have become so hardened that I could see Plancus and hear Laberius's verses in Caesar's games with great equanimity. Let me tell you that what I lack most is someone with whom to laugh at all this in an intimate, sophisticated way" (*Epistulae ad familiares* 12.18.2).[66]

Through the Looking Glass

The Romans had an inclination to think of things beyond measure as inverting themselves and yet carrying some part of their original tendency with them, creating paradoxes, creating monstrosities.

Horace complains in his sixth Epistle of the anomalies that result from moral absolutism. Beyond measure, the wise man becomes the fool; the moral man, immoral. "The *sapiens* is insane, the just man unjust when he pursues virtue itself beyond limits" ("Insani sapiens nomen ferat, aequus iniqui. / Ultra quam satis est virtutem si petat ipsam" [1.6.15–16]). The excessively grave or heavy becomes the *brutus*, the stupid, the stupefied. (As a synonym for *obstupuit* Festus offers "obbrutuit," from *brutus*, which was employed anciently as a synonym for *gravis* as well as *stupidus*.)[67] According to Cicero, the perfect wise man, exceedingly rare as he

[65] "Et enim ipsi di negare cui nihil potuerunt, / hominem me denegare quis posset pati? / . . . Eques Romanus e Lare egressus meo, / domum revertar mimus, ni mirum hoc die / uno plus vixi mihi quam vivendum fuit" (Macrobius, *Saturnalia* 2.7.3).

[66] "Equidem sic iam obdurui, ut ludis Caesaris nostri animo aequissimo viderem T. Plancum, audirem Laberi et Publili poemata. Nihil mihi tam desse scito, quam quicum haec familiariter docteque rideam."

[67] See Georges Dumézil, "*Maiestas* et *Gravitas*: De quelques différences entre les romains et les austronésiens," *Revue de Philologie*, 3rd ser., 25 (1951), pp. 7–28; Lucretius, *De rerum natura* 6.105–6; Horace, *Carmina* 1.34.9. The story of the elder Brutus is fascinating in this light. From the *stupidus* he becomes an icon of Roman *gravitas* (Plutarch, *Publicola*).

is, is a kind of freak, a *portentum* (*De divinatione* 2.28.61).[68] The master who relentlessly insists upon his superiority to his slave becomes a slave (Seneca, *Epistulae* 47.9). The paradox is a familiar one in Roman thought. Too much freedom becomes slavery (e.g., Tacitus, *Historia* 2.71). The "ultimate" law for the Roman was no law at all (i.e., "martial law," the *senatus consultum ultimum*). Too much justice was no justice at all: "summum ius summa iniuria" (Cicero, *De officiis* 1.10.33). The miser lacks all: "Many things are lacking to the poor man, but everything to the avaricious" ("Desunt inopiae multa, avaritiae omnia" [Seneca, *Epistulae* 108.9; cf. 94.43]). The Jews, too carefully distinguished from all other peoples, are indiscriminate (Tacitus, *Historia* 5.4–5).[69]

Inordinate refinements create monsters.[70] The decorum of the warrior, taken to its extremes, unmans one: the heightened demands of etiquette produce the hyperurbane person, the *perurbanus*—the fop—who ceases, by his extreme fastidiousness, to be a fit Roman warrior and becomes instead, like Seneca's dissolute Hostius Quadra, a *portentum*.[71] The "honorable" man was a sensitive man, but the excessively refined and thin-skinned Roman, exasperated by a table too carelessly set or a cushion in disarray, distressed if his bed of rose petals is crumpled, made queasy at a spot of dirt or of tarnish, shudders at the banging of a door or the rattle of bronze (*De ira* 2.25, 3.35).[72] At some point the discipline and distinctions of etiquette, grown excessively severe, implode. Indeed,

---

It is tempting to think that the linkage between the stories of Brutus the fool and Brutus the "heavy" is constituted by this Roman tendency to think of extremes as inverting, and by the opposite qualities implied in the word *brutus*.

[68] Compare the picture of the Stoic in Seneca's *Apocolocyntosis* 8, drawn from Varro's lost *Saturae Menippeae*: "rotundus . . . sine capite, sine praeputio." It is this closed sphere that the monstrous violates. "The grotesque ignores the impenetrable surface that closes and limits the body as a separate and completed phenomenon" (Bakhtin, *Rabelais*, p. 316; cf. pp. 281–83, 296, 317–18).

[69] E.g., the Jews are careful to avoid marriage or sexual intercourse with women of alien races, but among themselves, nothing is forbidden: "separati epulis, discreti cubilibus, proiectissima ad libidinem gens, alienarum concubitu abstinent; inter se nihil inlicitum." Excessive *religio* (scrupulousness) becomes *prava religio* or *superstitio* (Walter Otto, "Religio und Superstitio," *Archiv für Religionswissenschaft* 12 [1909], pp. 532–54; 14 [1911], pp. 406–22). *Magnus animus* (magnanimity) in its extreme comes to imply *despicientia rerum humanarum* (Ulrich Knoche, *Magnitudo Animi*, Suppl. vol. 27.3 of *Philologus* [Leipzig, 1935], pp. 49–50 and n. 220, p. 62 and n. 274, pp. 79ff. and n. 348).

[70] Cf. Seneca, *Controversiae* 10.4.17.

[71] E.g. Cicero, *Pro Caelio* 15.36 (Clodius "urbanissimus"), 28.67 ("lauti iuvenes"); *Ad Atticum* 2.14.2; 2.15.3 (The "perurbani" Gaius Arrius and Sebosus); see Ramage, *Urbanitas*, p. 65.

[72] Cf. *De providentia* 4.9–10; *De brevitate vitae* 12. These *fastidiosi* are not unlike the horrible *larvae* that are frightened away by the clang of bronze or iron (Lucian, *Philopseudes* 15). According to Martial, when you take the *mentula* out of the "light" poetry, you castrate it; you make the Priapus into a Gallus (1.35). In other words, when you become excessively fastidious, what you get is not the *durus* homo but the *mollis*.

the word *urbanitas*, connoting the peculiarly and essentially Roman (the "Romanness" of Romans), comes paradoxically to suggest detachment and cosmopolitanism ("urbanity" in our modern sense), as well as licentiousness.[73] Ovid, Maecenas, and Petronius, men of the period who devoted their lives to *urbanitas*, were not generally considered grave.[74] His refinement carried to an extreme, the urbane gentleman (*urbanus homo*) becomes the vagrant dandy (*scurra vagus*);[75] the excessively discriminating man becomes indiscriminate; the overly cultivated man becomes a buffoon.[76] According to Seneca, "All things are so mixed up by the most varied refinements that whatever ornaments were attributed to women, have become the burden of men—indeed, even of soldiers" (*Naturales quaestiones* 1.17.10).[77]

The creation of finer and more brittle categories does not so much foster inclusion as multiply "freaks," things that will not fit clearly into any particular category: Cleopatra, Spartacus, the *perurbanus*.[78] Florus does not know what to call a "war" against Spartacus: "bellum Spartaco duce concitatum quo nomine appellem nescio" (2.8.1–2). It is neither this nor that, neither serious nor comic; it is liminal. The emperor, so particularized, so unique and distinct from other men, becomes a freak or fool.[79]

[73] See Ramage, *Urbanitas*, esp. pp. 113 and 183n. 5; cf. pp. 101–2, 112, 126, 151. Words like *severitas*, *gravitas*, *comitas*, and *cultus* are forced to serve the function once played by *urbanitas*. See the examples from Pliny the Younger assembled by Ramage, op. cit., pp. 133–34.

[74] It is interesting, however, to notice the doubt raised about Petronius (cf. Tacitus, *Annales* 16.18), and to consider the prevailing tendency of the Romans to couple all forms of asceticism and license.

[75] See Horace, *Epistulae* 1.15.26ff.; Suetonius, *Vespasianus* 20 (the *urbanus* as *scurra* producing "infacetiae").

[76] Both Cicero and, following him, Quintilian, depict the *scurra* as indiscriminate in his ridicule, his attacks falling upon himself as well as others. The inability of the *scurra* to distinguish enemy and friend, self and other, deprives his wit of its strategic and competitive quality. See Cicero, *De oratore* 2.61.242, 247–48, 251; Quintilian, *Institutiones oratoriae* 6.3.82. According to Corbett (*The Scurra*, pp. 37, 74), the word *scurra* had, already in Plautus, implications of softness and lack of military form. Excessive confinement and restraint create the libertine (One thinks of Sade, Genet, Flaubert's Anthony, or the roused victims of encephalitic paralysis in Oliver Sach's *Awakenings*).

[77] "Omnia indiscreta sunt diversissimis artibus ut, quicquid mundus muliebris vocabatur, sarcinae viriles sint, omnes dico, etiam militares." See Seneca, *Epistulae* 114. Maecenas's excessively refined lifestyle makes him effeminate and reverberates in his "oratio portentosissima," with its ambiguity and inversions. It is filled with marvelous thoughts ("sensus miri") that, while often powerful, are nevertheless "enervati" (114.7–8).

[78] Just so, it is the need for clear and rigid distinctions between the sexes and between sexual roles that makes poor Herculine Barbin a freak. See *Herculine Barbin: Being the Recently Discovered Memoirs of a Nineteenth-Century Hermaphrodite*, trans. Richard McDougall (New York, 1980). The absence of festival and fantasy "has resulted in a deformed man" (Cox, *Feast of Fools*, pp. 16–17; cf. p. 73).

[79] For the king as monster, see Max Gluckman, "Rituals of Rebellion in South-East Af-

The more refined the patterns of speech the more ghastly and unnerving the slightest aberration.[80] As Erving Goffman points out, the higher one's status, the more "face" one has, the more finesse required to preserve it, the more ways one's "face" can be undermined or shown to be inconsistent.[81]

Envy is an emotion that is *always in excess*. It is, as J. Sabini and M. Silver observe, an emotion without a moderate or acceptable form.[82] Therefore envy is always *anceps*, paradoxical, liable to invert, "torqued." In this way, envy is exactly like the tyrant. They are monsters, and their antidote is monstrous.

Envy the *Pharmakon*

Privilege was most resented when it appeared "unearned," but all forms of excessive differentiation resulted in *invidia*.[83] Among the cosmic correctives for inequality that Horace applies to all distinctions in wealth and power is the paranoia that accompanies them: the suspended sword ruins the banquets of Sicilian tyrants; envy attends the new and splendid hall (*Carmina* 3.1). The master cannot sleep for fear of the violent malice of

---

rica" (1952), in *Order and Rebellion in Tribal Africa* (New York, 1963), pp. 110–45, esp. p. 134; Girard, *Violence and the Sacred*, pp. 252–53. The god, first and foremost, even more than the king, was the monster. "God's material form is grotesque" (Christian Morganstern, quoted by Wolfgang Kayser, *The Grotesque in Art and Literature*, trans. Ulrich Weisstein [New York, 1981 (orig. pub. 1959)], p. 205). "All sacred creatures partake of monstrosity" (Girard, *Violence and the Sacred*, p. 251). See Rudolf Otto, *The Idea of the Holy*, p. 40 (God as the "Ungeheuer" or "mysterium tremendum"); Harpham, *On the Grotesque*, p. 18; Northrup Frye, *Anatomy of Criticism* (Princeton, 1957), pp. 141–42. Cf. Augustine, quoting Seneca, *De civitate dei* 6.10.

[80] For monstrous speech in ancient Rome, see Edward Norden, *Die Antike Kunstprosa* (Darmstadt, 1958), vol. 1, pp. 277–81; Quintilian, *Institutiones oratoriae* 2.5.10ff., 5.12.17ff., 10.2.16–17, 12.10.73ff.

[81] Erving Goffman, "On Face-Work: An Analysis of Ritual Elements in Social Interaction," in *Interaction Ritual: Essays on Face-to-Face Behavior* (New York, 1967), pp. 13–14, n. 6.

[82] J. Sabini and M. Silver, "Envy," in *The Social Construction of Emotions*, ed. Rom Harré (Oxford, 1986), pp. 167–83.

[83] "Est enim hoc commune vitium in magnis liberisque civitatibus ut invidia gloriae comes sit et libenter de iis detrahunt quos eminere videant altius" (Cornelius Nepos, *Chabrias* 3). "Quam sit adsidua eminentis fortunae comes invidia altissimisque adhaereat" (Velleius Paterculus 1.9.6). "Numquam eminentia invidia carent" (ibid. 2.40.4). "Sed profecto sicut arborum altissimas vehementius ventis quati videmus, ita virtutes maximas invidia criminosius insectatur" (Fronto, *Principia historiae* 18 [ed. M.P.J. Van Den Hout]). "Envy is the tax which all distinctions must pay" (Ralph Waldo Emerson, quoted by Robert Nisbet, "Envy," in *Prejudices: A Philosophical Dictionary* [Cambridge, Mass., 1982], p. 108). Schoeck's *Envy* is a great storehouse of similar sentiments.

his army of slaves (Seneca, *Epistulae* 47.4–5).[84] Lack of modesty in success drove storms of *invidia* against Cicero (Seneca Rhetor, *Suasoriae* 6.24).[85] Ovid's proud, arrogant, and solitary Narcissus (so like the Hippolytus of Seneca's *Phaedra*) elicits envy, and this envy brings down upon him the complementary curse: may he want and never get what he wants; may he know himself.

Invidia was, thus, an equalizing force. Envy yearns for the equal opponent; it also creates the equal opponent, as the condition for honor.[86] When Caesar responded to news of the death of Cato by saying that "he had envied Cato's glory and Cato had envied his" (Valerius Maximus, 5.1.10), he was like the athlete who extends his hand to his defeated opponent at the conclusion of a hard-fought boxing match.

Io Saturnalia!

Martial confronts the rigidity of the repressive prudes, the "Catones," with the cry "Io Saturnalia!" (11.2). The sense of alienation that attends the perception of undue differentiation between people (and creatures and things) creates an intense need and yearning for equality, identity, mimesis. If Martial's pretended knight Phasis, lounging in the *equestria*, rejoices at Domitian's renewal of the *lex Roscia* and the strict segregation of the classes in the theatre ("Now we can sit more comfortably," Phasis says, "without being pressed, without being sullied by the mob"), the poet, in turn, exults when the arrogant imposter is ignominiously evicted from the fourteen rows and "reduced" to equality with those he scorned (Martial 5.8).[87] Just so, the extreme and imposed divisions of civil war drove the unhappy troops of Petreius to fraternize intimately with the forces of the enemy, Caesar—to the fury of their commander, as depicted in Lucan's epic (*Bellum civile* 4.168ff.).

The yearning for equality can be so great that the preserver of distinc-

---

[84] "No one is pleased with his lot who looks on that of another. Whence comes our anger even with the gods because someone else precedes us—forgetting how many follow, forgetting how much envy stalks the man who envies few" ("Nulli ad aliena respicienti sua placent. Inde diis quoque irascimur, quod aliquis nos antecedat, obliti quantum hominum retro sit, et paucis invidentem quantum sequatur a tergo ingentis invidiae" [Seneca, *De ira* 3.31.1]).

[85] The decemvirs who refuse to surrender their exalted position and refuse to hold elections bring down upon themselves an "invidiae tempestas" (Livy 3.38.6).

[86] "Envy is ever joyned with the Comparing of a Mans Selfe; And where there is no Comparison, no Envy" (Francis Bacon, "Of Envy," p. 29).

[87] Compare the story of Callistus and his master in Seneca, *Epistulae* 47.9.

tions must fight against the temptation within himself to dissolve them.[88] Seneca imagines the severe man having to block his ears with wax against the alluring arguments of those who would overturn the social and sexual restraints, the duties and *obsequia* (*Epistulae* 123.8–12). Similarly, in order to maintain "proper" distinctions in the distribution and quality of wine served at banquets, the cup bearers of Lucian's rich man, like the companions of Odysseus, must have their ears stuffed with wax (*Saturnalia* 32).

Equality tends to recede farther and farther away into the Golden Age or the City of Man.[89] Saturn's reign, according to Macrobius, was a time of happiness not only because universal plenty prevailed but because as yet there was no division into bond and free (*Saturnalia* 1.7.26).[90] Statius praises the Saturnalian celebration of Domitian as a new Golden Age, in large part, because of the indiscriminate intermingling of people of all levels and the enjoyment by everyone of the same food and service at a common banquet. "All the orders are fed at one table: the children, the women, the plebs, the knights, the senators. Liberty relaxes the demands of reverence" (Statius, *Silvae* 1.6, esp. 1.6.7–50).[91] Even the emperor shared in the banquet. The Stoics and, even more, the Cynics reacted to these excessive distinctions with cosmopolitanism and egalitarianism. Men inhabiting the City of God, like those inhabiting the Golden Age, are beyond class distinctions.

> What, finally, is an "equestrian," a "freedman," a "slave"? They are but names born of ambition and violence. One can leap to the sky from any little corner of the universe.[92]

[88] Even Juvenal, better known for his complaints that distinctions are not being preserved, also laments the inequality of wealth at Rome (*Satirae* 3).

[89] E.g., Seneca, *Epistulae* 47.4 + 14. It is interesting that Ovid's Polyhymnia, in her genesis, describes the distinctions and differentiations that succeeded chaos while asserting the equality of all honors ("par erat omnis honor" [*Fasti* 5.18]). Under Saturn's rule, the throne of god was sometimes occupied by some bold spirit "de media plebe" (5.19–20).

[90] The development of concepts of "humanity" and the cult of friendship also expressed this yearning for equality and identity in ancient Rome. According to Louis Dumont, in an aristocratic society one has a strong sense of personal ties—to ancestors, to relatives, to descendants—and a sense of temporal continuity and timelessness, but little or no sense of "humanity." In democratic or egalitarian societies one has a weak sense of personal ties, little sense of temporal continuity or relationship to ancestors or descendants, and a sense of living for the moment—but a stronger sense of "humanity" (*Homo Hierarchicus* [Chicago, 1979 (orig. pub. 1960)], p. 18). Cf. J. G. Peristiany, "Honour and Shame in a Cypriot Highland Village," in *Honour and Shame*, ed. Peristiany (Chicago, 1966), pp. 187–89.

[91] "Una vescitur omnis ordo mensa / parvi femina plebs eques senatus; / libertas reverentiam remisit." Compare Livy's wonderful description of the equality, indiscrimination, and harmony of the first *lectisternium*, or feast of the gods of 399 B.C.E. (5.13.7).

[92] Seneca, *Epistulae* 31.11.

Ambitio, the desire to distinguish oneself from one's peers, brings to a close the Golden Age of equality (Tacitus, *Annales* 3.26).

The greater the isolation and self-consciousness, the greater the yearning for the equal opponent. Lacking the equal opponent, one resorts to the mirror. Indeed, we hear that the mirror grew in value as "times got worse": in the Golden Age man saw himself reflected in calm pools and polished stones. As the world decayed, he began to see himself reflected in objects: a cup, a bronze object, a disc. Now, Seneca tells us, the mirrors are so desirable that they have surpassed in value the dowries of happier epochs (*Naturales quaestiones* 1.17.8). Taking to its extreme the tendency to substitute the mocking mirror for an equal opponent, the monster Caligula, a prodigy of isolation and self-consciousness, practices horrible grimaces at his own face in the mirror (Suetonius, *Gaius* 50).

Honey Mixed with Arsenic

Envy, yearning to abolish the distinctions it emphasized, was often, paradoxically, manifested by flattery and the giving of gifts.[93] So it was appropriate that Catiline's band of assassins planned to approach their victims on the Saturnalia in the guise of clients bringing gifts to their patrons (Diodorus Siculus 40.5).[94] Dio reconstructs the malice behind the honors offered to Caesar:

> Different men at different times kept proposing various extravagant honors, some exaggerating their flattery, some ridiculing. Others, and they were the majority, followed this course because they wished to make him envied and hated as quickly as possible that he might the sooner perish.[95]

The tongue of the bootlicker was drenched in venom. "The worst class of enemies are those who praise" ("pessimum inimicorum genus, laudantes" [Tacitus, *Agricola* 41]). Those who praise a man's virtues before a jealous emperor are difficult to distinguish from the informers. The motivation and the results of their praise are similarly deadly. "Caressing speech has its own poison" ("Habet suum venenum blanda oratio" [Publilius Syrus 251]). "The side where a man especially exposes himself to flattery is the side on which he is attacked" (Seneca *Quaestiones naturales* 4 praefatio 4).[96]

Envy was a monster for Horace, one with whom Augustus—and the

---

[93] "Praise and abuse are, so to speak, the two sides of the same coin . . . a two-faced Janus" (Bakhtin, *Rabelais*, p. 165).

[94] Plutarch, *Cicero* 18.2. (The conspirators planned to burn the city on the Saturnalia.)

[95] 44.7.2–3; cf. 44.8.4.

[96] The mind of Domitian was blinded and perverted by flattery (Tacitus, *Agricola* 43).

successful poet—were compelled to battle until death, like Hercules battling the hydra (*Epistulae* 2.1.10–12). The embodiment of envy, the flatterer/parasite, appeared as a standard grotesque figure in New Comedy, in the Roman *palliatae*, the Atellan and mimic farces. Some twisted or malicious trick was always expected to lurk behind his blandishments.[97] When he wore a mask, it was bald, with a huge nose, large ears, bulging eyes.[98] He was often played by the Dossennus, the hunchback.[99]

Toadies like Plancus and Villeius preyed on those they praised; they were, for Seneca, "experts in ensnaring their superiors" ("artifices ad captandos superiores").[100] They were like the legacy hunters ("captatores") who fawned on the elderly with the purpose of garnering their wealth.[101] Seneca's Satellius Quadratus is the flatterer (*"adrisor"*), and the nibbler (*"adrosor"*) of "the stupid rich"—and, needless to say, also their mocker (*"derisor"*).[102] To praise in excess was to "fascinare lingua" and expressed hostility.[103] Tertullian justifies the Christians' failure to flatter the emperor with an argument the Romans could understand: "I do not call the emperor God: I would not dare to mock him. And he himself would not wish to be so called; it would not be believed even in the ugliest and most pernicious adulation. If adulation does not blush at the lie, let it fear misfortune. It is a curse on the emperor to call him God before his apotheosis" (Tertullian, *Apologeticus* 33–34).[104] The superhuman honors

[97] E.g., Seneca, *Naturales quaestiones* 4 praefatio 12.

[98] Margarete Bieber, *Greek and Roman Theater* (Princeton, 1961), p. 100.

[99] Bieber, *Greek and Roman Theater*, p. 151. Horace, *Epistulae* 2.1.173 (speaking of standard types in Plautus): "Quantus sit Dossennus edacibus in parasitis." (*Edax* = devouring, gluttonous.) The roles of the learned man, the schoolmaster, and the philosopher (parasites all!) were also filled by the Dossenus in the Atellanae, according to Bieber, *Greek and Roman Theater*, p. 148.

[100] Vitellius conceals his hatred of Junius Blaesus with servile compliments, only to destroy him later (*Historia* 2.59, 3.38–39). Chapters 3–13 of the preface to book 4 of the *Quaestiones naturales* is given over to the dangers of flattery. See Horace, *Epistulae* 2.3.419–37.

[101] Horace, *Satirae* 2.5.45ff.; Petronius, *Satyricon* 116.7ff.; Juvenal, *Satirae* 10.201–2; cf. Seneca, *Epistulae* 123.11. "Fortuna cum blanditur captatum venit" (Publilius Syrus 197); "Heredis fletus sub persona risus est" (ibid. 258).

[102] The whole of the anecdote reported in *Epistulae* 27.5–8 is a sort of miniature mime, mocking the Trimalchio-like Calvisius Sabinus.

[103] I should add that refusing to praise at all could also be construed as envy. See Horace, *Carmina* 4.8.23–24 ("taciturnitas invida"), 4.9.33–34 ("lividas obliviones").

[104] Pushkin's envious Salieri, before pouring out the poison, proclaims, "You, Mozart, are a god and know it not! I know it" (Alexander Pushkin, "Mozart and Salieri," in *The Poems, Prose and Plays of Alexander Pushkin*, ed. Avrahm Yarmolinsky (New York, 1936), pp. 428–37. See the fascinating story of Herod's death by flattery (Josephus, *Antiquitates Judaicae* 19.8.2; cf. Acts 12:21–23). Plutarch imagines defending himself against the invidious praise of the people: " 'No god am I; why do you compare me to the Immortals?' . . .

heaped upon Caesar are like decorations heaped upon a corpse (Florus 2.13.92). As Nero was acutely conscious of the "flagrans invidia" that attended the privileges of the principate (*Annales* 13.4), he refused a temple to be dedicated during his lifetime not out of modesty, according to Tacitus, but out of fear that it would be interpreted as an omen of his death (Tacitus, *Annales* 15.74).[105] "Shepherds of Arcady," Vergil's Thyrsis implores, "crown with ivy your rising bard, that Codrus's sides may burst with envy; or, if should he praise me too much, crown my brow with foxglove, lest he harm the future bard with his evil tongue" (*Eclogae* 7.25–28).[106]

Tacitus remarks that no one could refrain from laughter when Nero, in his funeral oration for Claudius, praised the wisdom and foresight of the late emperor (13.3). Tacitus himself interprets Nero's words and actions as "tristitiae imitamenta," mimicries of sorrow (13.4). Our tendency might be to construe Nero's praise of Claudius as an instance of "ironic" or "insincere" flattery, but the Roman, acutely aware of the physics of envy, sensed the aggression in every form of blandishment.[107] It was always a poisoned sweet.

Cicero in his *De oratore* (2.51.208), like Plutarch in his *De se ipsum*

It is less invidious to be a Philadelphus or Philometor or Euergetes than a god or a son of a god" (*De se ipsum citra invidia laudando* 12 *Moralia* 543d–e).

[105] See the story told by the biographer of Septimius Severus in the *Scriptores historiae Augustae* (22.4–5): An Ethiopian soldier, famous among the *scurrae* and always a notable wit, approached him with a garland of cypress boughs: "You have been all things, you have conquered all things, now O Conqueror, be a god." ("Aethiops quidam e numero militari clarae inter scurras famae et celebratorum semper iocorum cum corona e cupressu facta eidem occurrit . . . 'Totum fuisti, totum vicisti, iam deus esto victor.' ") Severus in a rage ordered him to be removed. (Note: the cypress garland was a token of mourning.) See also Corbett, *The Scurra*, p. 73, for further discussion. Germanicus, the grandson of Augustus, was frightened by the excessively enthusiastic greeting given him by the Alexandrians of Egypt. Troubled by their acclamation of him as a god, he threatened to appear less often unless they restrained themselves (Friedrich Preisigke, *Sammelbuch griechischer Urkunden aus Ägypten* [Strassburg, 1915], vol. 1, no. 3924); McCartney, "Praise and Dispraise," p. 23.

[106] "Aut, si ultra placitum laudarit, baccare frontem / cingite, ne vati noceat mala lingua futuro." Pliny the Elder, *Historia naturalis* 7.2.16: "In eadem Africa familias quasdam effascinantium Isigonus et Nymphodorus tradunt, quorum laudatione intereant prata, arescant arbores, emoriantur infantes." (Cf. Aulus Gellius, *Noctes Atticae* 9.4.7–8.) Tertullian, *De carne Christi* 2.13: "Taceat et anus illa, ne fascinet puerum." Cf. *De virginibus velandis* 15.

[107] On hostile flattery, see Otto Jahn, "Über den Aberglauben des bösen Blicks bei den Alten," *Berichte der sächsischen Gesellschaft* 17 (1855), p. 39; Lafaye, "Fascinum," p. 983; Thomas Spencer Jerome, *Aspects of the Study of Roman History* (New York, 1962 [orig. pub. 1923]), pp. 282–83, 288–94; Elworthy, "Evil Eye," p. 611; McCartney, "Praise and Dispraise in Folklore"; Leslie Farber, "The Faces of Envy," *Review of Existential Psychology and Psychiatry* 1 (1961), pp. 133–34; Foster, "The Anatomy of Envy," pp. 172–74, 176–77, 182–83; Jankélévitch, *L'Austérité et la vie morale*, pp. 63–68.

citra invidiam laudando (12 *Moralia* 543d), assumes that the response to praise or boasting will be envy that must be systematically deflected or defused.[108] The *stips*, the gift one gave to the god, like that one gave to the beggar, was a sop thrown to envy.[109] It was a kind of "tip" or "kickback" given to those necessarily reduced by your increased honor. Aemilius Paulus lost one son five days before his great triumph and another three days later. He thought of his losses as a tax or sop to the gods for his victory, and thus as insurance for Rome's future (Plutarch, *Aemilius Paulus* 36).

Elworthy points out that "whosoever envies praises" ("laudat qui invidit") was so devoutly believed by the Romans that it became customary even for the speaker of praise or compliment to accompany his speech with a formula to exorcise malice, such as the words to the effect "may envy be absent from my words" ("praefiscini dixerim" = "absit invidia verbo").[110] For fear lest his praise harm Piso, the author of the *Laus Pisonis* has to qualify his promise to immortalize Piso with the words "si . . . fas est et deus ultor abest" (250–51).[111]

It was not simply affection for the dead, then, that caused the Romans to leave the refuse of dinner on the floor;[112] it was not simply compassion for the slave that caused the diners to leave scraps on their plates;[113] it was not only gratitude that brought little models of arms and legs, penises and breasts to the temples. There was hatred and fear behind all gifts, including those directed to the gods.

There was ill will in the *obsequia* of the client, in the admiration of the

---

[108] For example, the orator should emphasize that all the positive accomplishments of the person praised have been accompanied by compensating miseries, and that others are the beneficiaries of his successes (*De oratore* 2.51–52.207). Modesty was another strategic way of averting envy (Plutarch, *De se ipsum citra invidiam laudando* 12–14 *Moralia* 543d–544c). "Modesty is, in fact, a 'have your cake and eat it too character trait' " (Foster, "Anatomy of Envy," p. 176).

[109] "Les notables . . . se partagent entre la consommation ostentoire et la générosité ostentoire, espérant apaiser l'envie par des dons" (Veyne, *Le Pain et le cirque*, p. 309). For the working of "sop" mechanism in various cultures, see Foster, "The Anatomy of Envy."

[110] "Evil Eye," p. 611; for the variants *abaskantos*, "secure against enchantment," and *infascinate* (adv.), "without being bewitched," see F. Kuhnert, "Fascinum," in *P-W*, vol. 6.2, col. 2013.

[111] In a quotation from the lost *Setina* of Titinius, a lover exclaims, "Paula mea, amabo." Fearing that his words may injure her, he adds, "Pol tu ad laudem addito praefiscini." Charisius explains that the purpose was "ne puella fascinetur" (Charisius, *Ars Grammatica*, in H. Keil, *Grammatici Latini*, vol. 1, p. 212). Cf. Plautus, *Rudens* 458–61, *Asinaria* 491–93; Apuleius, *Florida* 16; Pliny, *Epistulae* 5.6.46; McCartney, "Praise and Dispraise," pp. 30–31.

[112] Cf. Robert, *Les Plaisirs*, p. 103.

[113] Cf. Horace, *Satirae* 2.6.66–67; Robert, *Les Plaisirs*, p. 104.

neighbor, in the adulation of the people.[114] Plutarch speaks of the invidious and exaggerated praise of the many: "huperphuon tinon legomenon epainon, hoia polloi kolakeuontes epiphthona legousin" (*De se ipsum citra invidiam laudando* 12 *Moralia* 543d). When Augustus summarily terminates the flattering clamor of the theatre audience precipitated by a mime uttering the words "O dominum aequum et bonum!" he is protecting himself not only from the envy of man and god invoked by praise but from the malice inherent in that very praise.[115] The anxiety of Augustus and Tiberius with regard to flattery is not just fear of calling down Nemesis from above. They are aware of flattery (even that which emphasized one's own deficiency or subordination) as a weapon of vengeance and a call for equality. In this context, it is clear why neither vituperation *nor* praise were allowed in the ancient Roman theatre, according to Cicero (*De republica* 4.10; Augustine, *De civitate dei* 2.9).[116]

The causal chain is simple: the Powers That Be are known to be envious; therefore, prosperity and glory are dangerous,[117] and security attends poverty and inconspicuousness.[118] The concepts of cursing by praise and blessing by ridicule and humiliation follow directly.[119]

[114] Cf. Seneca, *Phaedra* 981–84 ("Tradere turpi fasces populus / gaudet, eosdem colit et odit"). When Caligula held out the *digitus infamis* (the extended third finger used to drive away the evil eye) for Cassius Chaerea to kiss, this insult may have also been Caligula's way of signaling to Chaerea that he understood the malice in that kiss (Suetonius, *Caligula* 56.2). Caesar's failure to stand for the senate when they approached him with their extraordinarily flattering list of honors may have had a similar motivation (Suetonius, *Julius* 78).

[115] See Suetonius, *Augustus* 53; Orosius, *Adversus paganos* 6.22.4.

[116] "Kaitoi phesin [ho Katon] ev tini logo to epainein auton hosper to loidorein atopon eivai" (Cato frag. 77 [ed. Henry Jordan]).

[117] For the *invidia* of the gods and fortune, see, for example, Seneca, *Hercules furens* 385 ("sequitur superbos ultor a tergo deus"); *Epistulae* 8.3–4 ("munera ista fortunae putatis? Insidiae sunt"); Quintilian, *Institutiones oratoriae* 6 *praefatio* 10, cf. 4 + 8; Plutarch, *Quaestiones conviviales* 5.5 *Moralia* 679d–e; *Aemilius Paulus* 36; Statius, *Silvae* 2.1.120–24; 2.6.69–79; 4.8.15–19; 5.1.137–46; Jahn, "Über den Aberglauben des bösen Blicks," pp. 37–38, 56n. 106. For the relationship of hybris and nemesis to the physics of *invidia*, see Tertullian, *De virginibus velandis* 15: "Nam est aliquid etiam apud ethnicos metuendum quod fascinum vocant, infeliciorem laudis et gloriae enormioris eventum. Hoc nos interdum diabolo interpretamur: ipsius est enim boni odium, interdum deo deputamus. Illius est enim superbiae iudicium, extollentis humiles et deprimentis elatos. Timebit itaque virgo sanctior, vel in nomine fascini hinc adversarium inde deum."

[118] When Horace is at his Sabine farm, he is free from the "obliquus oculus," the envy that the low-born poet encounters in Rome, largely due to his friendship with the great Maecenas. At the farm, no one diminishes his happiness with the evil eye or poisons him with "odium obscurum" and backbiting ("morsus") (*Epistulae* 1.14.37–40). The insecurity of the court as opposed to the security and obscurity of country life is a constant theme in the literature of this period.

[119] L. Junius Brutus survives under the tyranny of Tarquinius Superbus by playing the part of a fool "secure in contempt" ("contemptu tutus" [Livy 1.56.7–9]). Horace knows he is

Correcting the Injustices of Finitude

> The monster is a being who has transcended chaos to recreate
> a cosmos; having plunged into the unfathomable *Urgrund*
> where all contraries are confounded, he has returned to the
> *apeiron* of Anaximander in an attempt to correct the
> "injustices" of finitude afflicting all beings living under the
> mandate of time. . . . [The monster] is, at once,
> fusion and refounding.
> (Brun, "Le Prestige du monstre")[120]

The more impossible, the more hopeless the bridging, the greater and more excruciating the yearning, the greater the possibility of fascination—and therefore the greater function afforded the monstrous and grotesque.[121] When people feel hemmed in and bound, the liminal, the ambiguous, the amorphous, the blurring of all distinctions become things of delight often associated with a primitive unity and harmony.[122] Rigid and

---

safe from envy when the neighbors laugh at "Farmer Horace" carrying sod and moving stones alongside his servant (*Epistulae* 1.14.37–40). Foster gives examples of the humiliation and defilement used by many societies to protect children ("Anatomy of Envy," p. 176). For the prophylactic effects of spitting or dirtying oneself or one's child, see Joannes Chrysostomus's homily *Epistola prima ad Corinthos* 12.7 (*Patrologia Graeca*, vol. 61, cols. 105–8); Theocritus, *Bucolici* 6.34–40; Kuhnert, "Fascinum," col. 2013; Elworthy, "Evil Eye," p. 613. Ritual abuse at a dinner party is accepted as inoffensive, while Horace's satires are assumed to be malicious ("lividus" and "mordax")—But it's *your* seemingly friendly words, your words of praise, retorts the poet, that are motivated by pure corrosive envy, "aerugo mera" (1.4.11–101).

[120] P. 307; cf. pp. 306, 310, 313–14. Compare Bakhtin on carnival (*Rabelais*, esp. pp. 24, 394, 410); Cox, *Feast of Fools*, p. 155.

[121] "It is no accident that the grotesque mode in art and literature tends to be prevalent in societies and eras marked by strife, radical change or disorientation" (Philip Thomson, *The Grotesque* [London 1972], p. 11). Sallust links poverty and envy with the desire for novelty and revolution in *Catilina* 37.3: "nam semper in civitate, quibus opes nullae sunt, bonis invident, malos extollunt, vetera odere, nova exoptant, odio suarum rerum mutari omnia student, turba atque seditionibus sine cura aluntur, quoniam egestas facile habetur sine damno."

[122] What Harry Stack Sullivan says about the envious man is interesting in this light. Sullivan points out that the envious often find momentary relief from the torment of invidious comparisons when released from the usual patterns of their lives: "Exceptions occur on occasions when, by accident or design, envious people fall into a position where there are no superior people, or people endowed with greater trappings of power and prestige than they. This is likely to occur when they are in a wholly novel environment. Then the envious person may be quite comfortable and give the impression of being what is ordinarily called 'a natural comfortable person to have around.' On such occasions he has a wonderful time, and he gets a lot of rest at night. Thus vacations are sometimes delightful for the intensely envious person unless they are fairly prolonged. If they are long enough so that he gets over

formalized behavior leads to an intense *desire* for, a delight in, the monstrous.[123] The monstrous, the grotesque, the obscene become associated with enormous vitality.[124]

The multiplication of distinctions and possibilities without fusion, without identity, creates the yearning for the monstrous union, the *coincidentia oppositorum*. In *The Two and The One*, Mircea Eliade discusses the hermaphrodite as the expression of the harmonization and reconciliation of all contradictions characteristic of the Golden Age (what Brun calls "la terre promise de l'ubiquité")[125]—and as the dissolution of categories, the pursuit of all possibilities, associated with the Apocalypse.[126] For Eliade, the *coincidentia oppositorum*, the eschatological symbol par excellence, discloses a nostalgia for a lost paradise, a primordial unity that precedes creation, a transcendental and powerfully creative androgyny.[127] As Victor Turner points out, in class or caste systems, the outcast,

---

the novelty with which he has been charmed, then the need for these prestige marks becomes more and more apparent. This is partly because envy represents a deficiency in the self and there is a corresponding alertness which the self controls, so that he alertly notes the evidences of his losing ground with strangers, and so on" ("Envy and Jealousy as Precipitating Factors in the Major Mental Disorders," in *Clinical Studies in Psychiatry*, ed. H. S. Swick et al. [New York, 1956], pp. 131–32). Cf. Victor Turner, "Passages, Margins and Poverty: Religious Symbols of Communitas," in *Drama, Fields and Metaphors*, pp. 239, 243, 254–55.

[123] "Ayant toutes les natures, et les plus contraires, quoi qu'il arrive, il y en aurait toujours une au moins qui serait satisfaite et je pourrais dire sans interruption: 'O monde, je veux ce que tu veux' " (Henri de Montherlant, "Aux fontaines du désir," in *Essais* [Paris, 1963], p. 242).

[124] "Energy and joy are the father and mother of the grotesque" (G. K. Chesterton, quoted by Harpham, *On the Grotesque*, p. 8; cf. pp. 7–8, 12, 17, 19). The classic statement of this idea is Bakhtin's *Rabelais*, passim, esp. pp. 90–91, 94, 307–8, 341, 352, 359, 370, 378, 407. See also Reich, *Der Mimus*, p. 23; Brun, "Le Prestige du monstre," pp. 303–4; Cox, *Feast of Fools*, pp. 59 ("Fantasy is a humus"), 69; Mary Douglas, "The Social Control of Cognition: Some Factors in Joke Perception," *Man* 3 (1965), pp. 361–75 and *Purity and Danger*, pp. 94–97, 161; Thomson, *The Grotesque*, pp. 15–16; Leszak Kolakowski, "The Priest and the Jester," *Dissent* 9 (1962), pp. 233–35. The word *satire* derives from the Latin *satura*, which has a range of meanings associated with fullness, fertility, abundance, being stuffed. See B. L. Ullman, "*Satura* and Satire," *Classical Philology* 8 (1913), p. 177.

[125] "The unusual seventeenth-century mystic Antoinette Bourignon started her career by fleeing from an impending marriage in the clothes of a male hermit. Among her later visions was that of a humankind created originally as androgynous, a state of whole perfection to which it would return at the resurrection of the dead" (Natalie Davis, "Women on Top," in *Society and Culture in Early Modern Europe* [Stanford, 1965], p. 145). The hermaphrodite as embodying all possibilities and as prefiguring the Apocalypse will be discussed in chapter 5.

[126] See Mircea Eliade, "Mephistopheles and the Androgyne; or, The Mystery of the Whole," in *The Two and the One*, trans. J. M. Cohen (Chicago, 1965), pp. 78–124. Eliade's division into positive and negative apocalyptics is a useful one, but I must point out that, for the envious, they are one.

[127] For the androgyne as symbol of the Golden Age, see Turner, "Passages, Margins and

the despised and rejected, are often assigned the symbolic function of representing humanity without status qualification or characteristics. "Here the lowest represents the human total, the extreme case most fittingly portrays the whole."[128]

The strictures of civilization create monsters, which then serve as remedies. One need only consider the origin and appeal of the "noble savages" of all times: the half-human, half-beast Enkidu, the *sylvani* and *fauni*, the Sasquatch, Tarzan the Ape Man. The monster of the mime, with his origins in agrarian fertility rites, carried with him some of the qualities of these "savages": he symbolized the triumph of rural *rusticitas* over *urbanitas*, of the wild over the tame, the boorish over the refined. (Notice that in both the ancient and the modern imagination the less than/ more than human wild creature is threatened and destroyed by the civilizing, limiting process.)[129] Richard Bernheimer accounts for the positive popularity of the Wild Man in the ancient, medieval and early modern period as arising, in part, from "the need to give external expression and symbolically valid form to the impulses of reckless physical self-assertion which are hidden in all of us, but are normally kept under control. . . . [T]he repressed desire for such unhampered self-assertion persists and may finally be projected outward as the image of a man who is as free as the beasts."[130] It is not surprising that, in a period where Romans themselves complain of being debilitated by excessive refinements and distinctions, when the wealthy build "paupers's huts," sleep on boards, eat the black gruel of the despised rustic, and write bucolic poetry, they would be attracted to the virile wilderness of grotesques.[131]

Poverty," pp. 244–45, 247; "Metaphors of Anti-Structure in Religious Culture," p. 286. See Paul's Letter to the Galatians: "Baptized into Christ, you have put on Christ: there can be neither Jew, nor Greek, nor bond, nor free, there can be neither male nor female, for you are all one man in Jesus Christ" (3.28); Douglas, *Purity and Danger*, pp. 157–58. It is interesting that, from a brief survey of the portents collected chronologically by Julius Obsequens for the years 190–12 B.C.E., it appears that the slaughter of the hermaphrodite ceases abruptly in the first century B.C.E.

[128] "Passages, Margins and Poverty," p. 234, cf. p. 239.

[129] Civilization makes an "idiot" of the feral child and a "madman" of the person unable to adjust to the strictures of society. See Jean-Marc-Gaspard Itard's account of *The Wild Boy of Aveyron*, trans. G. Humphrey and M. Humphrey (New York, 1932); Harlan Lane, *The Wild Boy of Aveyron* (Cambridge, Mass., 1979); Roger Shattuck, *The Forbidden Experiment* (New York, 1980); R. D. Laing, *The Divided Self* (Harmondsworth, Eng., 1965); Foucault, *Madness and Civilization*.

[130] Richard Bernheimer, *Wild Men in the Middle Ages: A Study of Art, Sentiment, and Demonology* (Cambridge, Mass., 1952), p. 3.

[131] Ramage refers to the "naiveté and helplessness arising from the overly sophisticated life of the city" (*Urbanitas*, p. 112). And Welsford remarks that royal courts (like the cities) delighted in naiveté and simplicity (*The Fool*, p. 149). The Roman cult of the animal, the child, and the "noble savage" stem, in part, from the helplessness resulting from complexity.

The Saturnalian Theatre

Fronto remarks in his *Principia historiae*:

> It seems to be one of the highest principles of political science that the emperor is not unconcerned about actors or other performers on the stage or in the circus, since he knows that the Roman people are held fast by two things, the corn-dole and shows; for an emperor's rule finds approval no less for the sportive [or "sports": *ludicra*] than for the serious [or "grave": *seria*]; there is greater damage if the grave, greater envy if the sportive is neglected. (18 [ed. M.P.J. Van Den Hout])[132]

Fronto asserts the importance of the spectacles, and particularly of the actors and performers, *for the mitigation of resentment*; the corn-dole and the spectacles are sops (and liable, as every form of generosity, to cause as much envy as they cure).[133] I would like to suggest that it was not simply the redistribution of wealth accomplished by giving shows but also the *matter* of the shows that served to direct and appease envy.

To begin with, it is important to consider that role playing itself was and is an important means of assuaging envy. The Romans of this period were extremely willing to picture the world as a stage, where one is allotted a role and therefore need not identify with it.

> Remember that you are an actor in a play, the nature of which is in the will of the playwright: if he wishes it to be short, it is short; if long, it is long. If he wishes you to play the part of a beggar, remember to act this part with all your powers; just so, if he should wish you to act the role of a cripple, a ruler, a private person [*privatus*]. For this is your part: to play well the role assigned to you; but the selection of that role is another's. (Epictetus, *Encheiridion* 17)[134]

One is a beggar or a prince by lot or fortune. Luck may have made one man a Caliban and another a Prospero; but if one envisages the world as

---

For the adoption of folk piety (and the mime) as one more self-indulgence of the courtly Roman upper classes, see Reich, *Der Mimus*, pp. 20–21.

[132] "Ex summa civilis scientiae ratione sumpta videntur, ne histrionum quidem ceterorumque scaenae aut circi aut harenae artificum indiligentem principem fuisse, ut qui sciret populum Romanum duabus praecipue rebus, annona et spectaculis, teneri; imperium non minus ludicreis quam serieis probari atque maiore damno seria, graviore invidia ludicra neglegi."

[133] See Veyne, *Le Pain et le cirque*, pp. 309–10, for the ingratitude and resentment caused by the very gifts designed to assuage *invidia*.

[134] Cf. Seneca, *Epistulae* 80.7; Marcus Aurelius 12.36; Arrian *apud* Stobaeus 4.33.28; Ariston *apud* Diogenes Laertius 7.160.

a stage, one can be as great a Caliban as a Prospero.[135] As an actor, the comedian Roscius was as highly esteemed as the tragedian Aesopus. The festival and the theatre with their deliberate Saturnalian inversions of reality were needed—and are needed—to demonstrate our understanding that *it might be another way.*[136] "The Feast of Fools," according to Cox, "exposed the arbitrary quality of social rank and enabled people to see that things need not always be as they are."[137]

The actor, as Erving Goffman remarks, can show a respect for others that he does not feel. As an actor, he can preserve an inner autonomy, "holding off the ceremonial order by the very act of upholding it."[138] Rather than being enslaved by dire compulsion, he can be liberated through collusion—like the gladiator, the Stoic *sapiens*, or the Christian martyr.[139] The worst humiliations of the gladiator and the martyr, the grotesque dwarf and the deformed buffoon could not only be borne but exulted in so long as they remained "spectacles."[140] The emperor Clau-

---

[135] An actor could be, Ariston suggested (op. cit.), as great a Thersites as an Agamemnon, or, the fragment of Arrian's homily indicates (op. cit.), as great an Oedipus at Colonus as an Oedipus the King.

[136] Bieber, in *The History of the Greek and Roman Theater*, explains this aspect of the actor's craft: "Dramatic art requires the actor to lay aside the personality with which he was endowed by birth and to feel himself as one who has abandoned the limitation of his own personality. He must lose his own identity and become a changed being, a demon, a god, or a hero" (p. 9).

[137] *Feast of Fools*, p. 5. Compare Bakhtin's remarks on the inversions of festival: "The carnival spirit offers a chance to have a new outlook on the world, to realize the relative nature of all that exists, and to enter a completely new order of things" (*Rabelais*, p. 34; cf. pp. 10, 81–82). Plautus's *Captivi* is a brilliant example of the physics of role playing in relationship to severe class distinctions and the vicissitudes of fortune. Fortune makes a slave of the rich man's son; it makes both the slave and the master into slaves. The slave of a slave plays the master of his master before his master. Cf. Turner, "Passages, Margins and Poverty," p. 260; Don Handelman, "Play and Ritual: Complementary Frames of Metacommunication," in *It's A Funny Thing, Humour*, ed. Antony J. Chapman and Hugh C. Foot (Oxford, 1977), p. 186; Douglas, "The Social Control of Cognition," pp. 361–75.

[138] Erving Goffman, "The Nature of Deference and Demeanor," in *Interaction Ritual: Essays on Face-to-Face Behavior* (New York, 1967), p. 58. The honor of Goffman's "fair player" is an expression of, and inconceivable apart from, the etiquette of the game. Regardless of antagonisms and differently assessed "social worth," regardless of victory or defeat, the "fair player" gains standing through careful adherence to the rules of the game ("On Face Work: An Analysis of Ritual Elements in Social Interaction," in *Interaction Ritual*, p. 11n. 5). "When performed voluntarily these indignities [i.e., ritual self-abasement] do not seem to profane his [i.e., the actor's] own image. It is as if he had the right of insulation and could castigate himself qua actor without injuring himself qua object of ultimate worth. . . . On the other hand, if he is forced against his will to treat himself in these ways, his face, his pride and his honor will be seriously threatened" ("On Face Work," p. 32).

[139] For role playing and freedom through collusion, see Cox, *Feast of Fools*, p. 145.

[140] Perhaps the willingness of the "freak" to display himself or herself in the modern period comes not only from economic necessity but also from the relief to the psyche of "play-

dius repeatedly explained that his humiliating stupidity had been a role deliberately and strategically assumed in order to survive under Caligula, like Brutus under Tarquinius Superbus or Khrushchev under Stalin (Suetonius, *Claudius* 38.3). Claudius the freak was a product of, and response to, the extreme power of Caligula.

In that the Saturnalia, like the "Feast of Fools," was a mechanism for mitigating envy, the king of the Saturnalia, like the kings and queens of the *festa stultorum*, were often elected by the toss of a die or some other game of chance.[141] Picturing the world as a game, particularly one of fate or chance, was in Roman thought closely related to picturing the world as a theatre. Gambling was a characteristic feature of the Saturnalia, and the "fixing of fortunes" was done at the New Year's celebrations concluding the Saturnalian festivities. Every name is tossed in the urn of Necessity. The crown, the host of clients, the fine name, the fancy hall, meet the lowly herd on terms of equality before the laws of adjustment inherent in the universe (Horace, *Carmina* 3.1).[142] Statius removes the sting of servile origins from the son of Claudius Etruscus (a former slave who became secretary of finances under Nero and a knight under Vespasian) and diverts the envy resulting from his transgression of social boundaries by attributing his fortunes to the universal domination of Fate, which governs every star, every deity, every king, and every kingdom. And Sulla, according to Plutarch, dispelled envy by always praising his luck, eventually proclaiming himself "the Fortunate" (*De se ipsum citra invidiam laudando* 11 *Moralia* 542f.). All inequalities, all distinctions are, in some sense, leveled by being equally under the compulsion of these inexorable laws (*Silvae* 3.3). In the face of fate, or Death the Equalizer, even kings were wont to see the world as a game or a play.[143] It is no mystery why

---

ing the freak" (and, in many cases, from being able to abandon that "role" after certain hours and rejoin a community of outcasts in which they are "normal"). Despite the cruel exposure of Joseph Merrick (the "Elephant Man") in the freak shows of Tom Norman and Doctor Frederick Treves, he displayed an ardent love of the theatre all his life. The "play" that made him a freak was also the "play" that allowed him to be a romantic hero. (See Michael Howell and Peter Ford, *The True History of the Elephant Man* [Middlesex, 1980] and David Lynch's wonderful film *The Elephant Man* [1980].) Both the role-playing and the oscillations it creates are "reality-sustaining." Cf. Erving Goffman, *Stigma: Notes on the Management of Spoiled Identity* (New York, 1963), p. 81.

[141] See Bakhtin, *Rabelais*, pp. 235, 238; Schoeck, *Envy*, p. 6.

[142] There is comfort in attributing one's low status to compulsion, necessity, the gods, the tyrant. Martial taunts the charioteers: "Go ahead now, spiteful, devouring envy [*livor edax*], excuse your failure by claiming that you were yielding to Nero [who favored the Greens]" (11.33).

[143] The relationship between the equalizations of death and the theatrical metaphor is particularly clear in Marcus Aurelius: "Mortal man, you have been a citizen of the great City; why does it matter to you whether for five or fifty years? For what is according to its laws is equal for every man [*to gar kata tous nomous ison hekasto*]. Why is it hard then, if

Augustus loved to gamble or (after examining himself in a mirror) closed his life with the question, "Have I acted well my part in the mime of life?" (Suetonius, *Augustus* 99).[144]

The "mime of life" (*mimus vitae*) was a kind of hilarotragedy offering solace to those oppressed by the feeling of being enslaved:[145] the king is but a slave dressed in finery (Seneca, *Epistulae* 80.4, 6–8).[146] When the Powers That Be are inflexible, when one cannot bend remorseless fate, when the brand of slavery or death is stamped upon the forehead, unreality can be a relief—and a revenge. If life is pictured as a game, then one can live in two worlds at the same time: a world in which one is engaged as a good player, a "good sport," and another in which one is detached and observing from a *punctum indifferens*. This *punctum indifferens* is the axis, the fulcrum, on which a life-preserving oscillation rests.

The monster, like the miracle, was the very essence of fortune. It revealed, with extraordinary poignancy, that "it might be another way." The birth of Siamese twins or a hermaphrodite, like the foal of a mule, revealed that there was no law that could not be overturned, no taboo that could not be transgressed. There was a play behind all "seriousness." To identify with the monster, like identifying with the actor or gambler, was to distance yourself from what appear insurmountable strictures on life. The Roman fascination with the monster, with the actor, with gambling and spectacles, often used as evidence (by ancients as well as moderns) of the moral laxness of the culture, are at the same time evidence for its excessive rigidity and inflexibility.

---

nature who brought you in, and no despot or unjust judge, sends you out of the City—as though the master of the show, who engaged a comic actor [*komodos*], were to dismiss him from the stage? 'But I have not spoken my five acts, only three.' 'What you say is true, but in life three acts are the whole play.' For he determines the perfect whole, the cause yesterday of your composition, today of your dissolution" (12.36 [Farquharson trans. with minor alterations]).

[144] Cf. Dio 56.30. On Augustus's "mimus vitae," see Otto Hirschfeld, "Augustus und sein Mimus vitae," *Wiener Studien* 6 (1884), pp. 116–19; Ulrich von Wilamowitz-Moellendorff, "*Res Gestae Divi Augusti*," *Hermes* 21 (1886), pp. 626–27. So Shakespeare's Macbeth begins his immortal soliloquy on the *mimus vitae* at the moment he is finally beseiged and trapped.

[145] Seneca resorts to the theatrical metaphor at a moment when he is feeling distressed at the thought of his own and others' slavery.

[146] Reich points out that although Seneca calls life a "mimus," he quotes from tragedy (*Der Mimus*, p. 72). I would suggest an explanation: just as, in the mime, the gods, kings and pompous characters are brought down to a level with the poor cook and ass, so in the *mimus vitae* the categories of tragedy and comedy dissolve: all life becomes a paradoxical hilarotragedy. A wonderful verse by the fourth-century pagan poet Palladas expresses this same combination of compulsion and play, tragedy and comedy, that the "life as theatre" metaphor suggests: "All of life is a stage and a game. / Either learn to play, setting aside all earnestness [*spoude*] or bear the pain" (*Anthologia Palatina* 10.72).

A univocal world is a tyrannical one. The insistence on the unique reality of "things as they are" aggravates rather than consoles the envious.
What Goffman labels "overinvolvement," the failure of participants in
an interaction to maintain a margin of disengagement, a sense of the spor-
tive qualities of the interaction, is "a form of tyranny practiced by children, prima donnas, and lords of all kinds."[147] The result, in Lucian's
Saturnalia, of the failure of the rich man to "play," to invert social roles,
is, for the poor man, one of both furious resentment *and a sense of unreality*. The poor man makes it clear that, as things are (i.e., without Saturnalia), life is not really life, festival is not really festival![148] Without
fictions there can be no reality.

The Alienation That Preserves

According to Florence Dupont, "Imitation—not in the Greek sense of
representation (*mimesis*)—but in the sense of mimic buffoonery, the play
of the comic double and of mirroring, was a fundamental component of
Roman culture. . . . Every form of imitation—whatever might be the object of this imitation: animal, profession, a famous person—caused the
Roman to laugh."[149] In the mime, asserts Seneca, aspects of the old, less
invidious relationship between master and slave still held (*Epistulae*
47.14). "The mime alone passed through every role and renders the man-
ifold one" (Manilius).[150] The mime exercised what Reich calls a "pro-
teischen Verwandlungsfähigkeit" (*Der Mimus*, p. 96).[151] He was, according to Plutarch, "many-faced," "multiform" ("polyprosopos").[152]
Habinnas, a guest at the dinner of Trimalchio, describes his household

[147] "Alienation from Interaction," in *Interaction Ritual*, p. 123.

[148] Lucian, *Saturnalia* 23. The person who does not suffer altered states, who is never
shocked, is liable to feel a sense of "unreality." Seneca makes this interesting observation:
"While all excesses are harmful, the most dangerous is unlimited good fortune: it stirs the
brain, it creates vain fancies in the mind and covers with darkness the boundary between
the false and the true" (*De providentia* 4.70). It is possible that the absence of "Saturnalia"
and its equalizations of status during the Industrial Revolution contributed to the sense of
"false consciousness" articulated by Marx. See Karl Mannheim, *Ideology and Utopia* (New
York, 1936); Herbert Marcuse, *One-Dimensional Man* (Boston, 1964).

[149] Florence Dupont, *L'Acteur roi: Le théâtre à Rome* (Paris, 1985), pp. 298–99.

[150] "Solusque per omnes / ibit personas et turbam reddet in uno." Related to the mime's
ability to change roles was the popular mimic theme of "radical changes of fortune." Antony's excesses upon getting hold of Pompey's estate remind Cicero of a character in a mime
"now needy, suddenly rich" (2 *Philippicae* 27.65).

[151] Cf. Hermann Reich, "Der Mann mit dem Eselskopf," *Shakespeare-Jahrbuch* 40
(1904), pp. 120–21.

[152] *Bruta animalia ratione uti* 19 *Moralia* 972f. (The starlings have voices "euplaston kai
mimelon"). See Seneca, *Epistulae* 11.7 for the many emotions displayed by the mime.

mime: "I had him taught by sending him to the *circulatores* [the wandering street mimes]. And so he has no equal, whether it be mule-drivers he wants to imitate, or the *circulatores* themselves; he can do a cobbler, a cook, a baker, he is a jack of all trades." He recites Vergil and imitates the sounds of trumpets (Petronius, *Satyricon* 68). The mime Vitalis recorded on his grave: "I so formed the faces, the bearing, and the words of the speakers that you would believe that many were speaking from one mouth."[153] "Faithless to his face" is how Tertullian brands the mime; molding it to resemble now Saturn, now Isis, now Liber (*De Spectaculis* 23).[154] In the tradition of the farce, whether the old Dorian burlesque, the Italian Phlyakes, the Oscan Atellanae, or the Roman mime, every distinction between persons, and between persons and gods, was subject to revaluation by these laughter-makers (*gelotopoioi*). "The mime adjusted the idealized figures of the mythical and Homeric gods and heroes to his own realistic and humorous type, bringing them down from their elevated station into intimate terms with all the other mimic *Lumpengesindel*" (Reich, *Der Mimus*, p. 29).[155] "The common people rejoice in jesters and buffoons [*aposkoptousiv kai loidoroumenois*], especially when they criticize what is held in high reverence" (Lucian *Revivescentes* 25).

The mime was everyman; he was, quite literally, the *vox populi*.[156]

Aut Rex aut Fatuus

R. W. Reynolds's very valuable article provides examples of the peculiar Roman manifestations of this grotesque *Umwertung* accomplished by the *derisor*:

[153] *Anthologia Palatina* 1173.

[154] Cf. Joannes Chrysostomus, *Commentarius in epistolam ad Ephesios, Homilia* 17, in *Patrologia Graeca*, vol. 62, cols. 119–20.

[155] Reich speaks of "die Umwertung aller idealistischen mythischen Werte durch den Mimus" (*Der Mimus*, p. 29; cf. pp. 81, 108, 111–13); cf. Tertullian, *Apologeticus* 15; Arnobius, *Adversus gentes* 4.35–36, 7.33; Boissier, "Le Mimus," p. 1907. Needless to say, this is a characteristic shared by mimes in many cultures. See James A. Boon, "Folly, Bali and Anthropology, or Satire Across Cultures," in *Text, Play and Story: The Construction and Reconstruction of Self and Society*, ed. Stuart Plattner and Edward M. Bruner (Washington, D.C., 1984), pp. 163–64; Geertz, *The Interpretation of Cultures*, pp. 139–40, on the Wayang clown Semar who is both buffoon and high god; James Peacock, *Rites of Modernization* (Chicago, 1968), on the function of the clown in the proletarian theatre of Indonesia (*ludruk*). "Machfoed, a pedicab driver, said ludruk clown humor is based on the idea of *nglètèk* (to reduce high to low, to peel away pretense). The clown's jokes reduce high status to low, culture to biological drives, *alus* (refinement) to *kasar* (crudeness), cosmopolitan to provincial" (Peacock, *Rites of Modernization*, p. 73).

[156] Boissier, "Mimus," p. 1907; R. W. Reynolds, "Criticism of Individuals in Roman Popular Comedy," *Classical Quarterly* 37 (1943), pp. 39, 41; Suetonius, *Galba* 13; Cicero, *Ad Atticum* 14.2 + 3 ("populi episemasia").

1. *The emperor as cinaedus.* The *cinaedus* was the mime who performed lewd and suggestive dances. Suetonius tells of an event that occurred at a performance of a mime during the reign of Augustus: "From his earliest youth [Octavian/Augustus] suffered from the various aspersions [of effeminacy] cast upon him. . . . Indeed, the whole people, together on a certain day for the games, applied to him with the greatest show of approval the insulting verse aimed at a Gallus [a castrated worshiper of Cybele] striking his orbital drum: 'Do you not see that a *cinaedus* now rules the world with his [middle] finger'?" (*Augustus* 68).[157]

2. *The emperor as old goat.* According to Suetonius, during Tiberius's extended retirement on Capri he pursued a Roman lady, Mallonia, with such cruel and disgusting attentions that she killed herself to escape him. "Whence it occurred that in the Atellan *exodium* [the comic farce that served as a short afterpiece in the theatre] in the next games, there was an allusion to him which was accepted with great approval by the people, and so was spread about: 'The little old goat licks daintily the *natura* of the roe' " (*Tiberius* 45).[158]

3. *The emperor as stupidus.* According to the biographer of the emperor, Marcus Aurelius's wife Faustina had an affair with a man named Tertullus. One day, when the emperor was present in the audience, the *stupidus* (the mime generally playing the cuckolded husband in the enormously popular adultery mimes)[159] asks another slave on the stage for the name of his wife's lover. The slave replies, "Tullus, Tullus, Tullus." The *stupidus*, pretending not to understand, questions him again. The slave replies, "I have already told you three times: Tullus" ("three times Tullus" = Tertullus [*Scriptores historiae Augustae, Marcus Antoninus Philosophus* 29]). "The consequent association, in the minds of the audience, of the emperor with the *stupidus* would," according to Reynolds, "add a special flavor to the jest."[160]

---

[157] "Prima iuventa variorum dedecorum infamiam subiit. . . . sed et populus quondam universus ludorum die et accepit in contumeliam eius et adsensu maximo conprobavit versum in scaena pronuntiatum de gallo Matris deum tympanizante: 'Videsne, ut cinaedus orbem digito temperat?' " See Reynolds, "Criticism," p. 40. The Galli, like the Christians and the Jews (indeed all persons and groups that sought to assert their moral uniqueness or superiority over others), were treated mercilessly by the mimes. The finger referred to in this passage is the third finger, which had several connotations. It was, of course, the *digitus infamis*, the finger used to insult and drive away bad spirits, and also the finger with which male homosexuals used to scratch their heads as both a signal of their sexual orientation and their availability.

[158] "Unde mora in Atellanico exhodio, proximis ludis adsensu maximo excepta, percrebruit: 'hircum vetulum capreis naturam ligurrire.' " (*Lugurrire* = to be dainty, to feed daintily upon, to lust after.) See Reynolds, "Criticism," pp. 41–42.

[159] Cf. Ovid, *Tristia* 2.497–506; Martial 5.61 (the cuckolded husband as Panniculus, a famous *stupidus*); Juvenal *Satirae* 8.196–97; Reich, *Der Mimus*, pp. 89–90. The "first mime," or *derisor*, played the adulterer. See Juvenal *Satirae* 6.42–44.

[160] See Reynolds, "Criticism," p. 43.

The monstrous double appeared not only on the stage but at funerals and in the streets. An *archimimus* both played the role of, and ridiculed, Vespasian at his funeral (Suetonius, *Vespasian* 19). Herod Agrippa, king of the Jews and friend of the emperor Caligula, was mockingly imitated by the Alexandrians of Egypt, as recorded by Philo. In the midst of general anti-Semitic discord, the crowd took "a wretched fool" from amongst their number, put a paper crown on his head and gave him a papyrus roll as a scepter. He accepted these insignia of royalty "as in a theatrical mime [*theatrikois mimois*]," while youths with rods on their shoulders stood around him "like mimic guards [*mimoumenoi doruphoroi*]" (*In Flaccum* 6).[161]

In this physics of envy, the fool—the *fatuus*, the *morio*, the *sannio*—are mirror images of the prince, as Diogenes the Cynic was the mirror of Alexander.[162] Seneca repeatedly equates the *fatuus* and the emperor in the *Apocolocyntosis*.[163] So, in the time of Claudius appeared a book entitled *The Rise of the Morio*, aimed at the emperor (Suetonius, *Claudius* 38.3) and insisting, in contradiction to Claudius himself, that his idiocy was not feigned. And Paul Graindor has published a photograph of a grotesque statuette of Nero the singer and cithar player (*citharoedus*) from the Museum of Cairo that resembles the hideous mascots kept as *ridiculi* to drive away the evil eye.[164]

Another of the figures caught in these fun house mirrors (like those popular distorting mirrors described by Seneca in the *Naturales quaestiones* 1.5.14, 1.6.5, 1.16.2–9) was the wise man or philosopher.[165] He,

---

[161] See Reich, *Der Mimus*, p. 576, and his "Der König mit der Dornenkrone," *Neue Jahrbücher für das klassische Altertum* (1904), pp. 705–33; Allardyce Nicoll, *Masks, Mimes and Miracles* (New York, 1963), p. 90. This story demonstrates the close link in the mind of Philo Judaeus between the Saturnalian mock king and the popular mime. Philo also connects the event with an Alexandrian and Egyptian propensity to envy (*In Flaccum* 5).

[162] Cf. Dio Chrysostomos, *Orationes* 4.66–69. It is interesting that in their conversation Diogenes compares the mighty Alexander to the ill-fated mock king of the Persian Secaea, a Saturnalian festival, implying that the glorious crown of the king sat on the head of a criminal condemned to death, and that death, furthermore, was brought on by the pretensions of the king. Dean A. Miller, in his "Royauté et ambiguité sexuelle" (*Annales: Économies, Sociétés, Civilisations* 26 [1971], pp. 639–52), mentions several late antique versions of this mirroring phenomenon: Symeon Stylites and the emperor Leo (p. 644); Symeon's disciple Daniel and the emperor (p. 645); Caesar and Christ (ibid.). It is possible to identify other such mirror images: Benkei and Yoshitsune; Sancho Panza and Don Quixote; the crucified thief and Lord Shingen in Kurosawa's psychologically profound *Kagemusha*. As Girard points out, the fool shares his master's status as an outsider (*Violence and the Sacred*, p. 12; cf. pp. 104–11).

[163] Cf. Suetonius, *Nero* 6.2; *Claudius* 8 (Claudius as *ludibrium aulae*).

[164] *Terres cuites*, pp. 35–36 and fig. 1.

[165] In Pliny's *Epistulae* (1.5.2) Regulus calls Arulenus Rusticus (a friend of Helvidius, son of Helvidius Priscus) a "Stoic Ape" ("Stoicorum simia").

like the king, found his freakish avatar in the *fatuus* or hunchbacked Dossenus. Seneca complains: "You know Harpaste, my wife's *fatua*. . . . I
particularly disapprove of these prodigies. Whenever I wish to enjoy a
clown, I am not compelled to look far—I can laugh at myself" (*Epistulae*
50.2).[166] In Lucian's *Lapithae* there appear as rival counterparts the buffoon Satyrion and the Cynic philosopher Alcidamus. "There is a con-
stantly recurring tendency," according to Enid Welsford, "to bring buffoons and learned men into connection with one another. Sometimes they
spar together, as do Philip and Socrates,[167] sometimes they are shown to
be indistinguishable from one another, as in the case of the Cynic Alcidamus and the buffoon Satyrion; though in this case it is the philosopher
who is the greater buffoon of the two."[168]

The image in the mirror was often a grotesque or monstrous one.
Midgets and dwarves were especially licensed to be mimics. Aulus Gellius
mentions with disgust the posturing and gesturing of men "of signal deformity and very ridiculous faces" who imitate actors. He compares the
revolting impression that they make to that of orators who express fine
but empty words (*Noctes Atticae* 11.13.10).

The equal opponent was replaced by the grotesque mimic. One of the
most striking examples of grotesque mimicry is the assignment of warrior
functions to animals, dwarves, and women. Pliny (*Historia naturalis*
8.2.5) mentions the pairing of elephants as gladiators, and we possess a
small terracotta statuette of a grotesque monkey-gladiator.[169] The dwarf-
warrior seemed to be a favorite of the Romans. Domitian paired bands

---

[166] "Harpasten, uxoris meae fatuam . . . ipse enim aversissimus ab istis prodigiis sum; si
quando fatuo delectari volo, non est mihi longe quaerendus; me rideo." One can compare
the aversion to fools expressed by Augustus (who nevertheless surrounded himself with a
retinue of fools, including the famous Gabba).

[167] See Xenophon's description of Philip the *gelotopoios* at the dinner party of Callias
(*Symposium*).

[168] Welsford, *The Fool*, p. 7. See Welsford's discussion of the ancient and medieval tales
of Marcolf and King Solomon (p. 38). The buffoon Buhlul treats Haroun-ar-Rashid much
like the Cynic Diogenes treats Alexander the Great (p. 81). For other comparisons between
the fool and the philospher, see Plautus's *Persa* (the comic parasite compares himself to the
Cynic philosopher at 123ff.); Lucian's *Philopseudes*; Corbett, *The Scurra*, pp. 24, 40–42,
64; Michael André Bernstein, "When the Carnival Turns Bitter: Preliminary Reflections
Upon the Abject Hero," *Critical Inquiry* 10 (1983), p. 293 (for both king = fool and wise
man = fool).

[169] Graindor, *Terres cuites*, pp. 63, 148–49, fig. 68. Graindor interprets the little grotesque as mocking the games. For the monkey charioteer, see Weber, *Die aegyptisch-griech-
ischen Terrakotten*, plate 37, p. 234, nos. 410–12. (Philo, *De animalia* 23 mentions an ape
driving four goats in the amphitheatre, shaking the reins, cracking the whip, shouting to his
team.) See *Anthologia Palatina* 6.312; John E. B. Mayor, *Thirteen Satires of Juvenal* (London, 1872), vol. 1, p. 435 (Juvenal, *Satirae* 5.153–55). For animals playing humans in fa-
blelike scenes: Graindor, *Terres cuites*, pp. 38–39, 60.

of dwarves in combat at his Saturnalia, "while the war-god Mars and bloody Virtue laugh" (Statius, *Silvae* 1.6.57–64).[170] In Lucian's *Lapithae* the scurrilous, misshapen ("amorphos") dwarf ("anthropiskos") buffoon ("gelotopoios") takes on and defeats the Cynic philosopher in battle (19).

Abuse That Empowers

Aeschrology, as Paul Veyne notes, "breaks through the envy" ("rumpitur invidia").[171] The laughter of his neighbors seeing "Farmer Horace" working in the field with his slave is taken by the poet as a comforting security against, and alternative to, *invidia* (*Epistulae* 1.14.37–40). Ritualized abuse and verbalized transgressions of all sorts have been and still are recognized prophylactics against the *invidia* of gods and men and a way of promoting fertility and power.[172] According to a line of Lucilius preserved by Nonius, "Obscene words avert the contentions of the gods" ("deum rixa vertat verba obscena").[173] Frazer gives examples from Greece, Rome, Estonia, the Carpathians, Berlin, and India of deliberately courting vituperation in order to gain good luck.[174] In Elizabethan England, according to Enid Welsford, a host would have a jester mock his or her guests to bring them good luck,[175] just as the Italians say, "In boca al lupe!" or we would say to an actor "Break a leg!"[176] This "fertilization

---

[170] Cf. Martial 14.213: "parma tibi, scutum pumilionis erit."

[171] "Le Folklore," p. 10.

[172] Mozley gives as two examples of the cursing at the sacrifice of Heracles Bouthoinas at Lindos, when the Dorians prayed for a bad hay harvest, and the advice of Stobaeus (5th century C.E.): "Blaspheme when sowing cummin; that is the way to make it grow well." "The idea," according to Mozley, "is that the gods are hostile on principle, and so you must ask them for the opposite of what you want." Cf. Pliny, *Historia naturalis* 19.36.120 (basil is sown with curses and lewdness; cultivators pray that their cummin will not come up); cf. Theophrastus, *Historia plantarum* 7.3.3, 9.8.8; Plutarch, *Quaestiones conviviales* 7.2 *Moralia* 700f–701a; Elliott, *The Power of Satire*, pp. 134–35. Compare the abuse between the hetaira and the student in the Mahavrata (A. B. Keith, *The Sanskrit Drama* [London, 1924], pp. 24–25); McCartney, "Praise and Dispraise"; Gluckman, "Rituals of Rebellion," pp. 110–45; Turner, *The Ritual Process*, esp. pp. 75–80.

[173] *Nonius Marcellus' Dictionary of Republican Latin*, ed. Wallace M. Lindsay (Leipzig, 1901), vol. 2, p. 566. Varro defines "obscene" as "that which should not openly be said except on the stage" ("obscaenum, quod nisi in scaena palam dici non debet" [*De lingua latina* 7.96]).

[174] James Frazer, *The Golden Bough*, 3rd ed. (New York, 1935), vol. 4, *The Magic Art*, pp. 278–82. In the account of Gluckman ("Rituals of Rebellion," esp. pp. 128–29), the abuse of the king is interpreted, by those who abuse him, as an expression of love for and protection of the king.

[175] *The Fool*, pp. 65, 67, 87.

[176] "Not many years ago in the neighborhood of Berlin, if you wished a hunter to have good luck, instead of saying so, you would tell him that you hoped he would break his neck,

through abuse" seems to have been the function of the Fescinnines, the ribald wedding songs of the Romans.[177]

Conclusions

Persius's first satire is an excellent example of the operation of the monstrous mimic and *derisor*. The *ressentiment* of the dependent poet/client unable to speak freely is here the subject of the satire (esp. 53ff.). Excessive differentiation of status—without sufficient compensation or relief—creates the intense desire on the part of the dependent to degrade the patron. The malice of the client toward the patron, whom he is compelled to accommodate and flatter face to face, like a parrot or magpie poet driven by the hunger in his belly, is expressed by the client's "making faces" and gesturing behind the patron's back. When the rich patrician's back is turned, the client gives him the evil eye; he makes "asses ears" and (like Medusa) hideous grimaces ("posticae sannae"), sticking out his tongue "as far as a thirsty Apulian dog." (In the same situation we might use the very same gesture or the *digitus infamis*.)[178]

The patron, demanding to "hear the truth" about himself from the client, knows full well that the unrelieved domination of the patron defines and limits that "truth." But within the "Saturnalia" of the satire, Persius, the *derisor*, dares to speak frankly.[179] "You want to know the truth? Okay—you're old, you're fat, you're bald and you're a fool."[180]

The speaker "Persius" concludes (like a good *curiosus*) by revealing a secret: "We all have asses ears." (We are all monsters.) Persius detests being a monster (just as Seneca hated the *fatui*, although he confessed himself to be one). But in the very act of revealing his secret shame and "speaking the truth," the client asserts the identity and equality between the patron and the client: we are all ridiculous monstrosities; we are all asses.

A similarly complex and suggestive vision of the role of the *derisor* and

---

or both his neck and his legs" (Elliott, *The Power of Satire*, p. 134). Johann Wolfgang von Goethe notes in his description of the carnival in Rome in 1788 that the apparent wishes for death that one person shouted at another in the street ("Sia ammazzato!") were meant to express joy and benevolence (Bakhtin, *Rabelais*, pp. 244–51, esp. pp. 248–49, 251).

[177] Horace, *Epistulae* 2.1.145–55. See Bieber, *Greek and Roman Theater*, p. 147.

[178] Caligula's practicing hideous faces in the mirror is simply the reverse of this phenomenon.

[179] Compare Martial's epigram directed at the bad host Zoilus (3.82).

[180] The failure of the philosophers to accept ridicule, their insistence on their dignity, inspires Lucian to use the theatrical metaphor and to compare them to the asses of Cumae dressed in lion's skins, to apes wearing heroic masks, bad actors, etc. (*Revivescentes* 31–36).

his relationship to social inequality and the dominance of the prince can be seen in the stories of Laberius. Compelled by Caesar to play the comic mime, the knight Laberius appeared dressed as a Syrian slave,[181] whom he represented as flogged by whips and beating a hasty retreat. He cried, "Oh Romans, we lose our liberty!" He followed this line immediately with another, however: "Many he must fear whom many fear!" ("Porro, Quirites! libertatem perdimus. / Necesse est multos timeat, quem multi timent.")[182] "And at those last words all the audience as one [*universitas populi*] turned their faces and their eyes to Caesar, indicating that it was his violence [or "want of self-restraint": *impotentia*] that was being assailed with this scathing jibe" (Macrobius, *Saturnalia* 2.7.5). This, according to Macrobius, was Laberius's revenge.

Laberius, taking on a *persona deformis*, dressing like a beaten slave, *emphasized* relative distinctions of status and power—and his own deeply resented loss of status. Nevertheless, even while he accentuates the loss of honor suffered by himself and his fellow Romans, he openly attacks this increased differentiation by asserting equality of power. In declaring that "he must fear many whom many fear," Laberius insists on an exact balance of power. According to Seneca, these famous words of Laberius, proclaimed in the midst of civil war, "caught the ear of the whole people as if utterance had been given to the people's voice": "Laberianus ille versus, qui medio civili bello in theatro dictus totum in se populum non aliter convertit, quam si missa esset vox populi adfectus" (*De ira* 2.11.3).[183]

The monster and the mocking mimic are related to political and social behaviors within a "physics of envy." To the extent that Rome had become a highly articulated and fragmentary culture in which hierarchy was both more elaborate and more rigid, envy hypostatized itself into the *derisor*, who was also its remedy, the negation of a negation.

---

[181] Publilius Syrus, a former slave, was Laberius's "unequal opponent" in the contest at Caesar's games (cf. Macrobius, *Saturnalia* 2.7.5–8).

[182] Macrobius, *Saturnalia* 2.7.4; *Comicorum Romanorum fragmenta*, ed. Ribbeck (Leipzig, 1855), frags. 125–26.

[183] See Reynolds, "Criticism," pp. 38, 44, and 38n. 8. Compare Seneca's protests against excessive status differentiations in *Epistulae* 47.1: " 'Servi sunt.' Immo homines. 'Servi sunt.' Immo contubernales . . . 'Servi sunt.' Immo *conservi*, si cogitaveris tantumdem in utrosque licere fortunae" (Cf. 47.17).

FIVE

ENVY (PART TWO)

STRIKING THE MONSTER

The extreme of freedom becomes the extreme of slavery.
(Cicero, *De re publica* 1.44.68)[1]

Nothing is more unequal than the resulting equality when
distinctions of class and dignity are confused,
disturbed, and confounded.
(Pliny, *Epistulae* 9.5.3)[2]

THE DEFORMED *scurra* Vatinius, like Rigoletto, was as much the target as the source of abuse (Tacitus, *Annales* 15.34).[3] Insofar as Vatinius was the butt and victim of derision he was playing a role the Romans often separated off from that of the *derisor*. If the *derisor* was the "first mime," the second mime (*mimus secundarium partium, mimos deuteros*) was the *souffre-douleur*, "the one who gets hit."[4] Gregory of Nazianzus speaks of the mimic fools as "used to knuckles": "Mimoi geloion, kondulois eithismenoi" (*Carmen* 8.85, in *Patrologia Graeca* vol. 37, col. 1583).[5] Johannes Chrysostomus refers to their "slapping one an-

---

[1] "Nimia illa libertas . . . in nimiam servitutem cadit."

[2] "Discrimina ordinum dignitatumque . . . quae si confusa turbata permixta sunt, nihil est ipsa aequalitate inaequalius." Similar sentiments are expressed by Pliny in *Epistulae* 2.12.5. See also Cicero, *De republica* 1.27.43.

[3] For the "Vatinian cups" ("calices Vatiniani") with their grotesque noses, see Juvenal, *Satirae* 5.46–47; Martial 14.96, 10.3.1–4.

[4] "Un des plus importants personnages était une sorte de Jocrisse (*stupidus*), avec des cheveux ras, dont tout le rôle consistait à recevoir des coups et à répondre des sottises" (Boissier, "Mimus," p. 1906). "Als Dümmling . . . mit dem glattrasierten Schädel, mit den Pausbacken, auf denen so herrlich die klatschenden Ohrfeigen sitzen . . ." (Reich, *Der Mimus*, p. 94, cf. p. 114nn. 2–4); Tertullian, *De spectaculis* 23: "[An deo] placebit et ille, qui voltus suos novacula mutat, infidelis erga faciem suam, quam non contentus Saturno et Isidi et Libero proximam facere insuper contumeliis alaparum sic obicit . . . ?" Cf. Juvenal *Satirae*, 8.188–92.

[5] Cf. *Nicobuli filii ad patrem carmen* 4.159: "mimon skieroisi hrapismasin" (*Patrologia Graeca*, vol. 37, col. 1517); Arnobius, *Adversus gentes* 7.33 ("delectantur, ut res est, stupidorum capitibus rasis, salapittarum sonitu atque plausu, factis et dictis turpibus, fascinorum ingentium rubore"); Asterius, *Sermo adversus kalendarum festum*, in *Patrologia Graeca*, vol. 40, col. 221 ("ton ezuremenon pros kondulon"; cf. Reich, *Der Mimus*, p. 125n. 5.

other" and tells how the mimic fool "is ashamed if he is not smacked in the service of the demos [*demosiai hrapizetai*]" (*Spuria de paenitentia*).[6] In an epigram Martial laments that the face of a dinner guest "was smashed with more noise than when Latinus smacks the cheap worthless face of Panniculus" (2.72).[7] In Epigram 5.61 Martial questions an acquaintance, Marianus, concerning the *crispulus* (a foppish or pretty boy) who is forever clinging to his wife: "Oh, Marianus, how you deserve the buffets of Latinus! You will be the successor, I fancy, to Panniculus."[8]

The monstrous *stupidus* arises in a universe irreconcilable with, and yet complementary to, the one I have discussed in the last chapter. The *stupidus* was the inverted mirror of the *derisor*, the *derisor* as seen from another perspective. The perception of the civil wars and the monarchy as permanently transgressing the *discrimina ordinum* brought into play a "physics" corresponding to René Girard's "Sacrificial Crisis": a collapse of the *sensus communis*, a shared system of categorizing and ordering.[9] It was a loss of a sense of common identity, and a sort of permanent civil war. In this civil war the monster, and especially his avatar, the grotesque *stupidus*, ranked among the principal and most effective sacrificial decoys and scapegoats required to preserve the "Roman." They were the recipients of many of the blows aimed at deformity in its broadest sense.

While the monsters spawned by inequality had the function of restoring equality, the monsters that issued from equality had the function of restoring distinctions. The first monsters struck down the taboo and the tabooed; the second expiated these transgressions. Embodiments of chaos and representatives of the society, the *stupidi* were types of the scapegoat.

---

[6] *Homilia* 37, in *Patrologia Graeca*, vol. 59, col. 760; cf. vol. 57, col. 426; Reich, *Der Mimus*, p. 116n. 3. For both Nazianzus and Chrysostomus, see Nicoll, *Masks, Mimes and Miracles*, p. 88.

[7]
Hesterna factum narratur, Postume, cena
quod nollem (quis enim talia facta probet?)
os tibi percisum quanto non ipse Latinus
vilia Panniculi percutit ora sono.

Compare the parasite Gnatho in Terence's *Eunuchus*: "at ego infelix neque ridiculus esse neque plagas pati possum" (244–45). The parasite who can endure the host who maintains social distinctions will next shave his head and offer it to be slapped (Juvenal, *Satirae* 5.170–72). The ridiculous parasite of Plautus's *Captivi* (472) is called "plagipatida" (slaphappy? hardheaded?); cf. *Mostellaria* 356; *Captivi* 88–90 ("Et hic quidem hercle, nisi qui colaphos perpeti / potes parasitus frangique aulas in caput, / vel ire extra portam Trigeminam ad saccum licet." See Corbett, *The Scurra* pp. 16, 19.

[8] "O quam dignus eras alapis, Mariane, Latini:/te successurum credo ego Panniculo." In *Pulcinella,* Dieterich (p. 239) reproduces a vase from southern Italy of a braggart soldier and an arms-bearer who, as Bakhtin points out (*Rabelais*, p. 201n. 6), remarkably resemble Don Quixote and Sancho Panza except that the antique figures both have enormous phalluses. There is a good chance that this is a depiction of the *derisor* and the *stupidus*.

[9] See *Violence and the Sacred*, esp. pp. 49, 93, 115.

"The railer who drives away evil may at the same time be made to take upon himself the accumulated evil of his people. He may be singled out as a *pharmakos*, a scapegoat, and be ceremonially beaten and exiled, if not slain."[10]

The Saturnalia out of Bounds

In Lucian's *Saturnalia* (2), the reign of Kronos is limited to seven days. Afterward he returns to being a private person and one of *hoi polloi*. "But during the seven days I, Kronos, have agreed not to conduct any business whatever, not even in politics. What I may do is drink and be drunk, shout, play games and dice, appoint masters of the revels, feast the servants, sing stark naked, clap and shake, and sometimes even get pushed headfirst into cold water with my face smeared with soot."[11]

Throughout the essay Kronos repeatedly emphasizes the brevity and limitations of his reign. Michael André Bernstein, compares Horace's *Satirae* 2.7 and Diderot's *Le Neveu de Rameau*:

> In Horace, as later in Diderot, such license is granted only once a year, and although [the slave] Davus is allowed to chastise and mock his master, both know that their normal roles are only temporarily suspended, not permanently dissolved. During the Saturnalia, each of the characters, master and slave, wise man and fool, speaks with a freedom whose operative condition is a precisely defined temporal span.[12]

Ritual has prescribed boundaries for the overthrow of boundaries.[13] Saturn, shaking off his shackles, is resigned in advance to resuming them.[14] Similarly with the theatre: license was granted to the stage, but even those defending the spectacles to Tertullian found them blameless only pro-

---

[10] See Elliott, *The Power of Satire*, p. 135; cf. Gilbert Murray, *The Rise of Greek Epic* (Oxford, 1907), pp. 185–87.

[11] Harmon translation.

[12] "When the Carnival Turns Bitter," p. 290.

[13] Particular temporal, formulaic, or psychic states may be the prerequisite of legitimate discourtesy. Concerning the Bacchanalia: "The ritual that allowed otherwise forbidden sexual couplings [and male transvestism (Livy 39.15.9)] was justified by the pretext of 'possession'" (Eva Cantarella, *Pandora's Daughters* [Baltimore, 1987], p. 127). The Ndembu, when about to launch into their agonistic "flyting" of the sexes first pronounce a formula which sets apart and excuses what they are about to say, and legitimizes the mention of matters that otherwise were "a secret thing of shame or modesty" (Turner, *The Ritual Process*, p. 78; cf. Cox, *Feast of Fools*, pp. 23–24).

[14] Lucian claims that Kronos was not shabby or in chains "as the painters show him, following the ravings of the poets" (*Saturnalia* 10). He recounts the popular story of Kronos as a god with compassion for the enslaved because he himself had been put in chains by Zeus.

vided that they preserved the fear of the gods and were limited to their time and place ("in tempore et suo loco") (*De spectaculis* 1.1). "Certain boundaries must be applied even to our play, so that that we do not wildly dissipate everything, and, carried away by our pleasure, fall into some turpitude" (Cicero, *De officiis* 1.29.104).[15] So Martial's famous claim, "My poetry is licentious but my life is upright" ("lasciva est nobis pagina, vita proba" [1.4.8]), is both a plea for Saturnalian freedom for his epigrams *and* an defense of that freedom on the grounds that it is confined to his compositions. His plea for indulgence is based on his observance of limitations.[16]

As the Saturnalia gained in popularity,[17] it gained in length, beginning with one and increasing to between three and seven days.[18] Concurrently, the medicine-show mimes and the *exodarii* who used to inhabit the entr'-actes and the territory outside the curtain[19] usurped the stage, driving off what we might call the "legitimate" theatre, the traditional comedy and tragedy. Furthermore, the *scurra* ceased to leave his sharp tongue and roisterous behavior behind at the close of the Atellan (the one farce in which the freeborn and even the noble participated without infamy),[20] and men like Ovid and Martial, neither acting or writing for the stage, claimed its liberties (e.g., *Tristia* 2.517–19).[21] For some it seemed as if the riot of the Saturnalia and the license of the theatre had transgressed their limitations and had ceased to be "the exceptions that proved the rule."

[15] "Ludendi etiam est quidam modus retinendus, ut ne nimis omnia profundamus elatique voluptate in aliquam turpitudinem delabamur."

[16] Cf. Martial 1 *praefatio* and 11.15; Catullus 16. For the importance of limitations in establishing the positive qualities of transgressions, see, for example, Cicero, *Pro Caelio* 18.43 and Juvenal, *Satirae* 8.163–66 (indulgence given to youth for a limited time); Seneca, *De tranquillitate* 17.9–10; Horace, *Carmina* 4.12; Ovid, *Tristia* 2.491–92 (one could speak the forbidden in verse in "smoking December"); Cicero, *De officiis* 1.40. 144 ("tanta vis est et loci et temporis").

[17] For the increasing popularity of the Saturnalia from the late Republic onward, see W. Warde Fowler, *The Roman Festivals of the Period of the Republic* (London, 1932), p. 270; Kay, *Martial*, p. 71.

[18] For the varying lengths of the Saturnalia, see Fowler, *Roman Festivals*, p. 268; H. H. Scullard, *Festivals and Ceremonies of the Roman Republic* (Ithaca, N.Y., 1981), p. 205; Kay, *Martial*, p. 71.

[19] For the mime taking place before the *siparium*, the *mimicum velum*, see Reich, "Der Mann mit dem Eselskopf," pp. 113–14.

[20] The actor in the Atellan did not have to take off his mask and reveal his identity; he could thus escape the disgrace of being seen on the stage. For the special status of the Atellanae, see Livy 7.2.12.

[21] See Reich, *Der Mimus*, pp. 52–53. Martial (1 *praefatio* and 1.4; 1.35; 3.86; 7.8; 11.2,6,15) uses as models and justifications for his scurrility a special "language of epigrams," the free indecencies of the Floralia, the triumph, the Saturnalia and the mimic theatre (Thymele, the *derisor* Latinus, and the *stupidus* Panniculus). Indeed, he calls his book "theatrum meum" (Martial 8 *praefatio*). Cf. Richlin, *The Garden of Priapus*, pp. 9–10.

It is December—and the city is in a great sweat. License is given to public wantonness. Everything echoes the noise of great preparations—as if there were any difference between the Saturnalia and any business day! There is so little difference that he does not seem to me to have been mistaken who said, "At one time December was a month—now it is a year." (Seneca, *Epistulae* 18.1)[22]

"There is a season for this furor. It is tolerable to be mad once a year." But now, Seneca complains, this nonsense goes on the Capitolium all year long![23]

The Rage for Order

How close together lie festival and warfare.
(Marcel Mauss, *The Gift*)[24]

The Romans deeply resented distinctions. They equally resented the absence of distinctions. The literature of this period is saturated with complaints that proper discriminations are not being observed. Cicero, in the *De oratore*, attacks the aristocratic *scurra* who does not resume his seriousness when the curtain has closed on the Atellan farce. He attacks the mimes and *scurrae* for ridiculing everything and anything, including themselves, without bounds and limits.[25] Livy complains that the license of the theatre has escalated to insanity (7.2.13), and Horace laments the progressive degeneration of the Fescinnines (*Epistulae* 2.1.139–54).[26]

---

[22] "December est mensis; cum maxime civitas sudat. Ius luxuriae publicae datum est. Ingenti apparatu sonant omnia, tamquam quicquam inter Saturnalia intersit et dies rerum agendarum. Adeo nihil interest, ut non videatur mihi errasse, qui dixit olim mensem December fuisse, nunc annum."

[23] Cf. Augustine, *De civitate dei* 6.10 (quoting Seneca): " 'Huic tamen,' inquit, 'furori certum tempus est. Tolerabile est semel anno insanire.' " In Lucian's *Revivescentes*, Philosophy claims not to be at all offended by the insults aimed at her by Comedy in keeping with, and customary at, the festival of Dionysius—quite the opposite! ("I am aware that no harm can be done by a joke. On the contrary, whatever is beautiful shines brighter and becomes more conspicuous, like gold cleansed in the minting.") The indignant philosophers protest, however, that while Aristophanes and Eupolis had made fun of them when it was permitted, Frankness abuses them without sanction of a holiday! (14). Cf. Elliott, *The Power of Satire*, p. 83.

[24] P. 80.

[25] *De oratore* 2.59.238–39; 2.67–68.274–754. Dupont, *L'Acteur Roi*, p. 299: "Aussi le mime apparaît-il comme celui qui est capable de faire rire n'importe qui à propos de n'importe quoi en n'importe quelle circonstance." See the epitaph for Vitalis (*Anthologia Palatina* 1173).

[26] For the rivalry and public riots generated by the mimes in this period, see Elaine Fant-

When the shocking did not lead to its own termination, it ceased, for many, to be cathartic.[27] Sadly, unstructured and unhierarchical social situations occasion malice and envy as surely as structured and hierarchical ones.[28] Sallust remarks, "To desire the same things and reject the same things—that indeed is firm friendship."[29] But wanting the same things also sharpened competitive envy; it produced what Cicero called a "communis ambitionis invidia" (*Pro Sulla* 1). "Desiring the same things" is both the basis of friendship and the source of malice because the desired things cannot be given to one unless taken from the other: "To want the same thing—which ought to have been the bond of love—is the cause of sedition and hatred. . . . What you desire is insignificant, but because it cannot be transferred to one without being stolen from another, it provokes those desiring the same things to contest and strife" (Seneca, *De ira* 3.34.3).

George Foster, in his important article "The Anatomy of Envy," finds that envy is characteristic of a worldview which emphasizes the loss of status relative to another's gain.[30] The Roman "physics of *invidia*" corresponds very well to Foster's "zero-sum game," the game in which the fortune of one is felt as the misfortune of another. "Profit cannot be made without loss to another," according to the mime-writer Publilius Syrus ("Lucrum sine damno alterius fieri non potest" [337]).[31] When the farm of the hardworking freedman Gaius Furius Chresimus was prosperous while those of his neighbors were not, the envious neighbors accused him before a Roman magistrate, the curule aedile, of charming their crops into his field (Pliny the Elder, *Historia naturalis* 18.8.41–43). "The envious man," according to Horace, "grows thin on the plenty of another"

---

ham, "Mime, the Missing Link," *Classical World* 82 (1989), p. 154n. 7; Friedländer, *Sittengeschichte*, vol. 2, pp. 144–47.

[27] For the threat involved to the current order, or to all order, in festivals of inversion, see Davis, "Women on Top," esp. p. 131: "I would like to argue . . . that comic and festive inversions could undermine as well as reinforce that assent [to traditional order]" (cf. p. 151). See also Richlin, *The Garden of Priapus*, p. 76; C. L. Barber, *Shakespeare's Festive Comedy* (Princeton, 1959), pp. 3–57; Turner, "Passages, Margins and Poverty," pp. 231–71; Bernstein, "When the Carnival Turns Bitter"; Emmanuel Le Roy Ladurie, *Carnival in Romans*, trans. Mary Feeney (New York, 1979). The revelers could get out of hand, like the Hell's Angels at the Rolling Stones' concert at Altamont.

[28] Leon Festinger, "A Theory of Social Comparison Processes," *Human Relations* 7 (1954), pp. 120–21, 125, 134; Alfred Schutz, "Equality and the Meaning Structure of the Social World," in *Collected Papers*, vol. 2 (The Hague, 1964), p. 267; Schoeck, *Envy*, esp. pp. 11, 17–20, 27 ("democratic envy"), 42, 62; Douglas, *Purity and Danger*, p. 103.

[29] "Nam idem velle atque idem nolle, ea demum firma amicitia est." (Sallust, *Catilina* 20.4).

[30] Pp. 165–202; cf. Max Gluckman, "The Magic of Despair," in *Order and Rebellion*, pp. 137–45, esp. p. 143; Schoeck, *Envy*, pp. 17–18, 39–40, 49.

[31] Compare Seneca's "ex multis paupertatibus divitiae fiunt" (*Epistulae* 87.38).

(*Epistulae* 1.2.57–59).[32] This "zero-sum game" can also be heard in Seneca's remarks on frustrated ambition:

> Unhappy immobility feeds resentment [*livor*] and they desire the destruction of all because they themselves cannot advance. From this aversion to the progress of another and desperation with regard to one's own, the mind, angry with fortune and complaining of the age, retreats into a corner and broods over its own misery, till it wearies and exhausts itself. (*De tranquillitate* 2.10–11)

Ambition cannot bear to see anyone before it or coming after it. The ambitious man is wracked by *invidia* on two fronts: he is envied, and he envies (*Epistulae* 84.11).

The greater the equality the more acute the competition and desire to distinguish oneself. The Roman aristocracy is no less competitive and obsessed with honors when we (and often they) can see them as empty and unearned and merely perquisites of the emperors.[33] On the contrary, the "loss of face" and the leveling of everyone to the status of "subject" acutely sharpened the yearning for distinctions—even empty ones!

Prolonged and enforced obliteration of status could be experienced, not as a liberation, but as the ultimate loss of honor or "being."[34] The Saturnalia, and festal inversions in general, could be perceived as expressions of *Faustrecht*, the naked war of all against all, when distinctions, when "common sense," is lost, and the naked power behind the "play" is revealed.[35] David Epstein points out that, in the disorders of the late Republic, when the frequent use of the *senatus consultum ultimum* (the senate's declaration of martial law, i.e., no law at all) made the boundaries of competition and the rules of the game unclear, *invidia* toward the winners increased.[36] "Cicero illustrated the grimness of his times by claiming

[32] "Invidus alterius macrescit rebus opimis."

[33] Compare the unintentionally poignant letter of Pliny the Younger on the tribunate (*Epistulae* 1.23).

[34] See, for example, Livy's description of the powerful reaction of the Roman consuls to the proposed *lex Canuleia*, which would allow intermarriage between patrician and plebeian: it would, they said, create monsters (Livy 4.2.5–6).

[35] For the Saturnalia as the Hobbesian "bellum omnium contra omnes," see Tacitus, *Historia* 3.83; Turner, "Metaphors of Anti-Structure in Religious Culture," p. 285; Jules Henry, *Jungle People* (New York, 1964), pp. 56–59. Festivals were notorious traps: Domitian's mock funeral banquet (Dio 67.9) is not funny to his guests because of Domitian's terrifying power; they feared a banquet like the one Cesare Borgia would give at Sinigaglia or Oliverotto at Fermo. After all, Romulus had raped the Sabine maids at the Consualia; the Republicans struck down Caesar in the theatre; the Catilinarian conspirators planned their assassinations for the Saturnalia; the Pisonian conspirators planned theirs for the circus (Tacitus, *Annales* 15.53; Livy 2.37).

[36] *Enmity in Roman Politics*, p. 54.

that the name of consul conferred more envy than prestige" (*Pro Sulla* 29
81).[37]

Lords of Misrule

The jaws of the great make Saturnalia all year long.
(Petronius, *Satyricon* 44)[38]

In Seneca's *Apocolocyntosis*, an unidentifiable deity discusses with Hercules the problem of making the dead Claudius into a god: "Even had he
sought this benefit from Saturn, whose month he, most Saturnalian of
princes, celebrated all year long, he would not have obtained it" (8). As
Sheila Dickison points out in "Claudius: *Saturnalicius Princeps*," Claudius was not only characterized by his love of sex, food, drink, and year-
round celebration (Suetonius *Claudius* 32–33), and by his restoration of
a day to the Saturnalia (Dio 60.25.8), but also, as depicted in Tacitus and
Suetonius, by his submission to the wayward wives and freedmen who
ruled in his stead.[39] I would add to this list of characteristics Claudius's
deformitas.[40] Claudius was the *rex stultorum* at a Saturnalia that never
ended.

Claudius was not alone of the emperors, the very symbols and often
the authors of excessive distinctions, to be branded patrons of indiscretion. The absence of restrictions on the powerful, like the excess of restrictions on their subjects, creates an inversion (Cicero, *De re publica* 1.42–
43; cf. 2.26): the creator and enforcer of rigid social distinctions is the
outrageous trangressor of them. Sulla, the wanton murderer, was the author of the *lex Cornelia de sicariis et veneficiis* (Seneca, *De providentia*
1.3.7–8). Livy's patrician Appius Claudius, under whose aegis the law of
the Twelve Tables was passed forbidding intermarriage between patrician
and plebeian, was prepared to arbitrarily degrade to slavery the plebeian

[37] Ibid., p. 49.
[38] "Nam isti maiores maxillae semper Saturnalia agunt."
[39] Sheila Dickison, "Claudius: *Saturnalicus Princeps*," *Latomus* 36 (1977), p. 646. Dickison believes that Tacitus modeled his Saturnalian themes on the plots of both earlier and
contemporary Roman comedy and draws comparisons between situations and themes in
Tacitus and Plautus. For a similar portrait of Nero's reign as a topsy-turvydom, see Philostratus, *Vita Apollonii* 5.7.
[40] Fantham ("Mime the Missing Link," p. 161) believes that Seneca, in emphasizing the
deformity of Claudius, the muscle-bound stupidity of Hercules, and the seizure and arrest
of the emperor at the end of *Apocolocyntosis* 11 and 13, is borrowing from the tradition of
the mime. (She speculates that the satire that we possess may have been based on an earlier
version staged as a mime at Nero's Saturnalia.)

Virginia, in order that he might violate her with impunity. Appius the lawgiver is Appius the man without *fides*.

Like the gods, those other august guardians of justice, the emperors lacked restraint.[41] As Judith Hallett demonstrates in her article "*Perusinae Glandes* and the Changing Image of Augustus," Augustus wore at least two masks at the same time: the guardian of social propriety and the adulterous libertine. Augustus the notorious prude is Augustus the rake and *scurra*.[42] As John D'Arms points out, Augustus paid careful attention to the rank and status of his guests, rigorously excluding freedmen from his table, and yet we know that the slave-dealer Toranius Flaccus was his frequent dinner companion.[43] Domitian, the defender of the virginity of the Vestals, is a lewd profligate; the man who reinforces the *lex Roscia* is also the patron of the grand and indiscriminate Saturnalia.[44] The peculiar and extreme bifurcation of Suetonius's imperial portraits reflects this Roman inclination to see the tyrant as the embodiment and propagator of both these divergent social tendencies.

Festival without End

This one evil was lacking to the ruined Trojans—to rejoice.
(Seneca, *Troades* 888–89)[45]

In this universe, celebration becomes a torment, a party one cannot leave.[46] Lucan's matron bids her sister Romans: Weep now! For when the civil war was won and the domination of Caesar or Pompey established, they would perforce rejoice. "Now you have the power to lament; while the fortune of the chieftains remains undecided; when one or the other shall have prevailed, you must celebrate" (*Bellum civile* 2.40–42).[47] The

---

[41] The gods or fortune are frequently pictured as the patrons of the Saturnalia out of Bounds (so throughout Lucan's *Bellum civile*).

[42] Judith Hallett, "*Perusinae Glandes* and the Changing Image of Augustus," *American Journal of Ancient History* 2 (1977), pp. 151–71. Compare the story concerning Julia's two dresses in Macrobius, *Saturnalia* 2.5.5.

[43] Macrobius, *Saturnalia* 2.4.28; D'Arms, "Control, Companionship, and Clientela," p. 340. D'Arms does an excellent job of detecting these contradictions.

[44] Nero was neurotically scrupulous with regard to the etiquette of competition but often totally indifferent to aristocratic Roman traditions: Suetonius, *Nero* 23–24; Philostratus, *Vita Apollonii* 5.7; Tacitus, *Annales* 16.4.

[45] "Hoc derat unum Phrygibus eversis malum / —gaudere."

[46] Cf. Tacitus, *Annales* 15.69; Petronius, *Satyricon* 72ff., and Dio's wonderful description of Domitian's horrible funeral banquet (67.9).

[47] "Nunc flere potestas, / Dum pendet fortuna ducum; cum vicerit alter, / Gaudendum est."

"Cicero" of declamation refuses to beg Antony for his life. If you live by the grace of Antony, he protests, "will you be free even to sigh?" (Seneca Rhetor, *Suasoriae* 6.4).[48]

This festal prison was not only a metaphor. The emperor Nero, while on tour, locked the doors of the theatres where he performed, allowing no one to leave for any reason. Exhausted with listening and applauding, spectators jumped from the walls or feigned death in order to be carried out of the auditorium (*Nero* 23.2).[49] At gladiatorial exhibitions, provided the sun was sufficiently hot, Caligula was wont to have the protective awning rolled back and to forbid anyone to leave, compelling the audience to watch decaying animals, "worthless" and aged gladiators, and fights between *patres familiarum* with marked debilities, thus deeply and doubly humiliating the audience (*Gaius* 26.5).[50] Dio tells this story about Domitian: "For though a heavy rain and violent storm suddenly arose, he let no one leave the spectacle, and though he himself changed into thick woolen clothes, he would not allow the others to change their attire, so that many fell sick and died" (67.8.3).

Seneca's bereaved Pastor has no choice but to put on the wreath and toast the emperor who has just butchered his son (*De ira* 2.33.3–6).[51] In this Saturnalia without end one is compelled to play-act.[52] "Every meal is a delight at the table of a king," asserts Harpagus, gnawing on his children's bones. The servant of the tyrant, he declares, must be prepared to laugh at the banquet of his king and the funeral of his dear ones (*De ira* 3.15.1–3).[53]

[48] "ne gemitus quidem tuus liber erit?" Cf. Cicero, 2 *Philippicae* 26.64.

[49] Vespasian all but lost his life for leaving the room and falling asleep during Nero's recitals (Suetonius, *Vespasian* 4.4; cf. Philostratus, *Vita Apollonii* 5.7). For the torment of the party that does not end: Petronius, *Satyricon* 72, 78 (Encolpius, Ascyltos, and Giton are unable to find a way out of Trimalchio's banquet). Not only can Beria, Malenkov, and Mikoyan not leave Stalin's endless banquets—they cannot *not* get drunk (*Khruschev Remembers*, p. 300). Compare the excruciating party in Luis Bunuel's *The Exterminating Angel* (1962).

[50] "Quoque paegniaris patres familiarum notos in bonam partem sed insignis debilitate corporis subiciebat." *Paegniarii*: gladiators who fought only for "the fun of it," the specialty acts of the arena.

[51] Cf. Suetonius, *Gaius* 27.4. Cicero, in a letter to Papirius Paetus (*Epistulae ad familiares* 9.26 [46 B.C.E.]), expresses the painfulness of rejoicing when all other options have been removed ("Gemitum in risus maximos transfero"). See Seneca, *Epistulae* 80.6–8, for the joyful face concealing the suppurating misery below.

[52] Role playing ceases to be a relief when there is no "time out." See Sheldon L. Messinger, Harold Sampson and Robert Towne, "Life as Theater: Some Notes on the Dramaturgic Approach to Social Reality," *Sociometry* 25 (1962), pp. 98–110.

[53] Complaints of being compelled to celebrate are closely related to complaints of being compelled by the tyrant to live. See Suetonius, *Tiberius* 61.5 ("Those who wanted to die were forced to live"); Seneca, *Troades* 574–77; *Medea* 19–20; *Thyestes* 247–48; *De providentia* 2.10; *Consolatio ad Marciam* 22.6. They are also related to ideas of *clementia* and

The tyrant as abettor of the war of all against all presides over the festal abolition of distinctions. During his reign of terror in 33 C.E., Tiberius litters Rome with the corpses of those he has ordered put to death for complicity with Sejanus: "The massacred lay, scattered or in heaps, of every age and sex, the illustrious with the obscure" ("iacuit immensa strages, omnis sexus, omnis aetas, inlustres ignobiles, dispersi aut aggerati" [Tacitus, *Annales* 6.19]).[54] According to Dio's description, Nero's public banquet and monumental debauch of 64 C.E. entailed not only riotous reveling but promiscuous mating: the slave was given free reign with the mistress in the presence of the master, and the gladiator violated the noble girl before the eyes of her father (62.15).[55]

At Antony's bacchanals in the villa of Varro, according to the indignant Cicero, freeborn youths, matrons and prostitutes freely intermingled: "ingenui pueri cum meritoriis, scorta inter matres familias versabantur" (2 *Philippicae* 41.105, cf. 27.65ff.]). The status-sensitive orator is even asked to share the festivities at the home of Eutrapelus with the former slave and mime Cythera (*Epistulae ad familiares* 9.26 [46 B.C.E.]).

The Little Tyrant was seen to operate on the same model as the gods and the emperors. Trimalchio invites his slaves to table, to the discomfiture of his guests (*Satyricon* 70–71), and the Trimalchio-like Zoilus toasts his *moriones* with Opimian, indulging his pets, his slaves, and his concubines over his invited guests (Martial 3.82). A client at the court of Antony and Cleopatra, Dellius the historian, complained that they (Antony's clients) were served sour wine, while the buffoon Sarmentus at Rome was drinking the rare and precious Falernian (Plutarch, *Antonius* 59.4).[56] Lucian's learned Greek must give way, in the household of the Roman grandee, not just to the dwarf reciting bawdy ionics, and to the lewd dancers,

---

indulgentia as methods of humiliating an inferior. See Seneca, *De ira* 3.19.5; Lucan, *Bellum civile* 2.114–18. For the sadistic *clementia* of the prince, see Plass, *Wit and the Writing of History*, pp. 161n. 7, 164n. 35.

[54] Keitel, "Principate and Civil War," p. 307; Tacitus, *Historia* 2.87. See Juvenal, *Satirae* 8.146–82 for the indiscriminate mingling of the taverns.

[55] Caligula, as patron of indiscretion, has the plebs occupy the seats of the knights in the theatre (Suetonius, Caligula 26.4). The author of the *Elegiae in Maecenatem* invokes the right of the powerful to justify his patron's freedom from the rules binding other men: "All things beseem the victor at the conclusion of war" ("omnia victores Marte sedente decent" [1.50]). Maecenas is free to sport and sleep on scented rose petals; he is free to discard conventional male dress and behavior—even to the point of submitting to a female tyrant (as Hercules submits to Omphale)—because he has been victorious in the civil war (the war against Cleopatra that is!). He is Augustus's friend. It is for the defeated to be limited (1, esp. 93–96). For an analysis of this phenomenon in Rome, see my "All Things Beseem the Victor; Paradoxes of Masculinity in Early Imperial Rome" (forthcoming).

[56] See H. D. Rankin, "Saturnalian Wordplay and Apophoreta in *Satyricon* 56," *Classica et Mediaevalia* 23 (1962), pp. 134–42. For Rankin the whole of the *Cena* is Saturnalian "in spirit and arrangement" (p. 136).

but even to the household pets (*De mercede*, esp. 27 + 34). Even the *morio* enjoys the favors of Martial's Marulla, who sleeps indiscriminately with the servants (while disdaining even her husband's friends or her neighbors) (6.39).

It is not just a Saturnalia, but rather the absense of all discrimination: there is neither order nor the traditional inversion of order—but pets, slaves, *moriones*, concubines, and kings are held in the same honor. It is, as Bernstein notes, "a carnivalization of values during which it is no longer a question of breaking down ossified hierarchies and stale judgments but rather of being denied *any* vantage point from which a value can still be affirmed."[57]

Absolute Whimsy

Complaints against the emperors are aimed not only against their excessive personal distinction—but against the arbitrariness with which, from their fulcrum of power, they can both overthrow and ordain differences of status. "Concerning that man in whom all power rests, I see nothing to fear, unless it be that all things are uncertain once law [*ius*] has been forsaken, and no one can insure a future dependent on the will—not to say whims—of another." (Cicero, *Epistulae ad familiares* 9.16.3 [46 B.C.E.]).[58]

Caesar's debasement of the knight Laberius met with indignation—but so did his equally arbitrary restoration of Laberius to the status of a knight.[59] When Laberius complained on stage that "the opinion of the *pedarius* [that is, the senator who expressed his judgment only in walking to one side or another in the course of voting] is a head without a tongue" ("sine lingua caput pedarii sententia est"),[60] he was expressing the indignation of those for whom the loss of status was felt as a mutilation. (When Caesar enlarged the number of senators to nine hundred he considerably weakened the power and voice of individual senators; he made it a less exclusive club and thus decreased its credit, giving power and prestige to "nobodies."[61]) But when the same Laberius, freed and rewarded by Caesar, attempted to take his place in the fourteen rows of the

---

[57] "When the Carnival Turns Bitter," p. 285. Cf. Juvenal, *Satirae* 8.183.

[58] "De illo autem, quem penes est omnis potestas, nihil video quod timeam, nisi quod omnia sunt incerta, cum a iure discessum est, nec praestari quicquam potest quale futurum sit, quod positum est in alterius voluntate, ne dicam libidine."

[59] Macrobius, *Saturnalia* 2.3.10, 7.3.8.

[60] Aulus Gellius, *Noctes Atticae* 3.18.9 = *Romani Mimi*, ed. Marius Bonaria (Rome, 1965), no. 109.

[61] Dio 43.47.3; Suetonius, *Julius* 41.1; Reynolds, "Criticism," p. 39.

equestria, he was rejected by those whose sentiments he voiced. "The knights," according to Macrobius, "felt themselves affronted by the violation of their order—both by Laberius's degradation and his offhand restoration: "violato ordine, et cum detrectatus est eques Romanus et comminus remissus." As he was passing Cicero in his search for a seat, the latter gibed, "I should have been glad to have you beside me were I not already pressed for room," intending by these words to reject the man, and at the same time to make fun of the new senate whose numbers had been unduly increased by Julius Caesar ("supra fas auxerat") [*Saturnalia* 2.3.10]).[62]

Res Publica in Extremis

We long ago lost the true words for things, it seems to me,
since to give away the possessions of others we call
"liberality"; to be audacious in crime we call "fortitude"; to
that extreme the Republic has come.
(Sallust, *Catilina* 52.11)[63]

Liquid disorder, like rigid order, results in a topsy-turvy universe. Each extreme turns back on itself. When it is Saturnalia out of Bounds, then comedy becomes sad. As Juvenal complains in *Satirae* 6.634: satire has taken the lofty tone of tragedy.[64] In this Saturnalia which is civil war, as in the war in Corcyra described so poignantly by Thucydides, the categories in which a society organizes the world are subverted. In the war of all against all, Cicero laments, those who fulfill their proper roles and respect authority are reproached as willing slaves (*De republica* 1.43); the members of a faction call themselves "the best men"; the license of the people is called liberty (ibid. 3.13).[65]

[62] The story is repeated in 7.3.8; cf. Seneca Rhetor, *Controversiae* 7.3.9.

[63] "Iam pridem equidem nos vera vocabula rerum amisimus; quia bona aliena largiri, liberalitas, malarum rerum audacia fortitudo vocatur, eo res publica in extremo sita est."

[64] Cf. Seneca, *De ira* 2.10.5: "Aut ridenda omnia aut flenda sunt."

[65] Cf. Tacitus, *Historia* 1.37; Dio 46.34.5. "Old men's wisdom and all the improving proverbs about truth, honesty and loyalty went out of date in the ruthless struggle when might again became right, as in the beginning of time. The meanings of words were now changed and perverted. The historian [Tacitus] propagated in his writings what he had learned from experience. It was a harsh and bitter doctrine, using for texts the moral precepts turned upside down" (Ronald Syme, *Tacitus* [Oxford, 1958], p. 196). "In times of peace and prosperity it [the political cant of a country] commands a wide measure of acquiescence, even of belief. Revolution rends the veil. . . . As commonly in civil strife and class-war, the relation between words and facts was inverted. Party-denomination prevailed entirely, and in the end success or failure became the only criterion of wisdom and patriot-

He Turannike Baskania

There was no one whose condition was so abject or fortune
so desperate that Gaius did not find some cause for
begrudging their happiness.
(Suetonius, *Gaius* 35.3)[66]

The envy created by the Saturnalia out of Bounds is not the malice of the parasite or would-be democrat. Those who envy now are those who cling to status distinctions and are tormented by the fear of losing them: the gods, the emperors, the Roman worthies, the free men. In English, when we do not use it as a synonym for *envy*, we use the word *jealousy* for this second form of *invidia*: the dread and anguish occasioned by the fear of losing something, someone, or some marks of status currently in one's possession. Latin, having only one word for both ideas, makes it easier to discern their interrelatedness.

The envy of the gods (or Fate or Fortune) is manifested in civil war, in death, and in the destruction of anything happy or exceptional. Whatever good fortune marks, there, according to Statius, the divine Invidia fixes her "torva lumina," her keen and staring eyes. The envious Fates straightaway wreak havoc on the healthy and the fine: the laden vineyards are blasted by the sirocco; the high corn rots in the rain; the storm clouds gather about the prosperous sails; the forest is gutted by fire; and the matchless beauty of Priscilla is snatched away from her (*Silvae* 5.1.137–53).[67]

The tyrant partakes of this divine jealousy. The *invidia* of the emperor

---

ism" (Ronald Syme, *The Roman Revolution* [Oxford, 1939], p. 154). See all of chapter 11 ("Political Catchwords," pp. 149–61) for a good discussion of the emptiness and completely arbitrary meaning of words in the civil war period. Cf. Seneca, *Epistulae* 14.9 (poverty becomes security in a land infested with brigands).

[66] "Nullus denique tam abiectae condicionis tamque extremae sortis fuit cuius non commodis obtrectaret."

[67] Cf. *Silvae* 2.1.120–24; 2.6.69–79; Ovid, *Amores* 2.6.25. For the envy of the gods causing death, see Quintilian, *Institutiones oratoriae* 6 *praefatio* 4,8,10; Jahn, "Über den Aberglauben des bösen Blicks," p. 56, and the (then) unpublished inscription quoted there: "Infelix mater tollit ad astra manus / incusatque deos, incusat denique Parcas" (p. 56n. 106). The "invida fatorum series" is one of the causes of the civil war (Lucan, *Bellum civile* 1.70). Plutarch recognizes competition as the source of envy, and his remarks could be applied to anyone possessing some mark of prestige, from gods and kings on down. Attempting to give an answer to the question "Why do men cover their heads when they worship the gods and uncover them when they meet those who are more powerful than they are (*hoi dunatoteroi*)?" Plutarch surmises that it is to protect the latter from the *invidia* of the gods, "that these men may not seem to demand the same honors as the gods, nor to tolerate or rejoice in attention like that bestowed on the gods" (*Quaestiones Romanae* 10 *Moralia* 266d).

will not allow him to tolerate any qualities in another which might lead to unfavorable comparisons.[68] According to Pliny the Younger, the virtues of Verginius Rufus made him suspected and resented by "certain of the emperors" (*Epistulae* 2.1.3).[69] The emperor Caligula could not tolerate any insult that might impair his own honor, while delighting in the humiliation of all and sundry (Seneca, *De constantia sapientis* 18.1). Most Saturnalian of princes, both Caligula and Nero were, nevertheless, suspicious and impatient of ambiguity and attacked mimes for uttering ambiguous little verses.[70]

This imperial envy leads to the institution of informers, the evil eyes of the emperors. The blind Catullus Messalinus, "a monster great and conspicuous even for our day," was a weapon aimed by Domitian at anyone of quality.[71] It is not surprising that Vatinius, the deformed buffoon and lowlife raised to influence and wealth by Nero, was one of Nero's informers, his *curiosus*, the living expression of the *invidia* of the emperor.[72]

A Wanton Wilderness

From this perspective the *coincidentia oppositorum* is nothing but an apocalyptic death-wish.[73] For those who perceive the world as a carnival gone awry, the monster is a disturbing, or even a disgusting, phenomenon, associated with corruption and pollution. Defying the limitations of any *genus*, the monster is a mongrel, the most appropriate possible vision of degeneracy and miscegenation. The *satyri*, the *incubi*, the *fatui ficarii* were associated, like the medieval Wild Men, with untamed sexual desires and the threat of sexual and genetic pollution (always fearful to the Roman).[74] Seneca's high-living Hostius Quadra, with his insatiable de-

---

[68] For *he turannike baskania*, see Marcus Antoninus 1.11; Ovid, *Amores* 2.6.25. "For to kings the good are more suspect than the bad, for the virtues of others are a cause of fear to them" ("nam regibus boni quam mali suspectiores sunt, semperque iis aliena virtus formidulosa est" [Sallust, *Catilina* 7.2]).

[69] Cf. Tacitus, *Agricola* 41.

[70] Suetonius, *Caligula* 27.4; cf. Reynolds, "Criticism," p. 41.

[71] Pliny, *Epistulae* 4.22.5–6; Juvenal, *Satirae* 4.113–22.

[72] Tacitus, *Historia* 1.37.5; *Dialogus de oratoribus* 11.2; Dio 63.15.1. Cf. Charles-Picard, *Augustus and Nero*, p. 90.

[73] Bernstein describes Céline's trilogy *D'un château à l'autre*, *Nord*, and *Rigodon*: "Now, instead of the annual ritual of licensed excess endured by the master in classical satires, history itself provides the Célinian Abject Hero with a global setting of pure destruction, one seemingly without temporal limits or effective restraints. The floor of the Café de la Régence has expanded to encompass a Europe brutalized by war and a France of collaborators, cowards, and toadying profiteers" (p. 301).

[74] See Bernheimer, *Wild Men*, p. 97. The wild men and women were considered especially erotic and especially dangerous because of their uncontrolled sexual passions (ibid., pp. 34,

sires, living beyond the limits of "nature" (*Naturales Quaestiones* 1.16), feasting on illusion with his fun house mirrors, is the portent, the monster of obscenity, who, like the "satanic hermaphrodite" of Mircea Eliade and Marie Delcourt, manifests an uncontrolled proliferation of erotic possibilities.[75] Rather than harmony, the monster symbolizes discord. Rather than simplicity, it symbolizes duplicity. Rather than relaxation, it symbolizes wantonness. So Vitruvius denounces the popular taste for "grotesques" in the late Republic:

> On the stucco are monsters rather than definite representations taken from definite things [*ex rebus finitis imagines certae*]. Instead of columns there rise up stalks; instead of gables, striped panels with curled leaves and volutes. Candelabra uphold pictured shrines and above the summit of these, clusters of thin stalks rise from their roots in tendrils, with little figures seated upon them at random. Again, slender stalks with heads of men and animals attached to half the body. Such things neither are, nor can be, nor have been. . . . For how can a reed actually sustain a roof, or a candelabrum the ornaments of a bagle, or a soft and slender stalk a seated statue, or how can flowers and half-statues rise alternately from roots and stalks? Yet when people view these falsehoods, they approve rather than condemn. (*De architectura* 7.5.3–4)[76]

54, 121–75). For the lascivious *fauni, sylvani,* and *incubi* see the articles "Ephialtes," "Fauni," and "Incubi" in W. H. Roscher's *Ausführliches Lexicon der griechischen und römischen Mythologie* (Leipzig, 1884–90); Augustine, *De civitate dei* 15.23. Bernheimer offers the story of the rape of Proserpine and her sojourn in the land of the dead as a version of the Wild Man abducting the human female. The Wild Man/abductor is a demon of death (p. 128). Bernheimer goes on to identify Orcus, the demon of death, as the oldest name of the Wild Man (p. 130). It is the absence of limits and categories associated with death that brings it into relationship with the monstrous and portentous Wild Man (as well as with the emperors).

[75] *The Two and the One,* p. 100; Marie Delcourt, *Hermaphrodite: Myths and Rites of the Bisexual Figure in Classical Antiquity,* trans. Jennifer Nicholson (London, 1961 [orig. pub. 1956]). The sympathies and interests of Delcourt, like those of Eliade, are with the hermaphrodite as symbolic of a transcendental unity. Delcourt finds the hermaphrodite (as embodied in sculpture, where its sexual attributes are multiplied rather than dissolved) to be "a meaningless trifle, designed to pander to pleasures of the more limited and circumscribed kind" (p. xii). For her, this hermaphrodite is a prison and not a liberation. Twins, like the hermaphrodite, can be manifestations of the primordial unity or portents of apocalyptic dissolution: A. R. Radcliffe-Brown, "A Further Note on Joking Relationships," *Africa* 19 (1949), pp. 133–40; *Structure and Function in Primitive Society* (New York, 1952), pp. 105–15; Girard, *Violence and the Sacred,* p. 58; Turner, *The Ritual Process.*

[76] E. H. Gombrich (*The Sense of Order* [Ithaca, N.Y., 1979]) commenting on Vitruvius's passage, notes "The reaction of exasperated helplessness provoked by hybrid creatures, part plant, part human, part fish, part horse, part goat. There are no names in our language, no categories in our thought, to come to grips with this elusive dream-imagery in which 'all things are mixed.' . . . It outrages both our 'sense of order' and our search for meaning. . . . 'What is the point?' The point is that there is no point. . . . Not only do the limbs of these

According to Horace, those painters and poets who allow wild to couple with tame, who partner a snake and a bird, a lamb and a tiger, who put a human head on a horse's neck or the torso of a woman on the tail of a hideous black fish have gone too far ("Ars Poetica"; *Epistulae* 2.3.1–14).

Persecuting the Monster

From this perspective the monsters are to be attacked. Martial ridicules the seven—he cannot bring himself to call them "children"—that Cinna's wife Marulla has given him: there is the curly-haired Moorish one, the flat-nosed and broad-lipped one, the blear-eyed one, the one with a brow of a lewd dancer, a *cinaedus* ("Feel free, Cinna, to use him as you use his father!"); and then there is the one with the pointed head and the donkey's ears (Martial's gesture in the direction of the family *morio*.) The poet continues his description of Marulla's offspring, ending with the quip, "You would have as big a herd as Niobe if Coresus and Didymus had not been eunuchs" (6.39). So Seneca rails against those who deliberately embrace the topsy-turvy universe, who *retro vivere*, who sleep all day and carouse all night (*Epistulae* 122); and Juvenal lambasts those who call the black slave "Swan," the dwarf "Atlas," the little deformed female "Europa," the mangy cur "Leopard" or "Tiger" or "Lion" (*Satirae* 8.32–38).[77] The way of righteousness is *simplex*, Seneca insists, the way of wickedness *multiplex*.[78] Things that are complicated, inverted, paradoxical are part of a warped revolt against "normal" restraints of custom. They are not a comfort or a solution; they make life harder. they

creatures defy our classifications, often we cannot even tell where they begin or end—they are not individuals. . . . Thus there is nothing to hold on to, nothing fixed, the deformitas is hard to 'code' and harder still to remember, for everything is in flux" (p. 268; quoted by Harpham, *On the Grotesque*, p. 42.) I owe to Harpham the juxtaposition of Vitruvius's text with Gombrich's commentary.

[77] Martial 5.57 (calling the slave "dominus").

[78] By contrast, for Petronius and Martial, "simplicity" was the category in which they put the absence of restraints—traditional courtesy being anything but simple (see Petronius, *Satyricon* 132.15 ["novae simplicitatis opus"]; Martial 1 *praefatio* ["iocorum nostrorum simplicitate"], cf. 11.15). For the complexity of "traditional" Roman speech in this period, with its use of irony, *schema*, and *emphasis*, see Frederick M. Ahl, "The Art of Safe Criticism in Greece and Rome," *American Journal of Philology* 105 (1984), pp. 174–208, esp. pp. 187–208. It is interesting that Juvenal, who generally directs his wit against transgressions of status and boundaries, seems to find the combination of rigid moralism and license still more horrifying than "simple" license. In *Satirae* 2 he makes it clear that he prefers the mannered gestures of the unabashed "pansy" to the complicated ruses of the pathic homosexual who observes all the proprieties; he praises the former's "simplicitas miserabilis" (2.15–21).

go against "nature" and so are like men rowing upstream (*Epistulae* 122, esp. 17).[79]

Saturnalia from the Saturnalia

Unbridled indiscrimination creates anomie which in turn calls up a "Saturnalia from the Saturnalia." At the funeral of Claudius, the joyous and lighthearted Roman people walked about like free men (Seneca, *Apocolocyntosis* 12). One of the thin, pallid, learned jurists, like Lazarus suddenly risen from the dead at the death of the emperor, accosts the blubbering pettifoggers ("causidici") with the words, "I told you the Saturnalia would not last forever" (*Apocolocyntosis* 12).[80] At the death of Nero, according to Suetonius, the common people ran about in the *pilleus*, the felt cap which was worn on the Saturnalia and by the manumitted (*Nero* 57) and which, together with a pair of daggers, appeared on the reverse of the coins issued by the tyrannicides in 42 B.C.E.[81] When the slaves of Seneca's monster Hostius Quadra murdered their lewd and profligate master, Augustus did not punish them. The usual severe measures against this threat to the Roman status system were suspended, but the ludicrous obscenities of the Hostius Quadra became the object of mimicry on the stage (Seneca, *Naturales Quaestiones* 1.16.1).

Dio tells a story that offers a wonderful paradigm of the "Saturnalia from the Saturnalia": When the emperor Claudius commissioned the senator Aulus Plautius to invade Britain, Plautius had difficulty inducing his army to advance beyond Gaul. The soldiers, indignant at being asked to carry on a campaign outside the limits of the known world, disobeyed their orders. But when the freedman Narcissus, dispatched by Claudius, mounted the tribunal and attempted to address them, they grew still more indignant and would not allow Narcissus to speak.[82] At once and with

---

[79] "Inter monstra numerare quod ancilla haberet matronae superbiam et matrona ancillae humilitatem" (Petronius, *Satyricon* 126.11).

[80] For the *causidici*, see Johan Huizinga, *Homo Ludens: A Study of the Play-Element in Culture* (Boston, 1950), pp. 77–88.

[81] H. A. Grueber, *Coins of the Roman Republic in the British Museum*, 3 vols. (London, 1910), East 68.

[82] The ambition, competition, and innovation encouraged in Roman social life were also infuriating. The transgressions of the presumptuous social climber, particularly the freedman, are attacked so frequently that I will give only one pertinent example. In the *Annales*, Tacitus depicts with disgust Nero's legate to Britain, the freedman Polyclitus with his prodigious train, a figure of terror to Roman soldiers ("militibus quoque nostris terribilis"). For the enemy, unacquainted with the exorbitant power that could be exercised by a mere freedman (and in whose breast freedom still burned!), Polyclitus was simply an object of ridicule (*Annales* 14.39.3).

one voice they shouted "Io Saturnalia!" and surrendered forthwith to their commander Plautius (Dio 60.19.1–3).

This anecdote is exceptionally interesting. It illustrates the indignation felt at the absence of distinctions even by those who had little hope of ever overcoming the limitations of birth and wealth and who suffered the most from these limitations.[83] For the soldiers, the same cry that signaled joyous liberation from restraint at the Saturnalia was employed to express resentment at the Saturnalia out of Bounds. ("This is a regular circus!" we might say.) The same easy equality of festival creates malice when it is perceived as out of its limits of place and time. The very men who mutiny against authority are repelled by this affront to tradition offered by the freedman—and the emperor. Submission to the general becomes a protest, a "carnival to end carnival."

Like Julius Caesar's baker, Hadrian's caterers, and the soldiers of Plautius, the common people sometimes clung to distinctions that emperors and aristocrats discarded. When the slave Giton bursts out in "unseasonable" laughter at the dinner of the freedman Trimalchio, it is the pretentious former slave and client of the host who shouts, "Io Saturnalia! What is it, I ask—the month of December?" and launches a blistering attack on the transgressor Giton (*Satyricon* 58).[84] A scholiast's gloss at Juvenal 5.1–5 informs us that the Etruscan *scurra* Sarmentus ("incertum libertus an servus") through his good looks and his *urbanitas* (the nature of which can be discerned from Horace, *Satirae* 1.5.52ff.) was able to insinuate himself into the circle of Augustus and Maecenas.[85] Encouraged by his high status at court, he attempted to pass as an equestrian, sitting in the first fourteen rows of the theatre. This "presumption" on the part of Sarmentus was met with a *populi dictum*: "Sarmentus has one *scriptum* [enrollment?], but the people would like to give him another. Let what is due to each be given: So Sarmentus would be burdened with heavy chains" ("aliud scriptum habet Sarmentus, aliud populus voluerat. / digna dignis: sic Sarmentus habeat crassas compedes").[86]

The social psychologist Leon Festinger explains the phenomenon of spontaneous hierarchization. Competition—and thus envy—is limited by

---

[83] Compare Dumont's descriptions of the fastidious status-consciousness of the Hindu Untouchable (*Homo Hierarchicus*, esp. p. 136).

[84] This comes immediately after a similar attack on Ascyltos for laughing "out of season."

[85] He was one of Augustus's "pets" ("deliciae": Plutarch, *Antonius* 59.4).

[86] Horace, the son of a freedman, attacks an upstart freedman, a tribune of the soldiers, for illegally usurping a place in the first row of the theatre (*Epodi* 4.15–16). According to Macrobius, Vatinius, "the cobbler" and *scurra*, was stoned by the people at a gladiatorial show that he gave (*Saturnalia* 2.6.1). Martial's playful attacks on Vatinius are his "Saturnalia from the Saturnalia" (3.16, 3.59, 3.99). See Meyer Rheinhold, "Usurpation of Status and Status Symbols in the Roman Empire," *Historia* 20 (1971), p. 281 and n. 25; Porphyrion's commentary on Horace, *Satirae* 1.5.51–55.

the creation of orders within a society: "And it seems clear that when such status distinctions are firmly maintained, it is not only members of the higher status who maintain them. It is also important to the members of the lower status to maintain them, for it is in this way that they can relatively ignore the differences and compare themselves with their own group."[87] The more anxiously competitive the situation, the more importance attached to victory, the more likelihood of the collusion—*of those who risk a loss of status*—in the formation of elaborate status differentiations.[88] The average athlete, for instance, is willing to put the extraordinary one "in a class by himself." The third-grader is willing and happy to be "outclassed" by the sixth-grader against whom he or she would otherwise be compelled to compete. The more fierce the competition, the more numerous the statuses accepted voluntarily. Clear and distinct differences in class or category can be a relief, allowing one to remove oneself, without loss of face, from an unhappy comparison of skills. So, in our culture, despite its democratic and egalitarian tendencies, we gladly divide up sports competitions into a myriad of hierarchical statuses, and we do not force the third-graders to compete with the seventh-graders, the high-school teams with the professionals, the "handicapped" with the "normal," etc. Hierarchy can allay as well as create despair, diminish as well as heighten envy, create a sense of inclusion as well as a sense of exclusion. ·

Punishing Humor

Laughter, the weapon of the transgressor, could also be turned against him. Miriam Griffin suggests that the Saturnalia of 54 C.E., less than two months after the death of Claudius, might have been the occasion for the reading of Seneca's *Apocolocyntosis* excoriating the Saturnalian prince.[89] The type of humor that sought to punish transgressions, to end the Saturnalia, is expressed frequently by Lucilius, Laberius, Juvenal, Persius, Tacitus, and often by Horace and Martial.[90] Plutarch commends a

[87] "A Theory of Social Comparison Processes," p. 136.

[88] Op. cit., pp. 129–33.

[89] Miriam Griffin, *Seneca: A Philosopher in Politics* (Oxford, 1976), pp. 130 and 129n. 3. See Fantham, "Mime, the Missing Link," p. 160.

[90] For moralistic ridicule: Horace, *Satirae* 1.3.19–33, 56–65; 2.1, esp. 62–70; Persius, *Satirae* 1, esp. 107–10; Juvenal, *Satirae* 1, Cicero, *De natura deorum* 1.93. When Laberius ridicules the senate for its weakness and composition, he is participating in the "Saturnalia from the Saturnalia." For the mime as moralist, see Seneca, *De brevitate vitae* 12.13. It is this type of Roman humor which is most easily perceived and identified by those who feel themselves threatened by the Saturnalia Out of Bounds and experience the loss of status as insecurity rather than liberation.

law of Thurii which allowed the mime to lampoon only adulterers and *curiosi* ("polypragmones") (*De curiositate* 8, *Moralia* 519b), and he praises New Comedy because it is uplifting and moralistic (*Quaestiones Conviviales* 7.8 *Moralia* 712b–d).

This limit-preserving laughter attacks *deformitas* in its broadest sense. The Romans "look askance at," they give the evil eye to *turpitudo* (foulness, disfigurement, obscenity, evil omen, inauspiciousness). The anomalous, the portentous (including, or especially, the monstrous emperor) are made the object of derision and ridicule. Cicero, in the *De oratore*, advocates as a particularly just and apt humor the kind that attacks *deformitas*: "Est enim deformitatis et corporis vitiorum satis bella materies ad iocandum" (2.59.239). Cicero sets only two limitations on attacking deformity: it should avoid that which is odious or pathetic in the extreme (2.59.238–39),[91] and it should be strategically advantageous to the wit, unlike the jokes of the mime or *scurra* (2.59.239).[92] For Cicero this type of competitive humor is the very antithesis of the indiscriminate humor which he associates with the mime and the *scurra*.[93] It is the old-fashioned warrior humor—a weapon designed to allow one to triumph in a contest with a worthy opponent such as one encounters in the court of law.[94] Wit operates within the context of a formalized and ritualized *agon* with rules and limitations.

Deformitas—the absence of correct form—is the one target assaulted with impunity. Paradoxically, it was often the monster and the grotesque mime who were called upon to do the attacking as well as the atoning. So the Roman nurse employed the hideous monster and mask—the *deformis*

[91] The extraordinarily pathetic could not, in general, be a worthy opponent, but even this rule could be waived if the pathetic object was also arrogant: Cicero, *De oratore* 2.237; Grant, *Ancient Theories of the Laughable*, p. 80.

[92] See Cicero, *De oratore* 2.248, 264, 266; Grant, *Ancient Theories of the Laughable*, p. 19 ("laughter has its origins in the contemplation of the ugly or defective"), pp. 24–25, 79–80.

[93] For the indiscriminate laughter of the mime and *scurra*, see Grant, *Ancient Theories of the Laughable*, pp. 49–50, 83–84, 87, 89, 93–96, 146. Ironically, Cicero was accused of just this type of indiscriminate humor (Plutarch, *Cicero* 27.1; Seneca Rhetor, *Controversiae* 7.9). Despite Cicero's attempt to distinguish the orator, who operated within a code, from the mime, who operated without (e.g., *De oratore* 2.274), it is clear that the mimes imitated the orators and vice versa. For the mimes mimicking the lawyers, see Orelli-Henzen, *Inscriptionum Latinarum selectarum collectio* (Zurich, 1828–56, no. 6188; Reich, *Der Mimus*, p. 152n. 2, cf. pp. 61–69; Grant, op. cit., pp. 88–89.

[94] For the tradition of agonistic vituperation in Rome, see Cicero, *De oratore* 2.236 (Cicero praises Cato for being "gravis in laudando" and "acerbus in vituperando"); Quintilian, *Institutiones oratoriae* 6.3.28; Plutarch, *Quaestiones conviviales* 2.1 *Moralia* 631d; Jerome, "The Use of Invective," chapter 4 of *Aspects of the Study of Roman History*, pp. 50–56; Grant, *Ancient Theories of the Laughable*, pp. 18, 73–76, 85; E. de Saint-Denis, "Evolution sémantique de *urbanus-urbanitas*," *Latomus* 3 (1939), pp. 4–25.

persona—to frighten their charges into behaving (Seneca, *De ira* 2.11.2).[95]

The Sacrificial Clown

The relationship between laughter, the well-being of the community, and the "sacrificial clown" is wonderfully expressed in Apuleius's *Metamorphoses* when poor Lucius, a stranger in Hypata, Thessaly (and a *curiosus*, searching out the secrets of the Thessalian witches) is made a "sacrifice" at the town's Festival of Laughter. He is brought before a kangaroo court, where he is bitterly humiliated, mocked, and threatened with death. Thoroughly unnerved and exhausted by his ordeal, he is then warmly congratulated and honored for having played the victim in their mime (2.32–3.11). This role, which may have once been carried out by the god,[96] the king as the god's substitute, or a substitute for the king such as the King of the Saturnalia, or even by the mascots or *sigillaria* (gifts given on the Saturnalia that included, in Martial's list, many human and figured grotesques),[97] is played by the monster and the grotesque mime. The benign god of the Saturnalia, the god acquainted with chains, was also a particularly bloody god who demanded human sacrifice.[98] The *Acts of Saint Dasius* tells us of the practice of the sacrifice of the King of the Saturnalia at the Moesian front even in the time of Diocletian. Chosen by lot, dressed in the insignia of his special status (probably as Kronos), and endowed with extravagant freedom, he was slain at the end of a month of debauchery.[99]

[95] For the *maniolae* or *maniae*, the bogeys used to frighten children into behaving, see Festus: "manias autem, quas nutrices minitantur parvulis pueris, esse larvas, id est manes quos deos deasque putabant" (Paulus ex Festo [ed. Lindsay], p. 114, lines 17–20); Juvenal, *Satirae* 3.172–76; Lucilius frag. 484–89M (= 524–29W); Horace, *Epistulae* 2.3.338–40; Lucian, *Philopseudes* 2; Jean-G. Préaux, "Manducus," in *Hommages à Albert Grenier* (Brussels, 1962), vol. 3 (= *Collection Latomus*, vol. 58), pp. 1285–88.

[96] Cf. H. S. Versnel, *Triumphus: An Inquiry into the Origin, Development and Meaning of the Roman Triumph* (Leiden, 1970), pp. 229–37.

[97] Were the *sigillaria*, like the *argei*, meant to be substitute sacrifices for humans? Or were they, in a certain sense, sacrificial gods themselves, the descendants of the *struppi* or *capita deorum* carried anciently in the *pompae*? (See Versnel, *Triumphus*, p. 260.) The divinity of the monsters of the *pompae* is affirmed by Festus (p. 114, lines 17–20 [Lindsay]). Was the little statuette that Nero honored above the gods a *sigillaria*?

[98] See L. Parmentier and F. Cumont, "Le Roi des Saturnales," *Revue de Philologie, de Littérature et d'Histoire Anciennes* 21 (1897), pp. 146–47, 151–52; Sextus Empiricus, *Hypotyposes* 3.208, 3.221; Rousselle, *Porneia*, pp. 148–49. Both the Greeks and the Romans tended to identify particularly "hungry" gods (like Moloch, Melkart, and the Zalmoxis of the Thracians and Scythians) with Saturn and the Saturnalia.

[99] Franz Cumont, "Les Actes de S. Dasius," *Analecta Bollandiana* 16 (1897), pp. 5–16.

The Stupidus

The Romans, whose lives centered, as T. P. Wiseman observes, around fascinating (and therefore debilitating and threatening) spectacles, were particularly fond of the second mime, the *stupidus* (i.e., the *stupefactus*, the stupefied, the fascinated one).[100]

"In *Maccus exil* a fragment of text preserves the typical lines: 'on the lintel I often cracked my wretched head; on the threshold I stubbed my toes.' "[101] The threshold was a most dangerous place. To trip on the threshold and crack one's head on the lintel, common and typical bad omens, were apt expressions for the functioning of the portentous *stupidus*. Like everything *turpis*, the mime and the monster were both ambiguous and ill-omened. To express his own and his friend's disapproval of the *scurrae*, the *cinaedi*, and the *moriones* of the elegant repast, Pliny labels them portents ("prodigia" [*Epistulae* 9.17.3]). Once labeled as portents, an expiation was called for. The most obvious and available victims were the portents themselves: the grotesques of the household, the streets, and the stage.

Petronius appears to have constructed his mock epic around the theme of the "Wrath of Priapus" against the *escaped scapegoat* Encolpius. The plot revolves, like that of Apuleius's mock epic, around the "sacrificial clown" and the expiation paid by the *curiosus*. Encolpius is compelled to compensate Domitilla for having seen something he should not have seen. Like Apuleius's Lucius or Euripides' Pentheus (the Athenian version of the sacrificial Saturnalian—here Dionysian—king), the ex-slave Encolpius is punished for looking.[102]

Despite Cumont's hesitations, the granting of special license and freedom to the same person who is to serve as the scapegoat is a well-known practice. Versnel (*Triumphus*, pp. 217–18, 249) discusses the Babylonian/Persian New Year's festival, the Secaea, which involved the reversal of social ranks and the serving of slaves by their masters. At this festival a criminal was granted the rights and dress of the king and tremendous freedom (including access to the king's harem) for five days. Afterward he was killed. See Berossos in Athenaeus, *Deipnosophistai* 14.639c; Dio Chrysostomos, *Orationes* 4.66–69; Strabo 11.8.4; Parmentier, "Le Roi des Saturnales," pp. 144–46; S. Langdon, "The Babylonian and Persian Secaea," *Journal of the Royal Asiatic Society* of *Great Britain and Ireland* (1924), pp. 65–72. For a comparable rite in Rhodes, see Porphyry, *De abstinentia* 2.54. For similarities with the Aztec festival of Tezcatlipoca, see Fray Bernardino de Sahagún, *Historia general de las cosas de Nueva España* (Mexico City, 1989), vol. 2, ch. 5; Georges Bataille, *The Accursed Share*, trans. Robert Hurley, vol. 1 (New York, 1988 [orig. pub. 1967]), pp. 49–51.

[100] *Catullus and His World*, p. 2. As Roger Caillois points out (*Man, Play and Games* [New York, 1976], p. 23), the goal of mimicry is to fascinate the spectator.

[101] Nicoll, *Masks, Mimes and Miracles*, p. 72.

[102] Reich ("Der Mann mit dem Eselskopf," pp. 126–27) suggests that both Apuleius and Petronius were borrowing from the mime.

The grotesque mimes functioned like the amulet and the mascot. In the *Quaestiones conviviales*, Plutarch explains that the *probaskania* (a name given to the various paraphernalia used to combat the evil eye) offered protection against envy by diverting, or catching, the gaze of the malicious by its *atopia*, its absurdity, singularity, strangeness (5.7 *Moralia* 681f–682a).[103] The monsters and Medusa's heads embossed on shields, the phallic bosses on horse's harnesses, the phalluses on the bathhouse walls, on baker's ovens, on lamps and braziers, the grotesque mascots, the wonderful polyphallic *tintinnabula* operated on this principle. Numerous representations link these particularly popular apotropaic images together. A charm reproduced by Dalmeyda, for example, depicts three mimes (one a grotesque) standing on a double penis.[104] The *geloion*, the *ridiculum* acted as a lure. According to Pollux, "It was the custom to hang or plaster up something ridiculous to avert envy" ("ethos en, geloia tina katartan e epiplattein epi phthonou apotrope" [7.108]). Phrynichus the Arabian explains that craftsmen used to hang up strange little humanoids to protect their businesses from the evil eye.[105] Augustus had his Gabba; Domitian, his pinhead; Trajan, his Capitolinus. Emperors, aristocrats, and other prominent people who surrounded themselves with grotesques, fools, and clowns, did so, in part, to protect themselves; these obscene or ridiculous creatures were, in the words of Enid Welsford, "reverse magnets or reverse lightning rods."[106]

Taking into account the sacrificial role of the *stupidus*, it is not surprising that martyrdom itself was a frequent topic of the mime in the Empire and that it was the *stupidus* who played the role of the Jewish or Christian martyr, or of Jesus himself.[107] There is much evidence, in addition, to suggest that the mimes went out of the way to make themselves vulner-

---

[103] E.g., *Priapea* 66. See Jahn, "Über den Aberglauben des bösen Blicks," p. 68; Elworthy, "Evil Eye," p. 612.

[104] "Mimus," p. 1902, fig. 5033. The desire to divert the look gave rise, as well, to the use of bright, shining ornaments of all kinds. The glittering helmet and fantastic headdresses of warriors can be attributed to this motive. See Lafaye, "Fascinum," p. 983; Elworthy, "Evil Eye," p. 611; Kuhnert, "Fascinum," col. 2011.

[105] *Anecdota Graeca*, ed. Immanuel Bekker (Graz, Austria, 1965 [orig. pub. 1814]), 30.5. The shield hanging on a shop, decorated with the image of a deformed Gaul (to which Julius Caesar Strabo compares his enemy Helvius Manca in Cicero, *De oratore* 2.266), probably served as a *probaskanion*.

[106] The biographer of Alexander Severus tells us that the emperor could make no use of all the male and female dwarfs, fools, worthless, chattering fellows, actors, and pantomimists collected by his predecessor, Elagabalus, so he gave them away to the people (*Scriptores historiae Augustae, Alexander Severus* 34.2). Cf. Welsford, *The Fool*, pp. 58–59, 61.

[107] Cf. Reich, *Der Mimus*, pp. 82n. 3, 93–4, 98n. 1. "In der That war ja, wie Paulus klagt, der griechisch-römischen Welt das Christentum eine Narrheit" (p. 94); cf. "Der Mann mit dem Eselskopf," p. 124.

able.[108] The shiny shaven pate identified the grotesque mime (*mimus calvus, moros phalakros*), as it did innumerable grotesques in the Roman world.[109] The misshapen dwarf clown of Lucian's *Lapithae* not only shaves his head but performs a dance in which he further distorts his body in order to make himself more ridiculous (Lucian, *Lapithae* 18). Likewise, the Roman mime cast aside even the protection from the evil eye of god and man afforded by the actor's mask.[110] They often, like many of the most ancient mimes, "dressed naked" (i.e., wore clothing meant to simulate nakedness). And on certain occasions they even appeared in the buff, such as at the Floralia, where female mimes danced nude.[111] Finally, the male mimes wore the universal lightning rod, the enormous exposed phallus. No character in all of Roman life was so carefully fashioned to attract the evil eye as the grotesque mime. They were the living amulets for an entire culture.

The mime's role as decoy may help to explain the value placed on the "natural" (as opposed to the "artificial," that is, clever) fool.[112] The "natural," like the *stupidus* made a more effective decoy precisely because he was so excruciatingly vulnerable, like Herriman's Krazy. Martial complains of a fool he had purchased: "He was said to be a *morio*. I paid twenty thousand for him. Give me back my money, Gargilianus—he has his wits [*sapit*]." (8.13).[113]

The clown or grotesque mime of the theatre had a doubly apotropaic function. On the one hand, as someone who appeared at intervals, like the modern circus or rodeo clown, or the clown of Javanese *ludruk*, he protected the audience from the fascination (the *fascinum*) which stupefies them: he "breaks the spell."[114] In addition, like the circus or rodeo

[108] Compare the modern rodeo clown who, without horse or weapons, courts those very animals endangering the cowboy hero.

[109] The shaven head was particularly identified with the *stupidus*. Cf. Dieterich, *Pulcinella*, p. 38; Reich, *Der Mimus*, pp. 66, 113 and n. 2, 116 and n. 3, 831–32; Joannes Chrysostomus, *Spuria de poenitentia*, in *Patrologia Graeca*, vol. 59, col. 760. (Chrysostomus emphasizes that hair would stand between the mime and shame.) See the delightful description of the buffeting of the bald-headed mime in Synesias, *Calvitii Encomium* 13.

[110] See Reich, *Der Mimus*, p. 28.

[111] For the nakedness of the mimes at the Floralia, see Valerius Maximus 2.10.8; Lactantius, *Divinae Institutiones* 1.20; Scholiast to Juvenal, *Satirae* 6.250; Augustine, *De civitate dei* 2.26; Reich, *Der Mimus*, p. 117.

[112] For the "natural," see Martial 6.39, 12.93, 14.210; Many of the instances of "family monsters" are *stulti, fatuui, nani, folli, sanniones*.

[113] "Morio dictus erat: viginti milibus emi. / Redde mihi nummus, Gargiliane: sapit."

[114] See Peacock, *Rites of Modernization*, ch. 11, esp. p. 166: The clown repeatedly breaks the verisimilitude of *ludruk* melodrama, inevitably appearing at the most gripping moment in a skit. Marginal to, or outside of, the story he is entering, he immediately lures the attention of both audience and orchestra, "bursts the bubble," and exposes the nonsense behind the sense. He thus insures the general disinclination of the Surabajan audience to fix its

clown, he protects the players from being fascinated by the audience (our "stage fright") by diverting the eyes of the audience and the malice of the gods onto himself. The baseball clown of opening day, and the team mascot, still play this "guardian monster" role. In many cultures, especially in the Mediterranean region, the hunchback continues to serve this function. Italians and Italian-Americans (especially gamblers) persist in carrying little hunchback figures (*gobbi, gobetti*) made of coral, mother-of-pearl, silver, or plastic as protection against the evil eye.[115]

Ascribing these functions to the extraordinary, the deformed, the monstrous was not an innovation of the Romans. The talismanic "mascot," the painting or statuette of the grotesque clown had a long pedigree. Already in the courts of the Hellenistic kings the monsters burst the limitations of ritual space and time. Dwarves abounded at the court of the Ptolemies.[116] The Greek polymath Athenaeus (late second century C.E.) connects the fashion with Greek Sybaris in Southern Italy.[117] The Romans, moreover, modeled their "mascots" on innumerable representations of the comic monster of the Greek and Italian theatre and on their masks.[118] The Roman version of the grotesques of the New Comedy (especially the parasite, the cook, and the slave) are difficult to distinguish from the Greek. "As a general principle," according to Margarete Bieber, "it may be right to consider the more grotesque figure as Roman."[119] It is not possible to say whether the grotesque mime is a reification of the apotropaic Little Monster or the Little Monster a reification of the types of comedy.[120]

---

attention. Peacock does not offer an explanation for this fostering of inattention, but he does describe the Indonesians' anxiety concerning their "national neurosis": *Latah*, involuntary and hypnotic imitation, a form of fascination. See p. 159 and n. 4, with pp. 37, 67–68, 242.

[115] See A.J.B. Wace, "Grotesques and the Evil Eye," *Annual of the British School of Athens* 10 (1903/4), p. 109; Richard Swiderski, "Italian Americans. From Folk to Popular: Plastic Evil Eye Charms," in *The Evil Eye*, ed. Clarence Maloney (New York, 1976), p. 37. Swiderski points out that the *gobbo* was a clown or jester in later European tradition; viz. Launcelot Gobbo and his father in Shakespeare's *Merchant of Venice*.

[116] *The Fool*, p. 58. The Hellenistic aristocrats also domesticated the mime, according to Reich (*Der Mimus*, pp. 29–30). As Margarete Bieber explains, many mimes lived at the court of Antiochus IV (187–63 B.C.E.), who liked to mingle and dance with them ("*Mima Saltatricula*," *American Journal of Archaeology* 43 [1939], pp. 640–44.)

[117] Athenaeus, *Deipnosophistai* 12.518; Navarre, art. "Nanus," in *D-S*, vol. 4.1, p. 1.

[118] Bieber's *Greek and Roman Theater* contains abundant illustrations of grotesque statues and representations modeled on the characters of Doric farce, Old and New Comedy, the Italian Phlyakes, Atellanae, etc.

[119] Bieber, *Greek and Roman Theater*, p. 92. Bieber attributes the hideous masks of comedy on the same principle: the coarser the features, the more likely to be Roman (loc. cit.; cf. pp. 150, 155). Barbara Hughes Fowler does not distinguish the Roman grotesque from the general category of Hellenistic grotesques. (*The Hellenistic Aesthetic* [Madison, Wis., 1989], esp. pp. 66–78).

[120] See G. Dalmeyda, "Mimus," in *D-S*, vol. 3.2, p. 1902. Gisela Richter ("Grotesques

When his fellow slaves first saw the humpbacked Aesop, according to the *Vita Aesopi*, they said that their master had bought him as "an amulet to protect his traffic in slaves [*probaskanion tou somatemporeiou*]."[121] The gentle, kindly humpbacked Crates was another living amulet or *apotropaion*.[122] Concerning Ascyltos of the prodigious genitals, Petronius remarks, "His parts were of such a size that you might think that he himself was simply the extrusion of a phallic amulet [= *fascinum*)]" ("Habebat enim inguinum pondus tam grande ut ipsum hominem laciniam fascini crederes" [*Satyricon* 92]).[123]

It is clear, as Dieterich, Reich, Navarre, Bieber, and Goldman attest, that many of the physically deformed became mimes, exposing their forms on the stage, in the street, and in private entertainments.[124] We possess many depictions of the deformed or grotesque as performers or members of popular mime troops: hunchbacked fluteplayers; grimacing, walleyed dancers (*saltatores*); naked ithyphallic clowns.[125] The living *probaskanion*, the animate *fascinum*, was more effective than that in clay or bronze.

There were places and points of passage where one was especially vul-

---

and the Mime," *American Journal of Archaeology* 17 [1913], pp. 149–56) believes that all these grotesque figures are all mimes.

[121] *Vita Aesopi* 3, p. 12. See B. E. Perry, *Aesopica*, pp. 211–41; *Babrius and Phaedrus*, Loeb Classical Library (Cambridge, Mass., 1965), pp. xxx–xlvi; Wace, "Grotesques and the Evil Eye," p. 109.

[122] See Jahn, "Über den Aberglauben des bösen Blicks," pp. 75–76 and n. 194; Apuleius, *Florida* 4.22., p. 101; Suidas, *Lexicon* (Hesychius 2341), "Krates" (Crates the man for whom all doors were open ["thurepanioktes"]); Plutarch, *Quaestiones convivales* 2.1 Moralia 632e. Jahn (p. 67n. 152) and Christian August Lobeck (*Aglaophamus* [Darmstadt, 1968 (1829)], p. 971) would put the statue of the lame Hephaestos which stood at the hearth in the category of *baskaniai* (*Scholia in Aristophanem*, ed. W.J.W. Koster [Groningen, 1962], part 4, fascicle 2 [*Aves* 436]).

[123] The bathers stand around and applaud Ascyltos. As Caillois points out, "Applause is not merely approval and reward. It marks the end of illusion and play" (*Man, Play and Games*, p. 49). To applaud (Latin *explaudere* or Greek *pternokopein*) is in itself apotropaic, in that it is designed to protect and "break the spell" on the audience as well as to reward and protect the performer. It was a response to the threat of fascination created by mimesis. The *scabellum*, or foot clapper, was also used to "break the spell" and signal the end of a theatrical piece; see Cicero, *Pro Caelio* 27.65.

[124] Dieterich, *Pulcinella*, pp. 36ff.; Reich, *Der Mimus*, p. 65 and n. 1; Navarre, "Nanus," p. 1 and fig. 5258; Hetty Goldman, "Two Terracotta Figurines from Tarsus," *American Journal of Archaeology* 47 (1943), p. 24; Propertius 4.8.41–42. Goldman believes that they were appreciated for their talismanic qualities; cf. Bieber, *Greek and Roman Theater*, p. 107.

[125] See Goldman's figs. 1 and 5 (p. 23); fig. 7 (p. 26). There is much to suggest that hideous masks were apotropaic: see Jahn, "Über den Aberglauben des bösen Blicks," p. 67 and n. 155. Jahn mentions an amulet in which a mask and phallus are conjoined. See also Elworthy, "Evil Eye," p. 612; *The Evil Eye*, pp. 147–48; C. A. Böttiger, "Über das Wort Maske und über die Abbildung der Masken auf alten Gemmen," in *Kleine Schriften* (Dresden, 1838), vol. 3, pp. 402–13.; Lobeck, *Aglaophamus*, vol. 2, p. 973.

nerable: corners, bridges, baths, doorways. The "liminal" areas of the world were highly charged, dangerous,[126] as were places like the stage and the rostrum where one was terribly exposed to the eyes of others.[127] Likewise there were articles and beings whose safety from the evil eye was especially critical for particular individuals: children, ships's prows, lamps, hearths, bakers's ovens, the tools and animals upon which one's livelihood depended. And there were parts and aspects of one's body which were terribly fragile, particularly vulnerable to the *invidia* of others: one's nakedness, one's back, one's bald head, one's big ears or nose, a woman's genitals, a man's large or exposed phallus, one's eyes. These were areas that were often protected by talismans and decoys.[128] But the most fragile thing of all was honor. That was, above all, the desperate object of the sacrifice of the monster—as it was of the gladiator.

Conclusions

In a poignant passage, Tacitus (*Annales* 13.15) describes a Saturnalian festival celebrated at the royal court. (That the setting is the Saturnalia signals, in itself, that the "physics of invidia" are being set into play.) At the same festival of inversion at which Seneca may have produced his *Apocolocyntosis* mocking the *rex* who was also a *fatuus*, his successor, the young prince Nero, is (not so paradoxically) chosen by lot to be King of Saturnalia. While he commands the others to perform acts which will not shame them, he singles out the child Britannicus ("the rightful heir") to sing, thinking that he will thus render the now doomed prince ridiculous and an object of scorn. The youth, instead of singing the anticipated comic ditty, sings a sad song about a man losing his patrimony and being driven from his homeland.[129] The fool's sad song becomes the "Saturnalia from the Saturnalia."[130]

[126] For some of the *limina* in Roman life, see Versnel, *Triumphus*, pp. 133–63.

[127] For the exposure to the evil eye of a woman participating in a parade, see Heliodorus, *Aethiopica* 7.2.

[128] The child was protected by the *bulla*, an amulet in the shape of a phallus or enclosing a model of a phallus. See Macrobius, *Saturnalia* 1.6: "inclusis intra eam remediis, quae crederent adversus invidiam valentissime."

[129] I am reminded of the powerfully moving scene at the end of the *Paths of Glory* (1957), Stanley Kubrick's saga of the First World War. The French soldiers, relaxing in a saloon after the painful experience of witnessing the sacrificial decimation of their own ranks, are offered a little German girl as a "treat." She is compelled onto the stage as an object of derision, but she sings a song of such innocent pathos that the laughter and ridicule cease to relieve either the soldiers or the movie's audience. Tears become the only relief, the "Saturnalia from the Saturnalia."

[130] Tacitus's plot resembles the accounts of the mimes who were allegedly converted to

Tacitus has imagined this miniature drama as arising from Nero's fierce feelings of resentment toward his stepbrother Britannicus, his rival for the throne. Status—indeed preeminence—is the issue. The rise of one necessarily entails the demise of the other. It is the perfect zero-sum universe which is the inevitable stage-setting for the most powerful dramas of envy. In this tiny masterpiece of a "mime," in which the inversion is inverted, the Saturnalia is perceived by the reader as a trap and not a liberation, the expression of the deadly malice of brother against brother and a farce directed by a deadly *princeps saturnalicius*. The distinction between comedy and tragedy dissolves, and the hero of the tale becomes the innocent "fool" Britannicus, "the one who gets slapped," the special object of the derision and malice of Nero, the tyrant and very embodiment of envy.

> **The vulture which explores our inmost nerves is not the bird of whom our dainty poets talk, but those evils of the soul, envy and excess.**
> (Petronius, quoted by Fulgentius)[131]

The Greeks and Romans speak of envy and insatiable desire as the most excruciating of all emotions.[132] According to Plutarch (*Quaestiones conviviales* 5.7 *Moralia* 681e), envy has an unparalleled ability to insinuate itself into the soul and contaminate it. When those subject to envy let their

---

Christianity in the course of playing the *stupidus* in the farces designed to mock the Christians, suddenly professing their "seriousness" during or after the performance. See the long discussion in Reich, *Der Mimus*, pp. 80–109.

[131] "Qui voltur iecur intimum pererrat / pectusque eruit intimasque fibras, / non est quem lepidi vocant poetae, sed cordis [mala] livor atque luxus" (*Mitologiarum Libri tres*, vol. 2, p. 45).

[132] Many of those who have studied envy regard it as one of the most primitive of emotions, and an emotion that is produced by the first imposition of limits and creation of comparisons. "It is perhaps the most primitive of primordial fears," according to David Gilmore (*Aggression and Community*, p. 166). The psychologist Marvin Daniels makes it still more basic: "I have seen my dog restless and upset when I petted another dog" ("The Dynamics of Morbid Envy in the Etiology and Treatment of Chronic Learning Disabilities," *Psychoanalytic Review* 51 [1964], p. 49; cf. Tourney and Plazak, "Evil Eye," p. 492). In Freud and Lacan it is predominantly associated with the role of the father and separation from, and competition for, the mother. It marks the end of the identity of child and mother and the beginning of self-consciousness. In René Girard's recasting of the Oedipus complex, envy and competition are even more elemental, with even the desire for the mother being the result of rivalry with the father. (The fantasied punishment for the child with Oedipal strivings is castration.) In contrast, for Schoeck, envy arises first in sibling rivalry. Note that the conditions predicated for the onset of envy reveal less about envy itself than about the theorist's tendency to regard equality or inequality as the more invidious social condition.

glance fall upon another, it is as if they were shooting poisoned arrows. So they are poisoned and poison in turn. "Sicilian tyrants could not invent a better torture," according to Horace.[133] It is an emotion which degrades just by its sensation, an autointoxication, a poison, like Nietzsche's and Scheler's *ressentiment*, an "evil secretion, in a sealed vessel of prolonged impotence."[134] The same formless frustration that drives Martial's Marulla to mate with the idiot drives Juvenal's Eppia to mate with the gladiator. These cruel and endless longings make idiots of us all (Seneca, *Epistulae* 15.9).[135]

The monster was the signal and evidence of *unacceptable* transgression, that is, transgression beyond the limits. So monstrous births and *portenta* both were, and attended, calamities. They were evidence of the god's envy, provoked by transgression into the god's sphere of the unlimited. They were also reminders of the god's unlimited and absolute powers and the divine superabundance of creative energy. (God could make a mule foal or give a calf two heads.) The portents are both the rejected of god and the agents and expressions of god's monstrous powers.

If the grotesque can be compared to anything, it is to paradox.

(Harpham, *On the Grotesque*, p. 19)[136]

The mimes were both the *thaumatopoioi* and the *gelotopoioi*, the "wonder-workers" and the "laughter-makers"; the ones who fascinated and the ones who broke the spell.[137] These complementary functions, those of the *derisor* and the *stupidus*, could be played by a single figure. The mime and, especially, the domestic buffoon often played both these roles alternately: his biting attacks (*dicacitas*) may have been graciously accepted

---

[133] "Invidia Siculi non invenere tyranni / Maius tormentum" (*Epistulae* 1.2.58–59).

[134] Albert Camus, *The Rebel: An Essay on Man in Revolt* (New York, 1956 [orig. pub. 1951]), p. 17. See Nietzsche, *Genealogy of Morals*, trans. Francis Golffing (New York, 1956 [orig. pub. 1887]); Max Scheler, *Ressentiment*, trans. William W. Holdheim (New York, 1961 [orig. pub. 1910]). The "psychical dynamite" of Nietzsche and Scheler is closer in its complex of emotional associations to ancient *invidia* than to the modern threadbare concepts of envy and jealousy.

[135] "Stulta vita ingrata est et trepida; tota in futurum fertur. . . . Quam tu nunc vitam dici existimas stultam? Babae Isionis? Non ita est; nostra dicitur." What makes us worse fools than Baba and Isio is that we are unable to be satisfied; our desires lead us always into stupid risks and fears.

[136] "Der Begriff des *paradoxon* ist . . . ein Aequivalent für *thaumasion* oder *apiston* 'wunderbar' [in the ethnography and literature of natural science of the Hellenistic period]" (Lefèvre, "Die Bedeutung des Paradoxen," p. 61n. 11).

[137] For scapegoating as a homeopathic system, see the remarks of René Girard in *Violent Origins*, ed. Robert Hammerton-Kelly (Stanford, 1987), p. 127.

and even welcomed, but he also functioned as the butt of ridicule. The fawning client and parasite of Horace's first epistle is an excellent example of the *derisor* playing the *stupidus* and repeating verbatim the words of his master (1.18.3–14),[138] and Juvenal refers to the insults heaped upon the *railleurs* Sarmentus and Gabba at the banquets of the mighty (*Satirae* 5.1ff.).

Often, however, these functions were given to pairs of mimes, resembling such comic teams as our own Abbot and Costello, Laurel and Hardy, or Herriman's wonderful Ignatz and Krazy. The attendant and comic double of the the *derisor*, the "second mime" often imitated the first; he was the mimic of a mimic. One of the most famous of these teams was that of the *derisor* Latinus and the *stupidus* Panniculus.[139] They were images of one another reflected in a distorting mirror.

The more unbearable the frustration, the distinctions, fixations, comparisons, and categorizations, the greater the yearning for reflection, mimesis, identity, and the greater the fear (and temptation) of fascination. If the "trick" mirror does not appear—if the monstrous mime does not come to the rescue, if there is no sameness but only difference—there is fascination and a loss of a world. The more complete the differences, the more insurmountable the distinctions, the greater the sense of loss.

Likewise, if there is only sameness, only identity, without difference and oscillating tension, there is no world, no self. But the more and finer the distinctions—the difference without the sameness, the sameness without the difference—the greater the gap falling between difference and sameness, the more extreme will seem the bridging of that gap, the fiercer, the more obvious, the more brutally self-conscious, the more ludicrous and obscene the play that will be necessary to preserve the world.

[138] The *stupidus* was a mimic of a mimic. Cf. Horace, *Epistulae* 118.14; Cicero, *Brutus* 243; Seneca, *De ira* 3.6.8. "Le stupidus, ou parasitus, qui ne manquait, nous dit-on, presque jamais à côté de l'acteur principal: il était sa doublure comique et faisait rire en copiant ses gestes et en parlant comme lui" (Boissier, "Mimus," p. 1906).

[139] Cf. Martial 1.4, 3.86, 9.28; Reich, *Der Mimus*, p. 93.

SIX

CONCLUSIONS

THE WIDENING GYRE

Neither does justice avail nor universal crime.

Fas valuit nihil aut commune nefas.

(Seneca, *Thyestes* 138)

IN THE *Naturales quaestiones*, Seneca compares the rainbow to the deceptions of the mirror, to the *speculi fallacia, simulacra, inanis verorum corporum imitatio* (1.15.7–17.1). At the same time he remarks that "mirrors were invented that man might know himself" (1.17.4).[1] Petronius's Circe, insulted by the impotence of "Polyaenus," reassures herself by looking in the mirror. "My mirror doesn't lie," she says (*Satyricon* 129). The mirror in Ovid's tale of Narcissus is a dissembler—and the one way through which Narcissus comes to know himself.

A "Roman" sense of identity, a sense of there being a "Roman" quality, depended on the existence of a "rerum concordia discors,"[2] a mirror in which fluctuated difference and sameness, boundaries and transparency. This willing embrace of ambivalence characterizes Otto Seel's "Morphologie des Römertums":

> Preservation of what is contradictory and opposed, rejection of systematic, conceptual simplifications and single meanings and, instead of that, desire to endure tension . . . a combination of pride and irony directed at oneself, of strong belief and sarcasm, of pomp and satire, [all of this] was part of the intellectual household of Roman culture from the beginning. The unclear situation and ambiguity of the dying Republic and of the principate greatly increased this state of affairs because of their conceptual and programmatic vagueness.[3]

The Romans did not conceive of their hierarchy and the patron/client system as a rigid, inflexible pyramid, a stairway set in cement, as we are

---

[1] "Inventa sunt specula ut homo ipse se nosset."

[2] I have taken this phrase from Horace, *Epistulae* 1.12.19.

[3] Otto Seel, *Römertum und Latinität* (Stuttgart, 1964), pp. 258–60 (from the chapter entitled "Römische Antithetik," pp. 211–45), quoted and translated by Plass, *Wit and the Writing of History*, p. 136n. 2.

wont to picture the medieval Great Chain of Being. Rather, it was envisaged as a mobile, fluid, dynamic system of relationships—personal and impersonal. It had its own "physics," a system of compensations, deterrents, and adjustments ever involving reversals and inversions. It was a system designed both to encourage the transgression of limitations and to discourage and compensate for these same transgressions.[4] It was—like the caste system described by Dumont and Srinivas and unlike the differentiated harmony described by Girard—forever being established.[5]

The stark tensions of Roman society—between fierce competition and fraternity, between distinction and identity, between violence and harmony, between hierarchy and collectivity, between the joy of being envied and the dread of the evil eye—could not be resolved but, under favorable conditions, channeled and organized. The reversal and obliteration of distinctions formed as vital a part of a system as the distinctions.[6]

Paradox and Reciprocity

We are accustomed to think of "truth" and categories as static, and to divide the world into "serious" and "festive," or into "ordered" and "disordered." "Order" is traditional and has the quality of being fixed, repeatable, stable, secure. The "festive" or "disordered" is opposed to the traditional order, to steadfast categories and definitions, even if it may

[4] For particular aspects of the Roman compensatory physics, see Dumézil, "*Maiestas* et *gravitas*," p. 24 and n. 2; Fugier, *Recherches sur l'expression du sacré*, pp. 28–29; Mikhail Bakhtin, "From the Prehistory of Novelistic Discourse," in *The Dialogic Imagination: Four Essays*, ed. Michael Holquist, trans. Caryl Emerson and M. Holquist (Austin, Tex., 1981), p. 58; Grant, *Ancient Theories of the Laughable*, p. 137.

[5] Compare the strangely fluid Hindu caste system as described by Dumont in *Homo Hierarchicus* and M. N. Srinivas in *Religion and Society Among the Coorgs of South India* (Oxford, 1952).

[6] It is possible to compare Rome with Dumont's India. The role of Tantrism in Indian social and religious life is especially interesting in this regard. Tantrism, with its indiscriminate and egalitarian antistructure, both inverted the dominant order and complemented and supported it. Rigid hierarchy and social stratification are often "supplemented" by festival: Parmentier, for example, remarks on the particular intensity with which the Saturnalia was celebrated among the Roman soldiers and their auxiliaries ("Le Roi des Saturnales," p. 148). See also Cumont, "Actes de S. Dasius," pp. 5–16, and Bishop Asterius's homily (ca. 400 C.E.) against the celebration of the New Year's festival (*Sermo adversus Kalendarum festum*, in *Patrologia Graeca*, vol. 40, cols. 215–26, esp. cols. 218, 221–22). For similar complementarities in Ashanti, Japanese, and British society, see Elliott, *The Power of Satire*, pp. 76–79; R. S. Rattray, *Ashanti Law and Constitution* (New York, 1969 [orig. pub. 1911]), pp. 326–27, cf. pp. 309–10, 372–73; Rattray, *Ashanti* (Oxford, 1923), pp. 151ff.; Turner, *The Ritual Process*, pp. 172, 178–81; Yoshida Mitsuru, *Requiem for the Battleship Yamato*, trans. Richard H. Minear (Seattle, 1985), pp. 18–24, esp. p. 24.

reinforce or permit them. Set categories and words with fixed meanings are the stuff of the more beneficial situation wherein humans have repressed the war of all against all.[7] At best the festive and disordered is seen as a temporary relief and complement to the benevolent monarchy of the fixed.

We tend, moreover, to think of the formal and restrained as dominant.[8] For Marie Delcourt, for example, what is cardinal is austere and reverent; shapeless buffoonery and license represent a degeneration.[9] Absurdity is a profanation, a sad sort of cicatrice on the majestically sober countenance of the divine. As Erving Goffman notes, modern Americans and Europeans expect consistency on "sacred occasions." "Serious matters" demand gravity and preclude laughter.[10] The serious is "sacred," the comic or ludic is "profane," and we are abashed by the mixing of the two. Ludic executions, mockery of the dead at funerals, and spilling of blood at the "games" offend us in part because they mix these two "fundamental" categories and appear, therefore, defiling, "decadent." (We have no Sterculus, no Acca Larentia, no Priapus—no gods of dung, no deified prostitutes, no deified penises.) Moreover, because they are so for us, we believe that the fixed, formal, repetitive aspects of the Roman rites are those that rendered them efficacious and acceptable to gods and man. The festive may have offered some *levitas*, some diversion from the wearisome *gravitas* of Roman life, but there was a necessary Roman order which these festal inversions served to reinforce or attack.[11]

[7] The architectural metaphor of "decadence" and "fall" imposes on ancient Rome our modern equation of stability with health.

[8] There are, of course, those who believe the most "real" or "original" state to be the "festive" or "disordered": Bakhtin's "Lower Stratum" is a kind of fat, fertile Tiamat; Nietzsche's lurid Dionysian is more elemental—if more unendurable—than the grave, stately, and redemptive Apollinian; Girard thinks of the "festive" as an episodic return to an original state of civil war, a "Sacrificial Crisis" of nondifferentiated chaos preceding a return to differentiated harmony. Most, however, like Vitruvius or Josephus (in *Against Apion*), have a venerable tradition which they oppose to innovation, an order which they oppose to artifice.

[9] *Hermaphrodite*, p. 14.

[10] Erving Goffman, *The Presentation of Self in Everyday Life* (Garden City, N.Y., 1959), p. 55. The whole of the author's discussion entitled "Maintenance of Expressive Control" (pp. 51–58) is relevant here.

[11] Richard H. Grathoff, in his introduction to *The Structure of Social Inconsistencies* (The Hague, 1970), discusses the historical reasons for our tendency to separate play and seriousness into very distinct and contextually inconsistent fields and both to marginalize play and to see it operating only in and against an encompassing, fixed, and unchanging "reality." Some of the factors which determine our "common sense" about the identity of, and relationship between, "seriousness" and "play" are the result of peculiar ascetic formulations (perceptible already in the ancient world, but given particular emphasis from the period of the Reformation through the Industrial Revolution); for example, the definition and

For us, the dwarf in his gladiator's panoply is like the grotesque miniature in the margins of a medieval illuminated manuscript—at best a decoration or ironic commentary, at worst a perversion. The pervasiveness of the gladiator and the monster in the late Republic and early Empire signals to us the disturbance of the authentic and solemn Roman order. When the street-corner mime with his hump and pointed head drives tragedy off of the stage, when the Romans engage in mock battles in the arena instead of real warfare in the field, when Nero goes on stage as Canace, there is, for us, a loss of the "sacred"—but we live in an age presided over by gods that do not envy.

The result of this perspective has been that the "impure," the monstrous, and the obscene have been, until recently, eliminated from our discussions of Roman life, and quite literally locked away from the ruins of places like Pompeii, Herculaneum, or Ostia Antica, leaving untouched, we believe, what is essential. The temple and the triumph and the funeral would not be changed in any fundamental way, we imagine, if the divine and the dead and the victorious were not mocked and parodied by the dwarf and the fool. The sacrifice of the "sacred" Christian martyr was unaffected by, and disconsonant with, the ignominious suffering of the gladiator; to compare them is to debase our very notion of sacrifice— sacrifice, of course, to a god who does not envy.

Our propensity to discredit or minimize the absurd, the portentous, the impossible, and the extreme, makes it hard for us to analyze—or even to perceive—the functioning *and misfunctioning* of elaborate compensatory systems and to deal with the layered but liquid ambiguities of ancient Roman life. Reciprocal systems are paradoxical by their nature, however, and a subtle appreciation of the untoward and the miraculous is necessary to grasp them. This book has been, in part, an attempt to reintroduce *disjunction* into our discussions of Roman life in order to enable us to deal more effectively not only with the emotional life of the ancient Ro-

---

the actualization of life as the dutiful submission to, and performance of, a set of prescribed, oft-repeated duties. The labor of a factory worker would be the extreme case of submission, for most of his or her waking life, to severely prescribed and endlessly repeated actions from which "play" (the oscillation of that "set" of operations and operating assumptions with other disconsonant ones) is severely restricted. The world of complex and conflicting contextual fields has been relegated to a very limited part of life and tends not to include, in its oscillations, much of the context of the "workaday" world. Cf. Cox, *The Feast of Fools*, pp. 15–16, 90, 141. Lucien Febvre's *La Religion de Rabelais* (Paris, 1942), especially ch. 3, and Bakhtin's *Rabelais* are two examples of the refreshing consequences, for Renaissance studies, of the rejection of this system of classification and reveal the degree to which our "common sense" concerning the necessary gulf between "seriousness" and "play" has created a history in which such a gulf has become an a priori assumption.

mans but with the whole world of social exchanges, including honor and sacrifice.

Dynamic Equilibria

Perchance, as for him who once ruled the Teuthrantian
kingdom, the same object will both wound and cure.
(Ovid, *Tristia* 2.19–20)[12]

The Romans, unlike ourselves, were deeply accustomed to thinking in terms of homeopathic systems.[13] "Like things are cured by like" ("similia similibus curantur"). This was true not only in sorcery and medicine but also in religion and law.[14] The physics of the universe was a physics of challenge and response, the principle "what goes up must come down" operating on every level of existence from the pantry to the cosmos. The Roman sense of order—indeed, the Roman sense of "reality," of "being"—came from motion, from oscillation and the stereoscopy produced by this movement. There was no "nature" without the obscene prodigy, no *gravitas* without *levitas*, no equality without hierarchy, no difference without sameness.[15]

---

[12] "Forsitan, ut quondam Teuthrantia regna tenenti, / sic mihi res eadem vulnus opemque feret." Ovid is comparing himself to Telephus, cured by the very weapon that had wrought him harm.

[13] For a mine of instances, see McCartney, "Verbal Homeopathy and the Etymological Story," *American Journal of Philology* 48 (1927), pp. 326–43; Rankin, "Saturnalian Wordplay and Apophoreta in *Satyricon* 56," pp. 134–42. One could cite also the Roman law against cursing in the Twelve Tables: a curse ("sacer esto") is used against a curse. Cf. Martial 9.96; Ovid, *Tristia* 1.1.99–100, 1.11.11–12, 2.266–76.

[14] The very nature of the sacred (*sacer, hagios*) is, for both the Greeks and Romans, highly paradoxical and implies both "blessed" and "cursed." In Euripides' *Ion*, Creusa has two drops of the Gorgon's blood: one kills, one cures. For homeopathic medicine and ritual violence, see Girard, *Violence and the Sacred*, pp. 37–38, 43, 95; Derrida, "Plato's Pharmacy" (the *pharmakon* as poison and antidote, both sickness and cure). The Roman justice operated on the *lex talionis*, the principle of equivalent vengeance (*par vindicta*).

[15] Handelman, in "Play and Ritual," expresses his awareness of the elaborate relationships that can exist between what we can, for lack of better words, call seriousness and play or better, ritual and play: "Ritual and play complement one another in the kinds of messages they communicate to the social order. Both are consistent and integral features of the cosmological equation that conceives of society, not only as a social order, but also as a moral one" (p. 185). For a careful attempt to describe and express the elaborate interaction of these different forms of consciousness and social interaction, see Don Handelman and Bruce Kapferer, "Symbolic Types, Mediation and the Transformation of Ritual Context: Sinhalese Demons and Tewa clowns," *Semiotica* 30 (1980), pp. 41–71. For Handelman, there is a great deal of what he calls "ordinary reality" that is neither ritual nor play. I would argue that the Romans did not have a concept of "ordinary reality" which fell outside of both

**Neither law nor love can be such when they are
implacably opposed; both are then hate.**
(Victor Turner)[16]

The threat to the Roman sense of order and reality came not from disorder (or from the tides of order and disorder) but from the absence of alteration, from fixity, from the divorce (or identity) of *gravitas* and *levitas*, the serious and the ludic. Or perhaps it would be more accurate to say that both *gravitas* and *levitas*, honor and dishonor dissolve when the poles are deadlocked—when there are no more inversions. The greatest threat to social and psychological life is from the absolute, from the end or absence of mobile relations between sets of behavioral assumptions. The *agelast*, the one who *never* laughed (like the grandfather of Crassus), was as much a monster as the one who laughed at everything;[17] *religio* (scrupulousness) unrelieved could lead to as atrocious crimes as *irreligio*.[18] The Roman cosmology, like that of Anaxagoras or Heraclitus, depended on the operation of reciprocal forces, a balancing act which required endless fine-tuning and the delicate adjustment of which was always threatened by extremes of fluctuation.

The major principles of adjustment were not fixity versus movement and restraint versus transgression, but rather "play" (or "agony") within limits versus "play" outside the limits. Movement within certain boundaries allowed for return or reciprocity and should be contrasted with movement to a place from which there was no return. In this "physics," just as every cure could be the disease, every gain constituted a deprivation.[19] (Consider the mime Publilius's aphorism on greed: "What he has is as much lacking to the avaricious as what he does not have" ("tam deest avaro quod habet quam quod non habet" [694; cf. Horace, *Epistulae* 1.2]). In the rites of Rome, as in the "Drum Songs" of the Greenland Eskimos or the "Dozens" of American Blacks, every "blessing by vituperation" could end in violence. Every cure was an infection.[20]

"ritual" and "play," that rather, the reality they experienced was the mediation between these social and psychological worlds.

[16] "Metaphors of Anti-Structure in Religious Culture," p. 294. See "Passages, Margins and Poverty," pp. 268–69.

[17] Pliny, *Historia naturalis* 16.19.79.

[18] See Lucretius's "tantum religio potuit suadere malorum" (*De rerum natura* 1.101). For *religio* as the transgression as well as the taboo, see Walter Otto, "Religio und Superstitio," pp. 532–54.

[19] Ovid's "eripit interdum, modo dat medicina salutem" (*Tristia* 2.266–69).

[20] When the unnamed pantomimist, imitating the mad Ajax, went wild, it was to the glee of the "unenlightened riffraff" and the consternation of the "enlightened." When this mad Ajax dared to sit down between two consulars, some laughed and some were horrified (Lucian, *Saltatio* 83).

The vendetta was, on the one hand, the balancing mechanism. On the other hand, the escalation of its violent fluctuations threatened the system with self-destruction. The vendetta was "unleashed" by excessive envy and unrestrained desire, which in turn resulted from the failure of the compensating mechanisms that protected the honor of the gods and man.

In any system of justice based on compensation, both justice and the absence of justice, both civic society and civil war are manifestations of the same principles of reciprocity—war and injustice being simply the extreme manifestation of the operation of these forces. The unjust is as much the extension and complement of the just as it is its opposite or negation. The disordered is as much the extension and complement of the ordered as its opposite or negation.

The Romans, like the Greeks, took great care to avoid the most extreme expressions of the vendetta by a carefully articulated system of sops and deterrents. Voluntary and preemptive adjustments, even when injurious to the self, were necessary and prophylactic.[21] The more display a man made of his wealth and status, the more essential was its redistribution;[22] the more extravagant the claims to superiority, the more liberal the payments made to envy. The acute opposition in Greek thought between the impetus to excel and admonitions to live unseen is repeated in Roman thought, for the person who advanced in status, who attained glory and dignity, invited exposure to the evil eye.

The more alienated the poles—the wilder the "swerve"—the more necessary and extreme the compensation required. Civil war and autarchy, the ultimate and monstrous manifestations of this reciprocal system out of control, required extreme and monstrous measures of expiation.

The Equal Opponent

No status differentiation in ancient Rome had meaning without being linked to identity and mimesis (however mocking).[23] There was, quite literally, no triumph without equality: any victory that was too easy, too

[21] For example, the "hybris" displayed by Antony in his merrymaking and raillery had in itself its own *pharmakon*, for he allowed others to ridicule him and transgress against him ("anthubrizein") in turn, and he enjoyed being laughed at as much as he enjoyed laughing at others (Plutarch, *Antonius* 24.7).

[22] Roman *liberalitas* was a system both of display and of "paying protection."

[23] Even within a highly differentiated and competitive culture, adherence to a certain code and to a certain concept of "normal" can provide a sense of community. The fact that the same things are generally acknowledged as monstrous and portentous can provide a group with a certain unity and coherence. Likewise, a common devotion to a set of behaviors, however infinitely divisive and competitive, like the caste system described by Dumont, creates some sense of sameness: we are all members of "A," even if "A" would seem to demand the alienation and distinction of every member of that group from every other.

"dustless," or that was won over an enemy with a humble and insufficient reputation ("hostium nomen humile et non idoneum"), such as slaves or pirates, was considered unsatisfactory.[24]

For the Romans, the most typical version of the mirror, and the most effective mechanism of adjustment, was the equal opponent, the *aemulus*: the most like and the most different. Profoundly anti-Roman but also profoundly equal and like, the equal opponent was the inverted image, the *antiperistasis*, the resistance that annealed. He offered, to use Sallust's expression, the "metus hostilis," the fear of the enemy that kept the Romans "on their toes."[25] By the period of the late Republic, Hannibal had become the model foe, the archenemy who taught the Romans to be Romans.[26] It is no surprise that the man whom Pliny chooses as the bravest of Roman heroes, Sergius, great-grandfather of Catiline, won his glory (at high cost) in battle with Hannibal.[27] Hannibal's code mirrored and reversed that of the Romans, as the Trojan code mirrored and reversed that of their Achaean adversaries. Accordingly, after the battle of Lake Trasimene, Hannibal, typically, sought to bury the fallen Roman general Gaius Flaminius with military honors as a tribute to his valor, and was only prevented from doing so by his inability to find the body (Plutarch, *Fabius Maximus* 3).[28]

One admired and scorned the equal opponent. War (like many other competitive arenas) offering an occasion for a high degree of discourtesy, the equal opponent was also someone whom one mocked, and whose very similarity to oneself was a form of mockery.[29] Appian states that one of the Lydi, the harpists and pipers who, on the Etruscan model, danced in regular order in the triumph, "wearing a purple cloak reaching to the feet and golden bracelets and necklace, caused laughter by making vari-

[24] See Aulus Gellius, *Noctes Atticae* 5.6.21.

[25] Marcus Aurelius 4.1; Sallust, *Bellum Iugurthinum* 41.2 ("metus hostilis in bonis artibus civitatem retinebat"). Cf. Appian, *Punica* 9.65.

[26] For the Carthaginians as the equal opponent, see Aulus Gellius, *Noctes Atticae* 10.27; Sallust, *Bellum Iugurthinum* 41.2–5.

[27] *Historia naturalis* 7.16.104–5.

[28] Compare Caesar's admiration for Vircingetorix (*Bellum Gallicum* 7.89.2).

[29] The mockery and the emulation are often indistinguishable. (Consider the ability of the Tupinamba, the Iatmul, or the Huron to honor *and/or* mock the captured enemy.) Hannibal mimicked the Romans by having his prisoners of war fight gladiatorial exhibitions, in imitation of Roman practice. Spartacus, the rebellious slave and gladiator turned general, celebrated the obsequies of his fallen officers with funerals like those of the Roman *imperatores*, compelling his captives to fight as gladiators over the graves of his fallen commanders (Florus 2.8.9). It is precisely because Spartacus was the unequal opponent that his actions seem more grotesque than those of Hannibal. Because of his lower status his actions appear, more clearly than in the case of Hannibal, those of a *derisor*. So Plutarch's Cleopatra and Ovid's Omphale, insofar as they are the "equal opponents" of Antony and Hercules, are also their *derisores*.

ous gesticulations, as though he were dancing in triumph over the enemy" ("schematizetai poikilos es gelota os eporchoumenos tois polemiois" [*Punica* 9.66]). The war of weapons and the war of words operated in tandem. One might viciously deride an enemy whom one feared and imitated. Just so, Plutarch's Romulus mocks the defeated king of the Veians against whom he had fought long and hard (Plutarch, *Quaestiones Romanae 53 Moralia* 277c). The obscene raillery that appears on the *Perusinae glandes*, the inscribed missiles aimed by both sides against the principals of the Perusine War, should not be construed as evidence that each side merely despised the other. It does mean, however, that each side attempted to "put down" the other's heroes, however feared or respected.[30]

The paradigm of the relationship between equal opponents on the battlefield was extended to every aspect of Roman life.[31] "While most of my war of words has been with these men [the Stoics], it is not because I hold them in especial contempt, but on the contrary, it is because they seem to me to defend their views with the greatest acuteness and skill" (Cicero, *De divinatione* 2.72.150). Martial will not condescend to a contest in ridicule between himself and Ligurra because the latter is too insignificant. "At bulls Libyan lions rush; they are not hostile to butterflies" (12.61). Contending with an unequal opponent, one risked loss of status even for one's victory. Dio cannot restrain the contempt and disgust he feels for Commodus's "victories" in the arena.[32] And Mucius Scaevola, according to Livy, was deeply ashamed of being blockaded by the Etruscans, whom the Romans had so often beaten in the field (2.12).

The same dismay and confusion occurred when the opponent was too much like oneself, as occurred in civil war. In the "Saturnalia" which was

---

[30] For the sexual badinage between L. Anthony and Octavian and their troops at the time of the Perusine War, see Hallett, "Perusinae Glandes"; Kay, *Martial Book XI*, p.111. For a medieval version of agonistic invective, see Richard C. Trexler's wonderful "Correre La Terra: Collective Insults in the Late Middle Ages," *Mélanges de l'École Française de Rome* 96 (1984), pp. 845–902.

[31] The law courts, above all, were the scene of the Roman agony of the wits. Trials were, as Huizinga points out, theatrical and verbal battles employing withering and excoriating invective (*Homo Ludens*, pp. 76–88). It was a delicate game; the abuse that vented, and thus prevented, malice could also create it. The "Drum Songs" of the Greenland Eskimo that released and cured the malice between tribes could also exacerbate it and lead to violence (ibid., pp. 85–86; Elliott, *The Power of Satire*, pp. 70–74). Likewise, the "Dozens" played by American Blacks was a release and catharsis that often ended in brawls, with the "loser" in the verbal exchange being the one who resorted to violence first. See John Dollard, "The Dozens: Dialectic of Insult," *The American Imago* 1 (1939), pp. 3–25; William Elton, "Playing the Dozens," *American Speech* 25 (1950), pp. 230–33; Elliott, *The Power of Satire*, pp. 73–74). For violent ritual abuse in the ancient Roman world, see Tacitus, *Historia* 2.21.

[32] Dio 73.15–20. Dio reports with disgust Commodus's slaying of beasts that were channeled to him, led up to him, or brought to him in nets.

civil war, one's opponent could not be sufficiently distinguished from oneself. Characteristic of the civil war (as of autocracy) was the absence of the equal opponent, the simultaneously like and unlike. Now the Romans fought with their slaves or with their brothers—or even with women, such as Cleopatra.[33] The more "unworthy" the opposition, the more "unequal" the persons to be brought into conjunction, the more the *mimesis* seemed ludicrous or obscene without being comforting.

It is hard to exaggerate the importance for the Romans of the concept of the equal opponent,[34] and the sense of malaise and even sickness that accompanied the absence of this particular form of mirror. With the loss of the equal opponent, according to Sallust, fate began to be cruel and to mix everything up (*Catilina* 10.1–4).[35] Without the equal opponent Rome is "dilacerata"; the dignity of the nobles and the liberty of the people turn to license and tear apart the Republic (Sallust, *Bellum Iugurthinum* 41.2–5).[36]

"Neither could Caesar bear a superior nor Pompey an equal" (Lucan, *Bellum civile* 1.125–26).[37] Here Lucan succinctly formulates the two sources of civil war: equality and status differentiation. They are identical to the two sources of envy. Caesar could not bear to be dominated; Pompey, who possessed the superiority, could not bear to lose it. In the late Republic the competition had grown so fierce that neither equality nor status distinctions were endurable.

Civil strife deeply disturbed Roman culture on every social level. And the conclusion of the civil war was also its consummation—the "sanctifying" of extremity, of absolutism. The institution of the monarchy represented the culmination and rigidification, and therefore the collapse, of the compensatory system, the end of republican constraints on competition (*par potestas* and *potestas ad tempus*). There were no opponents equal to the emperors—except in civil war. Dio remarks snidely that the gladiators who fought Commodus in the arena (like the fencing partners

[33] For Florus (2nd century C.E.), the disgrace of fighting with Spartacus made it a kind of Saturnalia gone amok: "bellum Spartaco duce concitatum quo nomine appellem nescio; quippe cum servi militaverint, gladiatores imperaverint, illi infimae sortis homines, hi pessumae auxere ludibriis calamitatem Romanam" (2.8.1).

[34] Those things for which Polybius (13.3.7) says the ancient Romans were praised—for declaring war, for rarely resorting to ambushes, and for looking to close one-on-one—are all manifestations of the desire, imputed to the ancestors, of seeking the "fair" fight.

[35] Compare the emotions of the Rutilians upon witnessing the unequal fight between Turnus and Aeneas (*Aeneis* 12.216–18).

[36] The emperor Vitellius and his army, believing they have no *aemulus*, indulge in cruelty, lust, and rapine, and give themselves over to foreign manners (Tacitus, *Historia* 2.73).

[37] "Nec quemquam iam ferre potest Caesarve priorem/Pompeiusve parem" Cf. Florus 4.2.

of Caligula or the musical competitors of Nero) somehow always lost (Dio 73.19.2–4). In peace, the monarch had status without agony. He was too differentiated. With the inception of the monarchy there is a sense that things can no longer be compensated for; they have gone too far; there is no turning them around—no inversion. Thus, everything is topsy-turvy; everything is inverted. It is no wonder that the prince—however much a proponent or even a precondition of peace—was seen as the very image and abettor of civil war.

> "Can there really be an antidote to Caesar?"
> (Suetonius, *Caligula* 29)[38]

Honor

The sad, keen emotions of the late Republic and early Empire give one a sense of a people that had "lost their way"—a "way" whose goal was honor. Honor was, for the Romans, synonymous with "being." It was not, as it is for us, some minor and dispensable aspect of life. The Romans were bereft of honor, a loss that was unbearable. And this loss of honor befell the Romans when, to use a phrase of Petronius, they had "Jupiter by the balls."

Honor was sacredness. It was also an emotion, the paradoxical *emotion of sacredness*, a compound of vitality and fragility, vulnerability and aggressiveness.[39] The Roman emotion of honor was not diminished but heightened by the civil war and the establishment of monarchy. The emotion of honor never played so large a role in Roman life as it did in this period, with a resulting aggravation of aggression and fragility. In fact, one could say that a sense of lost honor hypostatized violence and fragility.[40] A world without honor offered only violence to the point of numbness and fragility to the point of nihilism.

Status was a limited resource which could not be given to one without being stolen from another; the acknowledgment of another's superiority constituted a diminution of one's own.[41] For the triumvirs or the emperor

---

[38] "[Caligula] trucidaturus fratrem [Tib. Gemellum] quem metu venenorum praemuniri medicamentis suspicabatur: antidotum, inquit, adversus Caesarem?"

[39] It is easy to forget how much honor is connected to sensitivity and fragility. But even for us, the person with no shame is insensitive, "thick-skinned," impervious.

[40] There is no better example of this fury and fragility than the young poet Lucan—or his rival Nero.

[41] "It was believed at one time in Italy by the common people that one who gave an insult thereby took to himself the reputation of which he deprived the other" (Pitt-Rivers, "Honour and Social Status," in *Honour and Shame*, ed. J. G. Peristiany (Chicago, 1966), p. 24). See also, in the same volume, J. K. Campbell, "Honour and the Devil," pp. 150, 157, 166.

to gain preeminence was to deprive all others. In a more salubrious situation, honor and status were wedded forever in dialectical tension. To equate status with honor, to attribute "honor" without a contest, an agony, a "game," was to have no "honor" at all, or to cause it to appear as the polar opposite of status.

Roman honor cannot be comprehended apart from notions of reciprocity. We may think of status as static, but honor was, in ancient Rome, forever open to contest, enmeshed in a chain of challenge and response. It had to be tested; it required an agony and a spectacle.[42] Therefore the ludic, the spectacular, far from being peripheral, was for the Romans a necessary precondition of the sacred, of a person's most essential being. The stage and the arena, the ludic and the spectacular, were at the heart of Roman life.[43]

Goblins and Gladiators

Mirrors embody the logic of amulets . . . the talismanic
mirror demonstrates that amulets and their targets are at once
identical and different.
(Tobin Siebers, *The Mirror of Medusa*)[44]

The popularity, the "meaningfulness," of the gladiator and the monster in ancient Rome result from the radical bipolarization of equality and difference, license and asceticism, taboo and transgression. When *gravitas* and *levitas*, excess and deprivation, equality and status distinctions cease to abut one another, a chasm opens, a No Man's Land out of which the monster and the gladiator arise. They are the mirrors of the absolute, inhabiting the territory at, and outside, the limits within which a compensatory system could be maintained, the territory in which the categories employed by Roman culture to define and create itself are threatened with dissolution. They are animated metaphors for the most disturbed aspects of Roman life, allegories of the extreme.

[42] While Rome is a culture obsessed with honor on every level, very little has been written about Roman honor. I hope to correct this omission in a book on sacrifice and honor in Roman culture (in preparation).

[43] All of the thinkers who try to operate outside the limitations imposed by the strict segregation of "play" from "seriousness" and the marginalization of the former, suffer from the inadequacy of our vocabulary. Cf. Victor Turner, "Liminal to Liminoid in Play, Flow, and Ritual," in *From Ritual to Theatre: The Human Seriousness of Play* (New York, 1982), pp. 20–60. Our words are insufficient because, for instance, "play" can be "serious" and ritualized, and because the relationship between "seriousness" and "play" can itself be considered a type of play.

[44] Tobin Siebers, *The Mirror of Medusa* (Berkeley, 1983), p. 10, cf. pp. 59–63.

2. Marble bas-relief of a gladiator and assorted figures (including an eye and a *cacans*) designed to ward off fascination (Woburn Marbles).

As the mimics and mockers of all that is admired and exalted, and as the principal scapegoats and sacrificial figures of the culture, the gladiators and the monsters were also the chief heroes in the attempt to reestablish a fluctuating, compensatory system. At all times the monster played an important role in mechanisms of reflexivity, but never as great as in the period of the late Republic and early Empire. And, in a certain sense, the *retiarii* and the *Thraces* were not unlike the talismans that protected the bodies, the baths, and the bridges of the Romans.[45] Indeed, gladiators frequently appear in apotropaic amulets. The *tintinnabulum* discussed in chapter 2 is one example. Another is the apotropaic relief on the Woburn Marble, reproduced by Elworthy, showing both a gladiator and an obscene little *cacans*, besides an eye and an assortment of typical animals.[46]

Finally, the *compositiones*, the "engagements," of the gladiators and the *derisores* were an attempt (however mocking) to reconstruct the equal opponent, a system of challenge and response that was the condition of honor. The *geloia*, the *atopa*, the ludicrous, the deformed, and in particular the grotesque mime and obscene gladiator gained increasing and central importance in this period as a furious and desperate attempt to preserve the agony and the play through which a social world was constituted, and to fight "the evil eye" that threatened the very existence of their world.

In the period of the civil wars and the onset of the monarchy, the equilibria which allowed both fierce competition and relative equality to balance each other were deeply disturbed, resulting in an enormous sense of loss of status and identity. This loss was blamed either on the monstrous absence of defining distinctions or on the alienating excess of distinctions, on the severity of limitations or on their lack. The temptation was to resolve this excruciating schism through fascination—a leap into the abyss between them. The gladiator and the goblin baited the sky hook and the lure.

[45] Like the Japanese grotesque hero Benkei, he is both mocker and protector.

[46] F. T. Elworthy, *The Evil Eye* (New York, 1989 [orig. pub. 1895]), p. 137, fig. 24. Depictions of the gladiator on tombs and in mosaics and wall-paintings may have also helped to serve these purposes—as depictions of the rape of Europa by the bull/Jupiter explicitly served to deflect the evil eye of Juno. See Jocelyn M.C. Toynbee, "Life, Death and Afterlife on Roman-Age Mosaics," in *Jenseitsvorstellungen in Antike und Christentum: Gedenkschrift für Alfred Stuiber* (Münster, 1982), pp. 210–14. Toynbee believes that gladiatorial fights represented the *agon* of life. It is not inconsistent with her thesis to suppose that they also served as apotropaia.

MODERN WORKS CITED

Abraham, Karl. "Restrictions and Transformations of Scopophilia in Psycho-Neurotics; with Remarks on Analogous Phenomena in Folk-Psychology." Orig. pub. 1913. In *Selected Papers of Karl Abraham*, trans. D. Bryan and A. Strachey. New York, 1968.

Africa, Thomas. *The Immense Majesty: A History of Rome and the Roman Empire*. New York, 1974.

Ahl, Frederick. *Lucan: An Introduction*. Ithaca, N.Y., 1976.

———. "The Art of Safe Criticism in Greece and Rome." *American Journal of Philology* 105 (1984), pp. 174–208.

André, Jean-Marie. "Die Zuschauerschaft als sozial-politischer Mikrokosmos zur Zeit des Hochprinzipats." In *Theater und Gesellschaft im Imperium Romanum*, ed. Jüngen Blänsdorf, pp. 165–73. Tübingen, 1990.

Auguet, Roland, *Cruelty and Civilization: The Roman Games*. London, 1972.

Bakhtin, Mikhail. *Rabelais and His World*. Trans. Helene Iswolsky. Cambridge, Mass., 1968.

———. "From the Prehistory of Novelistic Discourse." In *The Dialogic Imagination: Four Essays*, ed. Michael Holquist, trans. Caryl Emerson and M. Holquist. Austin, Tex., 1981.

Barasch, Frances K. *The Grotesque: A Study in Meanings*. The Hague, 1971.

Barber, C. L. *Shakespeare's Festive Comedy*. Princeton, 1959.

Bataille, Georges. *Erotism*. Trans. Mary Dalwood. San Francisco, 1986. Orig. pub. 1957.

———. *The Accursed Share*. Trans. Robert Hurley. Vol. 1. New York, 1988. Orig. pub. 1967.

———. "Sacrificial Mutilation and the Severed Ear of Vincent Van Gogh." In *Visions of Excess*, trans. Allan Stoekl, Minneapolis, 1985.

Becker, W. A. *Gallus: Roman Scenes of the Time of Augustus*. New York, 1903.

Benedict, Ruth. *The Chrysanthemum and the Sword*. New York, 1946.

Benjamin, Jessica. "Master and Slave: The Fantasy of Erotic Domination." In *The Powers of Desire*, ed. Ann Snitow et al., pp. 280–99. New York, 1983.

Bernheimer, Richard. *Wild Men in the Middle Ages: A Study of Art, Sentiment, and Demonology*. Cambridge, Mass., 1952.

Bernstein, Michael André. "When the Carnival Turns Bitter: Preliminary Reflections Upon the Abject Hero." *Critical Inquiry* 10 (1983), pp. 283–305.

Bieber, Margarete. "Mima Saltatricula." *American Journal of Archaeology* 43 (1939), pp. 640–44.

———. *The History of the Greek and Roman Theater*. Princeton, 1961.

Boissier, Gaston. "Mimus," in Daremberg-Saglio, *Dictionnaire des antiquités grecques et romaines*, vol. 3.2, pp. 1903–7.

Bollinger, Traugott. *Theatralis Licentia: Die Publikumsdemonstrationen an den öffentlichen Spielen im Rom der früheren Kaiserzeit und ihre Bedeutung im politischen Leben*. Winterthur, 1969.

Bonelli, Guido. "Autenticità o retorica nella tragedia di Seneca." *Latomus* 39 (1980), pp. 612–38.

Bonfante, Larissa. "Nudity as a Costume in Classical Art." *American Journal of Archaeology* 93 (1989), pp. 543–70.

Boon, James. "Folly, Bali and Anthropology; or, Satire Across Cultures." In *Text, Play and Story: The Construction and Reconstruction of Self and Society*, ed. Stuart Plattner, and Edward M. Bruner, pp. 163–64. Washington, D.C., 1984.

Boren, Henry. *Roman Society*. Chapel Hill, N.C., 1977.

Böttiger, C. A. "Über das Wort Maske und über die Abbildung der Masken auf alten Gemmen." In *Kleine Schriften*, vol. 3, pp. 402–13. Dresden, 1838.

Bouché-Leclerq, Auguste. "Devotio," in Daremberg-Saglio, *Dictionnaire des antiquités grecques et romaines*, vol. 2.1, pp. 113–19.

Bremmer, Jan. "Scapegoat Rituals in Ancient Greece." *Harvard Studies in Classical Philology* 87 (1983), pp. 299–320.

Brisset, J. *Les Idées politiques de Lucain*. Paris, 1964.

Brun, Jean. "Le Prestige du monstre." In *Le Mythe de la peine*, ed. Enrico Castelli, pp. 301–22. Paris, 1967.

Büchner, Karl. *P. Cornelius Tacitus: Die historische Versuche*. Stuttgart, 1955.

Burkert, Walter. *Homo Necans*. Trans. Peter Bing. Berkeley, 1983. Orig. pub. 1972.

———. *Structure and History in Greek Mythology and Ritual*. Berkeley, 1979.

Caillois, Roger. *L'Homme et le sacré*. Paris, 1950.

———. *Man, Play and Games*. Trans. Meyer Barash. New York, 1976. Orig. pub. 1958.

Callahan, Steven. *Adrift: Seventy-Six Days Lost at Sea*. Boston, 1986.

Campbell, J. K. "Honour and the Devil." In *Honour and Shame: The Values of Mediterranean Society*, ed. J. G. Peristiany, pp. 141–70. Chicago, 1966.

Camus, Albert. *The Rebel: An Essay on Man in Revolt*. New York, 1956. Orig. pub. 1951.

———. *Caligula*. In *Théatre, récits, novelles*. Paris, 1962.

Cantarella, Eva. *Pandora's Daughters*. Baltimore, 1987.

Carcopino, Jerome. *Daily Life in Ancient Rome*. New Haven, 1940.

Céard, Jean. *La Nature et les prodiges*. Geneva, 1977.

Charles-Picard, Gilbert. *Augustus and Nero*. Trans. Len Ortzen. New York, 1968.

Cioran, E. M. *A Short History of Decay*. Trans. Richard Howard. New York, 1975.

———. *Drawn and Quartered*. Trans. Richard Howard. New York, 1983.

Clavel-Lévêque, Monique. *L'Empire en jeux*. Paris, 1984.

———. "L'Espace des jeux à Rome: Champs de lutte et lieux d'obtention du consentement." In *Mélanges offerts à la mémoire de Roland Fietier*. Paris, 1984.

Corbett, Philip. *The Scurra*. Edinburgh, 1986.

Coss, G. "Reflections on the Evil Eye." In *The Evil Eye: A Folklore Casebook*, ed. Alan Dundes, pp. 181–91. New York, 1981. Rpt. from *Human Behavior* 3 (1974), pp. 16–21.

Cox, Harvey. *The Feast of Fools*. Cambridge, Mass., 1969.

Cumont, Franz. "Les Actes de S. Dasius." *Analecta Bollandiana* 16 (1897), pp. 5–16.

Cuq, Edouard. "Sacramentum," in Daremberg-Saglio, *Dictionnaire des antiquités grecques et romaines*, vol. 4.2, pp. 951–55.

Dalmeyda, G. "Mimus," in Daremberg-Saglio, *Dictionnaire des antiquités grecques et romaines*, vol. 3.2, pp. 1899–1903.

Daniels, Marvin, "The Dynamics of Morbid Envy in the Etiology and Treatment of Chronic Learning Disabilities." *Psychoanalytic Review* 51 (1964), pp. 45–57.

D'Arms, John. "Control, Companionship, and *Clientela*: Some Social Functions of the Roman Communal Meal." *Échos du Monde Classique* 28 (1984), pp. 327–48.

———. "The Roman *Convivium* and the Idea of Equality." Forthcoming.

David, Jean-Michel. "Les Orateurs des municipes à Rome: Intégration, réticences et snobismes." In *Les 'Bourgeoisies' municipales italiennes aux IIᵉ et Iᵉʳ siècles av. J.-C.*, pp. 309–23. Paris/Naples, 1983.

Davis, Natalie. "Women on Top." In *Society and Culture in Early Modern Europe*, pp. 124–51. Stanford, 1965.

De Ghellinck, J. *Pour l'histoire du mot "Sacramentum."* Louvains, 1924.

Delcourt, Marie. *Hermaphrodite: Myths and Rites of the Bisexual Figure in Classical Antiquity*. Trans. Jennifer Nicholson. London, 1961. Orig. pub. 1956.

Derrida, Jacques. *Dissemination*. Trans. Barbara Johnson. Chicago, 1981. Orig. pub. 1972.

Descombes, Vincent. *Le Même et l'autre*. Paris, 1979.

Deubner, Ludwig. "Die Devotion der Decier." *Archiv für Religionswissenschaft* 8 (1904–5), pp. 66–88.

Dickison, Sheila. "Claudius: *Saturnalicius Princeps*." *Latomus* 36 (1977), pp. 634–47.

Dieterich, Albrecht. *Pulcinella: Pompejanische Wandbilder und römische Satyrspiele*. Leipzig, 1897.

Disalvo, Marilyn. "The Myth of Narcissus." *Semiotica* 30 (1980), pp. 15–25.

Dollard, John. "The Dozens: Dialectic of Insult." *The American Imago* 1 (1939), pp. 3–25.

Douglas, Mary. "The Social Control of Cognition: Some Factors in Joke Perception." *Man* 3 (1965), pp. 361–75.

———. *Purity and Danger*. London, 1966.

Dumézil, Georges. "*Maiestas et Gravitas*: De quelques différences entre les Romains et les Austronésiens." *Revue de Philologie*, 3rd ser., 25 (1951), pp. 7–28.

Dumont, Louis. *Homo Hierarchicus*. Chicago, 1979. Orig. pub. 1960.

Dupont, Florence. *L'Acteur roi: Le théâtre à Rome*. Paris, 1985.

Durkheim, Émile. *Suicide*. Trans. John A. Spauling and George Simpson. New York, 1951.

Eliade, Mircea. *The Two and the One*. Trans. J. M. Cohen. Chicago, 1965.

Elliott, Robert C. *The Power of Satire: Magic, Ritual, Art*. Princeton, 1960.

Elton, William. "Playing the Dozens." *American Speech* 25 (1950), pp. 230–33.

Elworthy, F. T. "Evil Eye," in *Hastings Encyclopaedia of Religion and Ethics*, vol. 5, pp. 608–15.

———. *The Evil Eye*. New York, 1989. Orig. pub. 1895.

Epstein, David. *Personal Enmity in Roman Politics 218–43 B.C.*, London, 1989.

Evans-Pritchard, E. E. *Nuer Religion*. Oxford, 1956.

Fantham, Elaine. "Mime: the Missing Link in Roman Literary History." *Classical World* 82 (1989), pp. 153–63.

Farber, Leslie. "Faces of Envy." *Review of Existential Psychology and Psychiatry* 1 (1961), pp. 131–40.

Febvre, Lucien. *La Religion de Rabelais*. Paris, 1942.

Fenichel, Otto. "The Scopophilic Instinct and Identification." *International Journal of Psychoanalysis* 18 (1937), pp. 6–34.

Ferenczi, Sandor. "On Eye Symbolism." Orig. pub. 1913. In *Sex in Psycho-analysis*, pp. 228–33. New York, 1956.

———. "On the Symbolism of the Head of Medusa." Orig. pub. 1923. In *Further Contributions to the Theory and Technique of Psychoanalysis*, ed. Rickman, trans. J. I. Suttie, p. 360. London, 1926.

Festinger, Leon. "A Theory of Social Comparison Processes." *Human Relations* 7 (1954), pp. 114–40.

Findlay, John. *Philosophy of Hegel*. New York, 1958.

Flam, Léopold. "Le Sacré et la désacralisation dans la pensée contemporaine." In *Le Pouvoir et le sacré*, pp. 179–86. Brussels, 1962.

Foster, George M. "The Anatomy of Envy: A Study in Symbolic Behavior." *Current Anthropology* 13 (1972), pp. 165–202.

Foucault, Michel. *Madness and Civilization*. Trans. Richard Howard. New York, 1973. Orig. pub. 1965.

———. *Language, Counter-Memory, Practice*. Ed. and trans. Donald F. Bouchard. Ithaca, N.Y., 1977.

———. *Discipline and Punish: The Birth of the Prison*. Trans. Alan Sheridan. New York, 1979.

Fowler, Barbara Hughes, *The Hellenistic Aesthetic*. Madison, Wis., 1989.

Fowler, W. Warde. *The Roman Festivals of the Period of the Republic*. London, 1932. Orig. pub. 1899.

Frazer, James. *The Golden Bough*. 3rd ed. New York, 1935.

Frend, W.H.C. *Martyrdom and Persecution in the Early Church*. New York, 1967.

Freud, Sigmund. *Three Essays on the Theory of Sexuality*. Trans. James Strachey. New York, 1975. Orig. pub. 1905.

———. "On the Universal Tendency to Debasement in the Sphere of Love." Orig. pub. 1912. In *The Standard Edition of the Complete Psychological Works of Sigmund Freud*. Trans. James Strachey, vol. 11, pp. 187–88. London, 1957.

———. *Totem and Taboo*. Trans. A. A. Brill. New York, 1912.

———. "Medusa's Head." Orig. pub. 1922. In *Collected Papers*, ed. James Strachey, vol. 5, pp. 105–6. New York, 1959.

Friedländer, Ludwig. *Darstellung aus der Sittengeschichte Roms*. 4 vols. 10th ed. Leipzig, 1964.

Friedman, Myra. *Buried Alive*. New York, 1973.

Frye, Northrup. *Anatomy of Criticism*. Princeton, 1957.

Fugier, Huguette. *Recherches sur l'expression du sacré dans la langue latine*. Paris, 1963.

Geertz, Clifford. "Religion as a Cultural System." In *The Interpretation of Cultures*, pp. 78–125. New York, 1973.

Gilman, Richard. *Decadence: The Strange Life of an Epithet*. New York, 1975.

Gilmore, David D. *Aggression and Community: Paradoxes of Andalusian Culture*. New Haven, 1987.

Girard, René. *Violence and the Sacred*. Trans. Patrick Gregory. Baltimore, 1977. Orig. pub. 1972.

Gluckman, Max. *Order and Rebellion in Tribal Africa*. New York, 1963.

Goethe, Johann Wolfgang von. *The Sorrows of Young Werther*. Trans. Elizabeth Mayer and Louise Bogan. New York, 1971.

Goffman, Erving. *The Presentation of Self in Everyday Life*. Garden City, N.Y., 1959.

———. *Stigma: Notes on the Management of Spoiled Identity*. New York, 1963.

———. *Interaction Ritual: Essays on Face-to-Face Behavior*, New York, 1967.

Goldman, Albert. *Elvis*. New York, 1981.

Goldman, Hetty. "Two Terracotta Figurines from Tarsus." *American Journal of Archaeology* 47 (1943), pp. 22–34.

Gombrich, Ernst H. *The Sense of Order: A Study in the Psychology of Decorative Art*. Ithaca, N.Y., 1984.

Goodman, Nelson. *Ways of Worldmaking*. Indianapolis, 1978.

Goody, Jack. *Cooking, Cuisine, and Class*. Cambridge, 1982.

Graindor, Paul, *Terres cuites de l'Égypte gréco-romaine*. Antwerp, 1939.

Grant, Mary. *The Ancient Rhetorical Theories of the Laughable*. University of Wisconsin Studies in Language and Literature no. 4, pp. 119–124. Madison, Wis., 1924.

Grant, Michael. *Gladiators*. New York, 1967.

Grathoff, Richard H. *The Structure of Social Inconsistencies*. The Hague, 1970.

Griffin, Jasper. "Propertius and Anthony." *Journal of Roman Studies* 67 (1977), pp. 17–26.

Griffin, Miriam. *Seneca: A Philosopher in Politics*. Oxford, 1976.

Grueber, H. A. *Coins of the Roman Republic in the British Museum*. 3 vols. London, 1910.

Guarino, Antonio. "I gladiatores e l'*auctoramentum*." *Labeo* 29 (1983), pp. 7–28.

Hackl, Anton. *Die spes als negativer Charakterisierungsbegriff in Caesars Bellum Civile, Ciceros Catilinariae, Lucans Pharsalia*. Diss., Innsbruck, 1962.

Hallett, Judith. "*Perusinae Glandes* and the Changing Image of Augustus." *American Journal of Ancient History* 2 (1977), pp. 151–71.

Hammerton-Kelly, Robert, ed. *Violent Origins*. Stanford, 1987.

Handelman, Don. "Play and Ritual: Complementary Frames of Metacommunication." In *It's A Funny Thing, Humour*, ed. Antony J. Chapman and Hugh C. Foot, pp. 185–92. Oxford, 1977.

Handelman, Don and Bruce Kapferer. "Symbolic Types, Mediation and the Transformation of Ritual Context: Sinhalese Demons and Tewa Clowns." *Semiotica* 30 (1980), pp. 41–71.

Harpham, Geoffrey Galt. *On the Grotesque: Strategies of Contradiction in Art and Literature*. Princeton, 1982.

Harris, William. *War and Imperialism in Republican Rome*. Oxford, 1979.

Henry, Jules. *Jungle People*. New York, 1964.

Herculine Barbin: Being the Recently Discovered Memoirs of a Nineteenth-Century Hermaphodite. Trans. Richard McDougall. New York, 1980.

Hirschfeld, Otto. "Augustus und sein Mimus vitae." *Wiener Studien* 6 (1884), pp. 116–19.

Hopkins, Jerry and Daniel Sugerman. *No One Here Gets Out Alive*. New York, 1980.

Hopkins, Keith. "Elite Mobility in the Roman Empire." *Past and Present* 32 (1965), pp. 12–26.

———. "Structural Differentiation in Rome (200–31 B.C.E.)." In *History and Social Anthropology*, ed. I. M. Lewis, pp. 63–79. London, 1968.

———. "Murderous Games." In *Death and Renewal: Sociological Studies in Roman History*, vol. 2, pp. 1–30. Cambridge, 1983.

Hopkins, Keith and Graham Burton. "Ambition and Withdrawal: The Senatorial Aristocracy Under the Emperor." In *Death and Renewal: Sociological Studies in Roman History*, vol. 2, pp. 120–23. Cambridge, 1983.

Howell, Michael and Peter Ford. *The True History of the Elephant Man*. Middlesex, 1980.

Huizinga, Johan. *Homo Ludens: A Study of the Play-Element in Culture*. Boston, 1950. Orig. pub. 1938.

Huxley, Francis. *Affable Savages*. New York, 1957.

Itard, Jean-Marc-Gaspard. *The Wild Boy of Aveyron*. Trans. G. Humphrey and M. Humphrey. New York, 1932.

Jahn, Otto. "Über den Aberglauben des bösen Blicks bei den Alten." *Berichte der sächsischen Gesellschaft* 17 (1855), pp. 28–110.

Jal, Paul. *La Guerre civile à Rome: Étude littéraire et morale*. Paris, 1963.

Jankélévitch, Vladimir. *L'Austérité et la vie morale*. Paris, 1956.

Janssen, L. F. "Some Unexplored Aspects of the *Devotio Deciana*." *Mnemosyne* 4 [34] (1981), pp. 357–81.

Jerome, Thomas Spencer. *Aspects of the Study of Roman History*. New York, 1962. Orig. pub. 1923.

Johns, Catherine. *Sex or Symbol: Erotic Images of Greece and Rome*. Austin, Tex., 1982.

Jörs, Paul. "Die Ehegesetze des Augustus." In *Festschrift Theodor Mommsen*, ed. Jörs, E. Schwartz et al., pp. 1–65. Marburg, 1893.

Kay, N. M. *Martial Book XI; A Commentary*. London, 1985.

Kayser, Wolgang. *The Grotesque in Art and Literature*. Trans., Ulrich Weisstein. New York, 1981.

Keitel, Elizabeth. "Principate and Civil Wars in the *Annals* of Tacitus." *American Journal of Philology* 105 (1984), pp. 306–25.

Keith, A. B. *The Sanskrit Drama*. London, 1924.

Kermode, Frank. *The Sense of an Ending*. Oxford, 1966.

Khrushchev, Nikita. *Khrushchev Remembers*. Trans. Strobe Talbott. Boston, 1970.

Kiefer, Otto. *Sexual Life in Ancient Rome*. London, 1934.

Kierkegaard, Soren. *The Sickness Unto Death*. Trans. Walter Lowrie. Princeton, 1941.

Klein, Melanie. *Gratitude and Envy*. New York, 1957.

Klingmüller. "Sacramentum." In Pauly-Wissowa, *Paulys Realencyclopädie der classischen Altertumswissenschaft*, vol. 1A.2, cols. 1667–74.

Knoche, Ulrich. *Magnitudo Animi*. Suppl. vol. 27.3 of *Philologus*. Leipzig, 1935.

Kolakowski, Leszak. "The Priest and the Jester." *Dissent* 9 (1962), pp. 215–35.

Kuhnert, F. "Fascinum." In Pauly-Wissowa, *Paulys Realencyclopädie der classischen Altertumswissenschaft*, vol. 6.2, cols. 2009–14.

Labhardt, André. "*Curiositas*: Notes sur l'histoire d'un mot et d'une notion." *Museum Helveticum* 17 (1960), pp. 206–24.

Lafaye, Georges. "Fascinum." In Daremberg-Saglio, *Dictionnaire des antiquités grecques et romaines*, vol. 2.2, pp. 983–87.

———. "Gladiator." In Daremberg-Saglio, *Dictionnaire des antiquités grecques et romaines*, vol. 2, cols. 1563ff.

Laing, R. D. *The Divided Self*. Harmondsworth, Eng., 1965.

Langdon, S. "The Babylonian and Persian Secaea." *Journal of the Royal Asiatic Society of Great Britain and Ireland* (1924), pp. 65–72.

Lane, Harlan. *The Wild Boy of Aveyron*. Cambridge, Mass., 1979.

Last, H. A. "The Social Policy of Augustus." *Cambridge Ancient History*, vol. 10, pp. 425–64. Cambridge, 1952.

Latte, Kurt. *Römische Religionsgeschichte*. Munich, 1960.

Layamon's Brut. Trans. Donald G. Bzdyl. Binghamton, N.Y., 1989.

Lefèvre, Eckard. "Die Bedeutung des Paradoxen in der römischen Literatur der frühen Kaiserzeit." *Poetica* 3 (1970), pp. 59–82.

Lieris, Michael. *Manhood*. Trans. Richard Howard. New York, 1963.

Leeman, A. D. "Das Todeserlebnis in Denken Senecas." *Gymnasium* 78 (1971), pp. 322–33.

Le Roy Ladurie, Emmanuel. *Carnival in Romans*. Trans. Mary Feeney. New York, 1979.

Levick, Barbara. "The *Senatus Consultum* from Larinum." *Journal of Roman Studies* 73 (1983), pp. 98–99.

Lintott, A. W. *Violence in Republican Rome*. Oxford, 1968.

Lobeck, Christian August. *Aglaophamus*. Darmstadt, 1968. Orig. pub. 1829.

Lowenthal, David. *The Past is a Foreign Country*. Cambridge, 1985.

Lutsch, Otto. "Die Urbanitas nach Cicero." In *Festgabe für Wilhelm Crecelius*, pp. 80–95. Elberfeld, 1881.

McCartney, Eugene S. "Verbal Homeopathy and the Etymological Story." *American Journal of Philology* 48 (1927), pp. 326–43.

———. "Praise and Dispraise in Folklore." In *The Evil Eye: A Folklore Case-*

book, ed. Alan Dundes, pp. 18–19. New York, 1981. Rpt. from *Papers of the Michigan Academy of Science, Arts and Letters* 28 (1943), pp. 567–93.

Mau, August and Francis Kelsey. *Pompeii: Its Life and Art.* New York, 1902.

Mauss, Marcel. *The Gift: Forms and Functions of Exchange in Archaic Societies.* Trans. Ian Cunnison. New York, 1967. Orig. pub. 1925.

Mayor, John E. B. *Thirteen Satires of Juvenal.* London, 1872.

Merquior, J. G. *Foucault.* Berkeley, 1985.

Messinger, Sheldon L., Harold Sampson and Robert Towne. "Life as Theater: Some Notes on the Dramaturgic Approach to Social Reality." *Sociometry* 25 (1962), pp. 98–110.

Michaelis, A. "Serapis Standing on a Xanthian Marble in the British Museum." *Journal of Hellenic Studies* 6 (1885), pp. 287–318.

Millar, Fergus. *The Emperor in the Roman World.* London, 1977.

Miller, Dean A. "Royauté et ambiguïté sexuelle." *Annales: Économies, Sociétés, Civilisations* 26 (1971), pp. 639–52.

Moeran, Brian. "The Beauty of Violence: *Jidaigeki, Yakuza* and 'Eroduction' Films in Japanese Cinema." In *The Anthropology of Violence*, ed. David Riches, pp. 103–17. Oxford, 1986.

Mommsen, Theodor. *History of Rome.* Trans. William Dickson. 4 vols. New York, 1886.

———. *Römisches Strafrecht.* Leipzig, 1899.

Montherlant, Henry de. "Aux fontaines du désir; Syncrétisme at alternance." In *Essais*, pp. 237–45. Paris, 1963.

Murray, Gilbert. *The Rise of Greek Epic.* Oxford, 1907.

Navarre, O. "Nanus." In Daremberg-Saglio, *Dictionnaire des antiquités grecques et romaines*, vol. 4.1, p.1.

Nicoll, Allardyce. *Masks, Mimes, and Miracles.* New York, 1963.

Nietzsche, Friedrich. *The Genealogy of Morals.* Trans. Francis Golffing. New York, 1956. Orig. pub. 1887.

Nisbet, Robert. *Prejudices: A Philosophical Dictionary.* Cambridge, Mass., 1982.

Norden, Edward. *Die Antike Kunstprosa.* 2 vols. Darmstadt, 1958.

Nutting, H. C. "*Oculos Effodere.*" *Classical Philology* 17 (1922), pp. 313–18.

Oakley, S. P. "Single Combat in the Roman Republic." *Classical Quarterly* 35 (1985), pp. 392–410.

Otto, Rudolf. *The Idea of the Holy.* Trans. John W. Harvey. New York, 1958. Orig. pub. 1917.

Otto, Walter. "*Religio* und *Superstitio.*" *Archiv für Religionswissenschaft* 12 (1909), pp. 532–54; 14 (1911), pp. 406–22.

Paoli, Ugo. *Rome: Its People, Life, and Customs.* New York, 1958.

Parmentier, L. and F. Cumont. "Le Roi des Saturnales." *Revue de Philologie, de Littérature et d'Histoire Anciennes* 21 (1897), pp. 142–53.

Peacock, James. *Rites of Modernization*, Chicago, 1968.

Peristiany, J. G. "Honour and Shame in a Cypriot Highland Village." In *Honour and Shame: The Values of Mediterranean Society*, ed. J. G. Peristiany, pp. 173–90. Chicago, 1966.

Pitt-Rivers, Julian. "Honour and Social Status." In *Honour and Shame: The Values of Mediterranean Society*, ed. J. G. Peristiany, pp. 21–77. Chicago, 1966.

Plass, Paul. *Wit and the Writing of History: The Rhetoric of Historiography in Imperial Rome*. Madison, Wis., 1988.

Pfligersdorffer, Georg. "Lucan als Dichter des geistigen Widerstandes." *Hermes* 87 (1959), pp. 344–77.

Pobee, John S. *Persecution and Martyrdom in the Theology of Paul*. Sheffield, 1985.

Praz, Mario. *The Romantic Agony*. New York, 1956.

Préaux, Jean-G. "Manducus." In *Hommages à Albert Grenier*, vol. 3 (= *Collection Latomus*, vol. 58), pp. 1282–91. Brussels, 1962.

Preisigke, Friedrich. *Sammelbuch griechischer Urkunden aus Ägypten*. Strassburg, 1915.

Radcliffe-Brown, A. R. "A Further Note on Joking Relationships." *Africa* 19 (1949), pp. 133–40.

———. *Structure and Function in Primitive Society*. New York, 1952.

Raditsa, Leo Ferrero. "Augustus' Legislation Concerning Marriage, Procreation, Love Affairs and Adultery." *Aufstieg und Niedergang der römischen Welt*, vol. 2.13, pp. 278–339. Berlin, 1980.

Ramage, Edwin S. *Urbanitas: Ancient Sophistication and Refinement*. Norman, Okla., 1973.

Rambaud, M. "L'Apologie de Pompée par Lucain." *Revue des Études Latines* 33 (1955), pp. 258–96.

Rankin, H. D. "Saturnalian Wordplay and Apophoreta in *Satyricon* 56." *Classica et Mediaevalia* 23 (1962), pp. 134–42.

Rattray, R. S. *Ashanti Law and Constitution*. New York, 1969. Orig. pub. 1911.

———. *Ashanti*. Oxford, 1923.

Rawson, Elizabeth. "*Discrimina Ordinum*: The *Lex Julia Theatralis*." *Papers of the British School at Rome* 55 (1987), pp. 83–114.

Regenbogen, Otto von. "Schmerz und Tod in den Tragödien Senecas." In *Vorträge der Bibliothek Warburg zur Geschichte des Dramas*, pp. 167–218. Leipzig, 1930.

Reich, Hermann. *Der Mimus: Ein litterar-entwicklungsgeschichtlicher Versuch*. Berlin, 1903.

———. "Der König mit der Dornenkrone." *Neue Jahrbücher für das klassische Altertum* (1904), pp. 705–33.

———. "Der Mann mit dem Eselskopf." *Shakespeare-Jahrbuch* 40 (1904), pp. 108–28.

Reinhold, Meyer. "Usurpation of Status and Status Symbols in the Roman Empire." *Historia* 20 (1971), pp. 275–30.

Reynolds, R. W. "Criticism of Individuals in Roman Popular Comedy." *Classical Quarterly* 37 (1943), pp. 37–45.

Richlin, Amy. *The Garden of Priapus: Sexuality and Aggression in Roman Humor*. New Haven, 1983.

Richter, Gisela. "Grotesques and the Mime." *American Journal of Archaeology*. 17 (1913), pp. 149–56.

Ricoeur, Paul. *The Symbolism of Evil*. Trans. Emerson Buchanan. Boston, 1967.

Robert, Jean-Noel. *Les Plaisirs à Rome*. Paris, 1986.

Robert, Louis. *Les Gladiateurs dans l'Orient grec*. Amsterdam, 1940.

Rorty, Richard. "The World Well Lost." *Journal of Philosophy* 69 (1972), pp. 649–65.

Roscher, W. H. *Ausführliches Lexicon der griechischen und römischen Mythologie*. Leipzig, 1884–90.

Rothman, G. *The Riddle of Cruelty*. New York, 1971.

Rousseau, Jean-Jacques. *The Confessions*. Trans. J. M. Cohen. Baltimore, 1954.

Rousselle, Aline. *Porneia: De la maîtrise du corps à la privation sensorielle*. Paris, 1983.

Rowell, Henry T. "The Gladiator Petraites and the Date of the *Satyricon*." *Transactions of the American Philological Association* 89 (1958), pp. 14–24.

Runciman, W. G. "The Sociologist and the Historian." *Journal of Roman Studies* 76 (1980), pp. 259–65.

Rutz, Werner. "*Amor Mortis* bei Lucan." *Hermes* 88 (1960), pp. 462–75.

Sabbatini Tumolesi, Patrizia. *Gladiatorum Paria*. Rome, 1980.

Sabini, J. and M. Silver. "Envy." In *The Social Construction of Emotions*, ed. Rom Harré, pp. 167–83. Oxford, 1986.

Sacks, Oliver. *Awakenings*. New York, 1973.

Saglio, E. "Deliciae." In Daremberg-Saglio, *Dictionnaire des antiquités grecques et romaines*, vol. 2.1, pp. 60–61.

Sahagún, Bernardino de. *Historia general de las cosas de Nueva España*. Mexico City, 1989.

Saint-Denis, E. de. "Evolution sémantique de *urbanus-urbanitas*." *Latomus* 3 (1939), pp. 5–25.

Saller, Richard P. *Personal Patronage Under the Early Empire*. Cambridge, 1982.

―――. "Patronage and Friendship in Early Imperial Rome: Drawing the Distinction." In *Patronage in Ancient Society*, ed. Andrew Wallace-Hadrill, pp. 49–62. London/New York, 1989.

Salomonson, J. W. *Voluptatem spectandi non perdat sed mutet*. Amsterdam, 1979.

Scamuzzi, Ugo. "Studio sulla *Lex Roscia Theatralis*." *Rivista di Studi Classici* 17 (1969), pp. 133–65, 259–319; 18 (1970), pp. 5–57, 374–447.

Scheler, Max. *Ressentiment*. Trans. William W. Holdheim. New York, 1961. Orig. pub. 1910.

Schneider, K. "Gladiatores." In Pauly-Wissowa, *Paulys Realencyclopädie der klassischen Altertumswissenschaft*, Suppl. vol. 3 (1918), cols. 760–84.

Schoeck, Helmut. *Envy*. Trans. Michael Glenny and Betty Ross. New York, 1966.

Schunck, Peter. *Römisches Sterben*. Diss., Heidelberg, 1955.

Schutz, Alfred. "Equality and the Meaning Structure of the Social World." In *Collected Papers*, vol. 2, pp. 226–73. The Hague, 1964.

Schwenn, Friedrich. *Die Menschenopfer bei den Griechen und Römern*. Giessen, 1915.

Scott, George Ryley. *Phallic Worship*. London, 1966. Orig. n.d.

Scullard, H. H. *Festivals and Ceremonies of the Roman Republic*. Ithaca, N.Y., 1981.

Seel, Otto. *Römertum und Latinität*. Stuttgart, 1964.

Seligmann, S. *Der böse Blick und Verwandtes*. 2 vols. Berlin, 1910.

Shattuck, Roger. *The Forbidden Experiment*. New York, 1980.

Sherwin-White, A. N. *The Letters of Pliny: A Historical and Social Commentary*. Oxford, 1966.

Siebers, Tobin. *The Mirror of Medusa*. Berkeley, 1983.

Smith, R. Spencer. "Voyeurism: A Review of the Literature." *Archives of Sexual Behavior 5* (1976), pp. 585–608.

Srinivas, M. N. *Religion and Society Among the Coorgs of South India*. Oxford, 1952.

Stekel, Wilhelm. *Sadism and Masochism: The Psychology of Hatred and Cruelty*. 2 vols., New York, 1929.

Straw, Carole. *Gregory the Great: Perfection in Imperfection*. Berkeley, 1988.

Sullivan, Harry Stack. "Envy and Jealousy as Precipitating Factors in the Major Mental Disorders." In *Clinical Studies in Psychiatry*, ed. H. S. Swick et al., pp. 128–44. New York, 1956.

Sullivan, J. P. *The Satyricon of Petronius: A Literary Study*. London, 1968.

———. *Literature and Politics in the Age of Nero*. Ithaca, N.Y., 1985.

Swiderski, Richard. "Italian Americans. From Folk to Popular: Plastic Evil Eye Charms." In *The Evil Eye*, ed. Clarence Maloney, pp. 28–41. New York, 1976.

Syme, Ronald. *The Roman Revolution*. Oxford, 1939.

———. *Tacitus*. 2 vols., Oxford, 1958.

Thomson, Philip. *The Grotesque*. London, 1972.

Tourney, Garfield and Dean J. Plazak. "Evil Eye in Myth and Schizophrenia." *Psychiatric Quarterly* 28 (1954), pp. 478–95.

Toynbee, Jocelyn M.C. "Life, Death and Afterlife on Roman-Age Mosaics." In *Jenseitsvorstellungen in Antike und Christentum: Gedenkschrift für Alfred Stuiber*, pp. 210–14. Münster, 1982.

Trexler, Richard C. "Correre La Terra: Collective Insults in the Late Middle Ages." *Mélanges de l'École Française de Rome* 96 (1984), pp. 845–902.

Turnbull, Percival. "The Phallus in the Art of Roman Britain." *Bulletin of the Institute of Archaeology* 15 (1968), pp. 199–206.

Turner, Victor. *The Ritual Process. Structure and Anti-Structure*. Ithaca, N.Y., 1969.

———. *Dramas, Fields, and Metaphors*. Ithaca, N.Y., 1974.

———. *From Ritual to Theatre: The Human Seriousness of Play*. New York, 1982.

Ullman, B. L. "*Satura* and Satire." *Classical Philology* 8 (1913), pp. 172–94.

Versnel, H. S. *Triumphus: An Inquiry into the Origin, Development and Meaning of the Roman Triumph*. Leiden, 1970.

———. "Two Types of Roman Devotio." *Mnemosyne* 29 (1976), pp. 365–410.

Veyne, Paul. *Le Pain et le cirque*. Paris, 1976.

Ville, Georges. *La Gladiature en Occident des origines à la mort de Domitien*. Rome, 1981.

Wace, A.J.B. "Grotesques and the Evil Eye." *Annual of the British School of Athens* 10 (1903/4), pp. 103–14.

Wagenvoort, H. *Roman Dynamism*. Oxford, 1947.

Wallace, Anthony F. C. *The Death and Rebirth of the Seneca*. New York, 1972.

Weaver, P.R.C. "Social Mobility in the Early Roman Empire: The Evidence of the Imperial Freedmen and Slaves." *Past and Present* 37 (1967), pp. 3–20.

Weber, W. *Die aegyptish-griechischen Terrakotten*. Berlin, 1914.

Webster, Paula. "The Forbidden: Eroticism and Taboo." In *Pleasure and Danger*, ed. Carole S. Vance, pp. 385–98. Boston, 1984.

Welsford, Enid. *The Fool: His Social and Literary History*. New York, 1961. Orig. pub. 1935.

Wilamowitz-Moellendorff, Ulrich von. "*Res Gestae Divi Augusti*." *Hermes* 21 (1886), pp. 623–27.

Wiseman, T. P. *Catullus and His World*. London, 1985.

Wooten, C. *Cicero's Philippics*. Chapel Hill, N.C., 1983.

Wissowa, Georg. "Devotio." In Pauly-Wissowa, *Paulys Realencyclopädie der klassischen Altertumswissenschaft*, vol. 5, cols. 277–80.

Yavetz, Zvi. *Plebs and Princeps*. London, 1969.

Yoshida Mitsuru. *Requiem for the Battleship Yamato*. Trans. Richard H. Minear. Seattle, 1985.

INDEX

aboulie, 53

abnormal, the, 71, 96, 102, 105, 135n, 160–62, 164, 180. *See also* natural, the

absolute, the, 101–3, 118–19, 137, 156, 174, 181–82, 184–87. *See also* alienation; envy; idealization

abundance. *See* excess

adultery, 50, 65, 69, 116, 139, 161, 165

agon. See contest; desire for the same things; equal opponent

actor or acting, 29–30, 34, 39–40, 60–66, 76–77, 119, 133–36, 140–41, 143n, 148, 154, 166, 168n, 179. *See also* hypocrisy; mime; theatre

alienation, 56–58, 98–100, 103, 105, 116, 123, 125, 137, 182

alternation. *See* reciprocity

ambiguity. *See* categories; paradox

amor mortis, 24, 31–32, 41, 46, 51n, 59–60, 73n, 154n, 159. *See also* conflagration; death

amulet, 96–97, 140, 168–72, 187, 189. See *fascinum*

animals, 50, 53n, 56–57, 67–68, 73, 86, 88, 132, 136–37, 139, 141, 143, 154, 156, 161, 172–73, 184n, 189. *See also* monsters; pets

anomie, 52n, 162

apathy, 7, 21, 34, 56, 58–62, 65, 67, 69, 71, 75n, 85, 98, 100–101, 104–5, 119, 121, 136, 153n. *See also* fascination; numbness; stupefaction

apocalypse, 49, 54–56, 59, 69–70, 104n, 130–31, 150n, 159–60n. *See amor mortis*; civil war

applause, 87, 154, 171n

arena. *See* games; gladiator

asceticism, 3, 14, 18–21, 33–34, 48, 70–80, 112, 115–16, 121n, 124, 132, 178n, 187. *See also* gladiator; severity

audience, 17–24, 27, 33–36, 56, 62–64, 87–91, 104, 119, 129, 139, 144, 154, 169n, 170–71n

austerity. *See* asceticism

auto-fascination, 92, 100. *See also* fascination

banquet, 19, 21, 33, 50–51, 61, 64, 72, 108–12, 115n, 118, 122, 124, 130n, 141n, 151n, 153–55, 167, 175; laws of the, 109–11, 115n

beauty, 14, 56, 63, 79–81, 87–88, 92, 98–99, 158, 163

being, sense of. *See* reality

boredom, 51–53, 55n, 58, 71–72. *See also* apathy; frustration

buffoon, the, 72, 89, 107–9, 121, 134, 137–38, 141–43, 155, 159, 174, 178. See also *derisor*; fool; ridicule; *scurra*

burning, as metaphor, 69n, 72n, 80, 91–93, 98

cannibalism, 51, 60, 68, 78, 90, 94–95, 154

castration, 72–73, 75n, 96–98, 120n, 139, 173n

categorization, 6–7, 78, 101–2, 111, 113–14, 116, 119–25, 130–32, 134–35, 137, 144, 146, 149, 157, 160–61, 175–89; absence, confusion or transgression of, 7, 49, 71, 78, 85–87, 91, 99, 101, 106–7, 114, 121, 124, 129–34, 138–41, 143n, 146, 149, 151–65, 173, 177–78, 185; elaborate or excessive, 107, 115–16, 120–24, 131–32, 136, 143–44. *See also* hierarchy

catharsis, 98; absence of, 67, 69n, 150, 185. *See also* frustration

Catones, 111, 112n, 123. *See also* indignation

chance, 13, 63–64, 89, 137n. *See also* fortune, gambling

chaos. *See* conflagration; indiscrimination

cinaedus, 72, 139, 161, 167

civil war, 3, 27–29n, 36–39, 46, 50, 69–70, 95, 103–4, 114, 117, 123, 130n, 144, 146, 153, 155n, 157–58, 173, 178, 182, 184–86, 189; envy as, 95. *See also* conflagration

class. *See* categorization; hierarchy

client, the, 28–30, 39, 58, 77, 109–10, 117–18, 124–25, 128, 143, 146n, 155, 174, 176. *See also* humiliation